Phases of the Moon

Phases of the Moon

A Cultural History of the Werewolf Film

Craig Ian Mann

EDINBURGH
University Press

For the Monster Squad

Edinburgh University Press is one of the leading university presses in the UK. We publish academic books and journals in our selected subject areas across the humanities and social sciences, combining cutting-edge scholarship with high editorial and production values to produce academic works of lasting importance. For more information visit our website: edinburghuniversitypress.com

Edinburgh University Press Ltd
The Tun – Holyrood Road
12 (2f) Jackson's Entry
Edinburgh EH8 8PJ

Typeset in Monotype Ehrhardt by
IDSUK (DataConnection) Ltd

A CIP record for this book is available from the British Library

ISBN 978 1 4744 4111 7 (hardback)
ISBN 978 1 4744 4112 4 (paperback)
ISBN 978 1 4744 4113 1 (webready PDF)
ISBN 978 1 4744 4114 8 (epub)

Every effort has been made to trace the copyright holders for the images that appear in this book, but if any have been inadvertently overlooked, the publisher will be pleased to make the necessary arrangements at the first opportunity.

Cover image by Mute: www.mutecult.com

Contents

Figures

Acknowledgements

One dark afternoon in the 1990s (when I was nine or ten years old), a friend invited me to his house to watch horror films, having convinced his parents to buy a VHS box set containing *Bram Stoker's Dracula* (1992), *Mary Shelley's Frankenstein* (1994) and *Wolf* (1994). We watched the latter, in which Jack Nicholson turns feral and urinates on James Spader's shoes. I borrowed the tape and didn't give it back for a decade. In the following years, I watched as many werewolf films as I could. So my first thanks go to Ryan Watson – who sussed the fine art of convincing his parents to buy horror films for him at an impressively young age.

The seed of this book was planted in my undergraduate dissertation, written at Sheffield Hallam University in 2010, which was inspired in equal part by a lifelong love of werewolf fiction and Shelley O'Brien's module on the American horror film. I'm grateful to Shelley for thinking that writing about werewolf films was a good idea in the first place and her supervision of both that dissertation and the thesis that formed the basis of this book. A huge thank you is due to the director of my doctoral studies, Sheldon Hall, who has continually challenged me to make my work better; constantly encouraged me in furthering my professional development; provided many obscure films; answered my tiresome and often inane questions at all hours of the day and night (I'm not actually sure when it is that he sleeps); read first (and sometimes second . . . and third . . .) drafts of almost everything I have ever written; and offered a spellchecking service that money couldn't buy. I also owe a great deal of gratitude to Gillian Leslie and Richard Strachan at Edinburgh University Press for all their help, guidance and, perhaps most importantly, patience.

Writing this monograph would have been considerably more difficult without the help and support of several individuals who have provided material that would otherwise have been difficult to obtain: thanks to Angela Quinton of Werewolf-News.com for maintaining an incredibly useful website; to the late Peter Hutchings – a giant in horror studies – for providing his contribution to the collection *She-Wolf* (2015), and to the editor, Hannah Priest, for several other chapters; to Lowell Dean for granting early access to *WolfCop* (2014); to Simon Brown for providing his conference paper on *Silver Bullet* (1985) and his endless kindness; to Kieran Foster for digitising *The Werewolves of Moravia*; to Stacey Abbott, Chi-Yun Shin and Iain Robert Smith for their vital examiners' comments on my thesis; a second thanks to Stacey for graciously agreeing to pen a foreword to this book; and a huge thank you to Dave Huntley for producing some jaw-dropping cover art. Thanks are also due to others who have offered so many forms of help and encouragement along the way: Sergio Angelini, Liam Ball, Kev Bickerdike, James Blackford, Jon Bridle, Louise Buckler, Jake Burton, Leah Byatt, Andy Cliff, Chris Cooke, Jon Dickinson, Liz Dixon, Larry Fessenden, Liam Hathaway, Chris and Lisa Hopkins, Dawn Keetley, Murray Leeder, Kurt McCoy, Mike Mann, Joe Ondrak, Jon Robertson, Caitlin Shaw, Suzanne Speidel, Eric J. Stolze, Chris Suter and Johnny Walker. Special thanks are due to Stella Gaynor, Shellie McMurdo, Laura Mee and Tom Watson; they know why.

I can't offer enough thanks to my mother, Gillian Mann, who has always supported me and has made untold sacrifices with no (well, very few) complaints; did everything she could to fuel my love for movies from a very young age; and even encouraged my passion for horror films – unless it was *The Exorcist* (1973), which was for many years kept in an ominous black box on the top shelf of the video cabinet. Finally, thank you to Rose Butler, who was the primary sounding board for the majority of ideas in this monograph, for listening to me complain during frustrating spells of writer's block, watching a great many films of somewhat questionable quality and spending several years silently tolerating my tendency to turn nocturnal during writing periods (along with a number of other bad habits). I hope you found what you were hunting for.

*

An earlier version of Chapter 3 was previously published in 'Horror Studies' 10.1 (2019).

A section of Chapter 5 was previously published with Arrow Video's 2019 release of *An American Werewolf in London* (1981).

Foreword: Monsters Everywhere

Monsters are everywhere and our continued fascination with them – expressed by dressing up as Dracula or Morticia on Halloween, watching Danny Boyle's stage adaptation of *Frankenstein* (2011), or indulging the carnivalesque pleasure of a zombie walk – shows that monsters continue to have cultural value; to have meaning. They speak to our fears and our desires. They embody our past and our future. They express our psyche and our politics but that meaning, like the monster that embodies it, is not fixed. Together they shift and change, responding to a plethora of influences and contexts. Drew Barrymore's twenty-first-century liberated zombie of Netflix's serialised sit-com *Santa Clarita Diet* (2017–) has little in common with the mind-controlled zombies enslaved by Bela Lugosi in the horror film *White Zombie* (1932). The aristocratic vampires of Universal Studios' *Dracula* (1931), *Dracula's Daughter* (1936) and *Son of Dracula* (1943) are a world apart from the working class, damaged vampires of *Martin* (1977), *The Hamiltons* (2006) and *The Transfiguration* (2016).

Nina Auerbach famously opened her groundbreaking *Our Vampires, Ourselves* (1995) with the statement 'we all know Dracula, or think we do, but as this book will show, there are many Draculas – and still more vampires who refuse to be Dracula or to play him'. She argued that there was a vampire for every generation. Her work took an interdisciplinary approach to consider the cultural meaning of the vampire across literature, film and television, much like Gregory A. Waller's *The Living and the Undead* (1986). Others have followed similar paths in relation to a range of folkloric and literary monsters. David J. Skal's *The Monster Show: A Cultural History of Horror* (1994) offers a rich overview of the history of monsters throughout popular culture, from freak shows to stage and screen to gothic literature and comic books.

Tanya Krzywinska examines the cinematic legacy of witchcraft and magic in *A Skin for Dancing In: Possession, Witchcraft and Voodoo in Film* (2000). Kyle William Bishop's *American Zombie Gothic: The Rise and Fall (and Rise) of the Walking Dead in Popular Culture* (2010) offers a pains-taking reading of the zombie as a monster from the Americas, tracing its evolution from Haitian folklore, a product of a history of colonialism and slavery, to post-Romero contemporary American cinema and television. Roger Luckhurst examined the cultural fascination of the myth of the Mummy in *The Mummy's Curse: The True History of a Dark Fantasy* (2012) and followed this with a rich global cultural history of the zombie in *Zombies: A Cultural History* (2015). As these books attest, monsters are indeed everywhere.

When I started work on my book *Celluloid Vampires: Life after Death in the Modern World* (2007), which began its life in 1997 as my doctoral the-sis, I was most influenced by Waller and Auerbach's work on the vampire. I sought to follow their lead but with a specific focus on the cinematic afterlife of the vampire. I was struck by how few scholarly works on vam-pires, or other monsters for that matter, focused exclusively on film. I therefore decided to examine how developments within cinema shaped the vampire but also how the cinematic vampire was shaped by industrial, cultural and social contexts of the twentieth century. Not a creature that embodied the past returned to haunt the present, but a monster born of the modern world. With the growing popularity of vampire and zombie film and television in the twenty-first century, I took a similar approach in *Undead Apocalypse: Vampires and Zombies in the 21st Century* (2016).

The werewolf, a shapeshifter by nature, is potentially even more muta-ble than the undead and yet has received far less scholarly consideration, despite a folkloric and cinematic history as rich as the vampire. While Hannah Priest's *She-Wolf: A Cultural History of Female Werewolves* (2015) and Samantha George and Bill Hughes's *In the Company of Wolves: Were-wolves, Wolves and Wild Children* (2020) offer an interdisciplinary exami-nation of the werewolf, little attention has been paid to the history of the werewolf in its cinematic form until Craig Ian Mann's *Phases of the Moon: A Cultural History of the Werewolf Film*.

As Mann so eloquently demonstrates, when Universal began mak-ing what would become their horror classics in the 1930s, the werewolf joined the pantheon of Universal monsters, after Dracula, Frankenstein's creature, the Invisible Man and the Mummy, first in *Werewolf of London* (1935) and then to even greater success with *The Wolf Man* (1941). While *Werewolf of London* offered a stunning transformation sequence that sig-nalled the genre's close affinity with cutting-edge special effects, it was Lon Chaney Jr's incarnation of the cursed Larry Talbot in *The Wolf Man* that became as iconic to the werewolf myth as Lugosi was for Dracula and Karloff for Frankenstein's creation. The werewolf is in many ways one of the most brutal of monsters and yet, following Chaney's lead, they often evoke the greatest sympathy, presented as being as much a victim as a monster.

But, like the vampire, there is not one werewolf but many werewolves – and these early successes for Universal opened the door to a century's worth of re-imaginings of the monster. Some werewolves are cuddly and comic, like Michael J. Fox's *Teen Wolf* (1985), while others are virile and hyper-masculine, like Jack Nicholson's *Wolf* (1994); some invite sympathy and identification, such as David Kessler in *An American Werewolf in London* (1981), while others still, like the pack in *Dog Soldiers* (2002), are unknowable. There are werewolves for every generation, speaking to a diverse and complex range of social, cultural, political and industrial histories that shaped and moulded this shapeshifter into new forms and new narratives. It is to these histories of the cinematic werewolf that Mann turns, offering a rich and comprehensive analysis of the werewolf movie from the first cinematic forays into the genre with *The Werewolf* (1913) and *The White Wolf* (1914) to twenty-first-century horror films such as *Late Phases* (2014) and *Wildling* (2018).

Mann's discussion of 100 years of cinema deliberately moves beyond the perception of the werewolf as representing the beast within to show how this shapeshifter has transformed with the times, articulating, embodying and responding to, sometimes contradictory, socio-cultural and political histories. Written with a passion for the genre alongside a historian's keen eye for cultural meanings, *Phases of the Moon* shows us how the cinematic werewolf, like so many monsters, has much to tell us about ourselves, our past and our present. Filled with insight and encyclopaedic knowledge of all things lycanthropic, Mann gives the reader plenty to chew over. Sit back and enjoy. It's time to howl at the moon.

Stacey Abbott

Introduction: Bark at the Moon

A full moon looms over a dark forest in the blackest night and, somewhere deep amongst the overgrown trees, something howls.

It is a scene as familiar as that of a vampire lurking deep in the catacombs of a Transylvanian fortress; as ingrained in popular culture as the image of a patchwork monster rising from the dead amongst crackles of electricity; as enduring as a Pharaoh escaping his sarcophagus to take revenge on those who have disturbed thousands of years of peaceful rest. Such a story instantly brings to mind the image of a werewolf, a mainstay of horror fiction that has become synonymous with a feral beast, savage and uncontrollable.

A basic definition for the mythical creature termed a werewolf is a human being who, either purposely or against their will, transforms into a wolf. Certain accounts depict a partial transformation into a monstrous hybrid of human and lupine features while others depict a complete anatomical transition from human to wolf. Outside of this basic definition, fictional depictions of werewolves often adapt existing mythology, established by other werewolf tales in several media, or create their own. The circumstances of transformation, the effect this transformation has on the individual, how much humanity remains once transformation is complete and whether the condition can be considered a blessing or a curse are all narrative elements that have changed frequently. And there are multiple names for such a monster: werewolf, wolf-man, shapeshifter, skinwalker and lycanthrope are the most common in the English language. However, even with so many variations of the myth in existence, the basic concept of the werewolf itself remains deeply ingrained in popular culture, especially in Europe – where the fear of werewolves reached its peak during the Early Modern period – and nations historically colonised by European peoples.

This study is dedicated to the werewolf in cinema, with a particular emphasis on that genre that has become so synonymous with tales of werewolfism: horror. From *The Wolf Man* (1941) to *WolfCop* (2014) via *I Was a Teenage Werewolf* (1957), *Werewolves on Wheels* (1971) and *An American Werewolf in London* (1981), it presents a history of the werewolf film from its origins in the silent era to contemporary examples. In doing so, it explores the monster's cultural significance, making the case for it as a product of its times: a mutating metaphor that can be seen to shift and evolve in tandem with the fears and anxieties particular to its historical moment. This, of course, is not an unusual approach to monsters in cinema, but it is a significant departure from existing academic work on the werewolf film.

For scholars, the werewolf has long been associated with the 'beast within'. Since the nineteenth century, the monster has come to be closely associated with this concept, and the phrase is still employed widely in academic responses to werewolf fiction. It is designed, of course, to emphasise the psychological dimension of 'werewolfism' or 'werewolfery' – or 'lycanthropy', a term that is itself problematic due to its clinical connotations – and to suggest that the affliction is symptomatic of a war between the civil and bestial sides of the human self. It is now often used as a universal explanation for the enduring appeal of the werewolf across several media and even the sole source of its thematic significance. As Anne Billson argues in a discussion of contemporary werewolf films, 'Werewolves may seem less versatile in metaphorical terms than vampires or zombies, which these days can symbolise just about anything . . . The werewolf, on the other hand, is basically just the beast within.'[1]

Historically, Billson has not been alone in this view. The werewolf, especially in cinema, has not been widely studied; however, a considerable proportion of the existing writing on the subject uses psychoanalysis as a framework through which to form its conclusions. For example, Reynold Humphries suggests that *Werewolf of London* (1935) is an allegory for castration anxiety,[2] and that *The Wolf Man* (1941) uses its protagonist's monthly transformations as a metaphor for menstruation, leading to a climax in which 'The father kills the son for not being man enough, according to the dominant values he represents.'[3] Meanwhile, James B. Twitchell argues that the werewolf myth is a precursor to the themes of duality and sexual violence raised by Robert Louis Stevenson's *Strange Case of Dr Jekyll and Mr Hyde* (1886). He argues that the werewolf is best understood as 'a skin changer, a pagan turncoat who did for generations of Europeans what Mr Hyde does for us: he provided first the frisson of a metamorphosis gone awry, and then the shock of ensuing bestial aggression'.[4]

Similarly, in *The Curse of the Werewolf: Fantasy, Horror and the Beast Within* (2006), Chantal Bourgault du Coudray posits that the werewolf film generally articulates a deep-seated fear of the beast within by figuring werewolfism as symptomatic of repressed masculine aggression. She argues, for example, that *The Wolf Man* 'consolidated the werewolf of the cinema as psychologized and masculine' and 'explores the consequences of a failure to "discipline" the "beast within" for male power and identity';[5] suggests *The Werewolf of Washington* (1973) delivers an 'unequivocal' message that 'normative masculinity is vulnerable to the onset of sudden crisis';[6] and asserts that the infamous transformation scene in *The Howling* (1981) emphasises 'the masculinity of the werewolf's body'.[7]

The allure of using psychoanalysis to explain the enduring popularity of the werewolf is not difficult to comprehend. The words 'lycanthrope' and 'lycanthropy' are clinical terms, and psychosis leading human beings to believe they have the ability to transform from human to lupine form has been considered a disease of the mind for thousands of years.[8] Early werewolf films actively play on the monster's psychological dimensions; the silent *Wolfblood* (1925), for example, never reveals whether its apparent werewolf is a literal monster or simply a broken man who is suffering from terrible delusions. It concerns Dick Bannister (George Chesebro), the manager of a logging company who receives a blood transfusion from a wolf after a serious accident in the Canadian wilderness. Following a spate of wolf attacks around his camp, Bannister comes to believe he is a werewolf. By the film's end it is heavily implied that he is simply delusional: a lycanthrope rather than a werewolf. Similarly, *The Wolf Man* devotes much of its running time to exploring the inner turmoil of its werewolf protagonist as he tries to discern if he is a wolf-man or a madman.

It might seem that these are themes that have always been at the heart of werewolf fiction – and, if that were true, it would certainly explain the dominance of psychoanalysis in studies of the werewolf in cinema. But in fact the idea of the 'beast within' developed only in the 1800s, while the werewolf myth itself is thousands of years old. As Leslie A. Sconduto explains in her monograph *Metamorphoses of the Werewolf: A Literary Study from Antiquity through the Renaissance* (2008), the earliest reference to a werewolf in ancient literature is in fact 'in the Akkadian *Epic of Gilgamesh*, a collection of mythic tales which circulated in the region of southern Mesopotamia'.[9] Thereafter, werewolves appear in Ovid's *Metamorphoses*, authored in AD 8, and Petronius's *The Satyricon*, which was circulated during the reign of Nero. In the centuries following these initial accounts, the werewolf myth proliferated throughout Europe.

With the fall of the Roman Empire and the coming of Christianity, the Church was forced to reconcile a popular belief in creatures such as werewolves with religious doctrine. As Sconduto notes, 'seen as remnants of pagan beliefs and practices, the werewolf legends inherited from antiquity threatened Christian notions of divinity, creation and salvation'.[10] Sconduto asserts that Christian writers found it important to re-evaluate the myths inherited from antiquity in an attempt to deny the existence of werewolves or otherwise propose that the appearance of metamorphosis could be achieved only through demonic trickery.[11] In short, early clerical writings stressed that the idea of a man transforming into an animal was either impossible or illusionary.

However, the efforts of clerics to quell a popular belief in werewolves failed, and the werewolf thereafter became a prominent figure in medieval literature. To illustrate changing attitudes to the monster, Sconduto highlights several texts from the twelfth and thirteenth centuries in which men are transformed into wolves as punishment for their sins. The werewolves in these tales retain their human minds and souls, forced to roam the earth as wolves in atonement.[12] In a further attempt by clerical writers to rationalise metamorphosis in the context of Christianity, then, these tales suggested 'God is using metamorphosis to carry out his divine vengeance . . . to make visible his authority over mankind'.[13] Such stories were likely inspired by a similar account of metamorphosis included in the Bible, in which God turns the Babylonian king Nebuchadnezzar into an animal in order to punish him.[14] Thereafter, medieval writings would come to feature sympathetic, noble and sometimes tragic werewolves who play a part in narratives designed to deliver a Christian message, often condemning a sin or endorsing a virtue; for a time, the werewolf became the hero of its narrative. For example, Sconduto argues that Marie de France's *Bisclavret* – written sometime between 1160 and 1178 – is a lesson on the importance of loyalty.[15] Sconduto goes on to analyse three other medieval texts in detail, outlining how they condemn cardinal sins such as pride and lust or endorse Christian notions of virtue, such as personal sacrifice.[16] What is common amongst these medieval tales is that the werewolf comes to embody Christian values, while his antagonist is often a wicked woman who seeks to betray or outwit him. In many ways, then, these stories reinforce not just Christian doctrine but the Church's patriarchal control.

The depiction of werewolves radically changed during the Early Modern period, as Europe was gripped by a widespread fear of witchcraft and the supernatural. As Brian P. Levack attests: 'roughly from 1450 to 1750, thousands of persons, most of them women, were tried for the crime of witchcraft. About half of these individuals were executed, usually by burning.'[17] Perhaps the first writing that documents a change in the Church's position on the occult is the *Malleus Maleficarum* – or *The Hammer of Witches* – originally penned by Heinrich Kramer in 1486. The text directly contradicts the clerical writings that followed the decline of the Western Roman Empire: 'instead of stating that it is blasphemous to believe in the existence of witches and their ability to fly and transform themselves, he declares that witches really exist and that it is heretical to believe the opposite'.[18] It is probable that the *Malleus Maleficarum*, like many medieval werewolf stories, was intended to reinforce Christian patriarchy; its focus is almost entirely on female witches and it has since been noted by scholars that it is a fundamentally misogynistic text which aided heavily in the oppression of women.[19] However, a patriarchal subtext is perhaps the only thing that the *Malleus Maleficarum* has in common with earlier werewolf writings of the Middle Ages; for the most part it can be seen to serve as a counterpoint to the idea of the werewolf as noble victim.

Designed to aid inquisitors and to serve as a theological basis for heresy trials, Kramer's text took hold in Europe and helped to develop a wide-spread belief in satanism and black magic. Of course, this also had implications for the Church's stance on metamorphosis and werewolfery: 'in addition to affecting attitudes regarding witchcraft, the text shaped opinion about werewolves, for belief in witches and their ability to transform themselves into animals also made the belief in werewolves permissible'.[20] As the witch-hunt began, the noble medieval werewolf was replaced by 'a rough, dirty peasant who savagely attacks, kills, and then eats his victims, who are usually children'.[21]

Furthermore, these werewolves were not confined to the pages of literature. They were, to an extent, real: court records detail the trials of individuals who were accused of werewolfism during the witch-hunt. For example, Peter Stumpp – or the 'Werewolf of Bedburg' – was accused of werewolfery in 1590; an account of his trial and execution can be read in its entirety in *The Werewolf* (1933), a study of the mythical creature penned by the occultist Montague Summers.[22] The perceived threat posed by werewolves escalated in the Early Modern period to the point that between 1520 and 1630, 30,000 cases of suspected werewolves were recorded in France alone.[23] How many of the accused were executed is unclear. As Ian Woodward states, 'the mind literally quails at the thought of how many innocent people went to their deaths for no other reason than the fact that a vindictive neighbour had trumped up some wild allegation of werewolfery against them'.[24]

The Enlightenment later saw scholars reject superstition in favour of logic and reason, and it became widely accepted that those souls accused of werewolfism during the witch trials had been suffering from a form of psychosis known as 'lycanthropy'. It was reasoned that literal metamorphosis was impossible – or at least unproven. That these supposed werewolves suffered from delusions was a far more logical conclusion. A 1988 study found that lycanthropy does indeed exist as a symptom of severe psychosis in some patients,[25] but due to the sheer number of people executed it seems unlikely that all Early Modern 'werewolves' suffered from it. Nevertheless, this remained the dominant belief until the nineteenth century, when other explanations for a historical belief in literal wolf-men were explored by scholars.[26] For example, Sabine Baring-Gould contended that suspected werewolves may have been monsters of a different type: serial killers. He stated: 'Startling though the assertion may be, it is a matter of fact, that man, naturally, in common with other carnivora, is actuated by an impulse to kill, and by a love of destroying life.'[27]

Thus the Enlightenment brought an end to both the werewolf trials and a popular belief in literal wolf-men. Of course, sightings of feral beasts are occasionally reported (such as Wisconsin's 'Beast of Bray Road' or East Yorkshire's 'Old Stinker') and, as Woodward has noted, there are still some secluded regions in Europe where a belief in werewolves may persist.[28] For the most part, though, a widespread fear of men with the power to transform into wolves was quelled by Enlightenment reasoning. The werewolf was not revived until the 1800s, when it became a prominent figure in popular literature as writers, influenced by the works of scholars such as Baring-Gould, began to explore the werewolf as a subject for fiction in the gothic novel and the penny dreadful.[29]

However, renewed scholarly interest in the werewolf myth is not the only reason for the werewolf's assimilation into nineteenth-century culture. Bourgault du Coudray attests that the development of romanticism also contributed to the re-emergence of werewolfism as an inspiration for literary works. The romantic movement rejected the steadfast rationalism of the Enlightenment, instead seeking to embrace mysticism and the occult as cultural influences for art and literature. As a result, creatures of myth that had long been disregarded as the product of outdated superstition – such as the vampire and the werewolf – were resurrected.[30] Bourgault du Coudray argues that it was the meeting of Enlightenment and romantic ideas that gave new life to the werewolf myth and also informs much of the subtext of nineteenth-century werewolf fiction:

> the Gothic has been read primarily as a discourse about identity and/or subjectivity, a reading that has emerged from a theoretical focus on the ways in which the Self is constructed through processes of "Othering." Such theoretical work has represented a convergence of Enlightenment and romantic concerns; on the one hand, the focus on identity formation maintains an Enlightenment emphasis upon the individual's relationship to society and community; and on the other, the focus on subject formation perpetuates the romantic emphasis on inner experience . . . The werewolf is uniquely positioned to describe and clarify this relationship, because it is implicated in processes of identity formation and subject formation.[31]

In short, Bourgault du Coudray suggests that werewolf fiction of the nine-teenth century alternates between sociological and psychological interpre-tations of the werewolf myth.[32] These ideas came to be represented in works which either connected werewolfism with a social 'Other' – largely in connection with race, class and gender – or explored the inner turmoil of afflicted individuals forced to reconcile with their monstrosity. She sug-gests that George W. M. Reynolds's *Wagner the Wehr-Wolf* (first serialised in 1846–7 and later published in its entirety in 1857) is one of the first works of fiction to pioneer the concept of the beast within by suggesting that the werewolf 'could not always be safely confined to an externalised Other; on the contrary, it implied that the affliction might also emanate from within the Self or Same'.[33]

These psychologised werewolf narratives are heavily influenced by developments in psychiatry and particularly a growing scholarly inter-est in the unconscious mind, concerned as they are with 'subjectivity or inward experience'.[34] As Bourgault du Coudray suggests, the nineteenth century saw the human mind theorised as an opposition between con-scious (civil) and unconscious (bestial) components, and 'as the prolifera-tion of werewolf literature . . . in the nineteenth century indicates, this conceptualisation of the psyche was by no means confined to psychia-try; it permeated the culture as thoroughly as Charles Darwin's theory of evolution'.[35] These concepts were consolidated in the work of Sigmund Freud, whose theories have since become a touchstone in the study of the arts in the form of modern psychoanalysis. As such a great deal of gothic werewolf fiction was informed by these burgeoning ideas, and films such as *Wolfblood* and *The Wolf Man* continued to reproduce them. And, of course, they have been echoed in scholarly responses to werewolf fiction. As Bourgault du Coudray recounts,

> The fields of film studies and literary criticism are perhaps those discourses that have most enthusiastically embraced the perspectives of psychoanalysis and they are, of course, the two bodies of theory that have had the most to say about the genre of horror and the theme of the werewolf.[36]

The dominance of psychoanalysis in the study of the werewolf is there-fore easily explained, and none of this is to say that such approaches are unwelcome. In fact, the highly accomplished analyses published by the likes of Twitchell, Humphries and Bourgault du Coudray have formed the basis for further study of the werewolf in cinema. But it is vitally important to remember that the beast within is a nineteenth-century invention; as Sconduto's work illustrates, the meaning of the werewolf myth shifted over many centuries before the monster was psychologised in gothic fiction, and has endured for over 100 years since the end of the Victorian era. Furthermore, even the werewolf fiction of the 1800s was not solely concerned with the beast within; though she does not explore the werewolf's sociological dimensions beyond the nineteenth century, Bourgault du Coudray provides an in-depth discussion of female werewolves as a form of 'Othering' in her discussion of gothic werewolf fiction.[37] Her observations are echoed by Stefan Dziemianowicz, who suggests that it is in the Victorian era that 'female werewolves begin to gain currency' in stories that – like the werewolf tales of the Middle Ages – use female monsters to reinforce patriarchal values.[38] Dziemianowicz references Clemence Housman's *The Were-Wolf* (1896), in which a woman seduces men before slaying them in wolf form, as an example of the werewolf being used to illustrate the apparently 'predatory nature of females in non-traditional roles'.[39]

Given its evolving depiction over several centuries, then, it is odd that the werewolf has come to be associated with a single interpretation – particularly one that was most clearly evident in werewolf fiction published over a century ago. Moreover, it is troubling that the beast within has since worked to narrow perceptions of the monster's metaphorical potential. For example, in a 2014 article for popular horror magazine *Fangoria*, writer Craig Anderson echoes Billson's suggestion that the werewolf is 'basically just the beast within'.[40] In discussing the contemporary werewolf film, he muses: 'are werewolves, as central characters, passé . . . Are they simply too limiting, the Dr Jekyll and Mr Hyde conflicting nature overplayed and now infertile as subject matter?'[41] Here, then, Anderson perpetuates an idea originally championed by Twitchell: that the werewolf film is simply in the business of replicating the Jekyll-and-Hyde formula, primarily through the same 'conflicting nature' that is strongly associated with the beast within.

This is a particular problem in film studies. Published as early as 1979, Woodward's account of the werewolf in history and folklore, *The Werewolf Delusion*, explores the correlation between the geography of werewolf trials and the spread of rabies epidemics to provide an empirically evidenced explanation for a historical belief in werewolves. Similarly, Sconduto's work has framed seminal works of werewolf literature in the context of specific cultural moments to chart the shifting depiction of werewolves in relation to the development of the Christian Church. More recently, Willem de Blécourt's edited collection *Werewolf Histories* (2015) has provided vital cultural context for historical beliefs in werewolves across Europe, in countries such as Denmark, Estonia, Germany and Italy amongst others.[42]

Meanwhile, the werewolf's significance in film and television has been largely overlooked. Hannah Priest's *She-Wolf: A Cultural History of*

Female Werewolves (2015) contains many illuminating essays on the female werewolf as a cultural metaphor, but only a handful of its chapters concentrate specifically on film. Similarly, Kimberley McMahon-Coleman and Roslyn Weaver's *Werewolves and other Shapeshifters in Popular Culture: A Thematic Analysis of Recent Depictions* (2012) draws out interesting social and cultural subtexts related to gender, sexuality, race, disability and even substance abuse in a number of werewolf texts across several media but, as its title suggests, it limits its scope to contemporary case studies.

Of course, academics have discussed some individual werewolf films and television shows in relation to their cultural contexts. For example, David J. Skal has interpreted *The Wolf Man* as a product of wartime,[43] while *I Was a Teenage Werewolf* (1957) has been extensively studied in relation to the juvenile delinquency moral panic of the 1950s by Peter Biskind and Mark Jancovich.[44] More recently, Robert Spadoni has examined *Werewolf of London* as a coded commentary on attitudes to homosexuality in the 1930s; Simon Bacon has suggested a number of werewolf films, including *The Wolf Man* and *An American Werewolf in London*, figure the werewolf as a metaphor for a social underclass; and Lorna Jowett has discussed issues of gender and class in a number of recent American television shows featuring werewolves.[45]

But such accounts of the werewolf in film and television are few and far between, particularly in comparison to cultural studies of other classic monsters. See, for example, Nina Auerbach's landmark work *Our Vampires, Ourselves* (1995) or Stacey Abbott's *Celluloid Vampires: Life after Death in the Modern World* (2007), both of which make the case for the cinematic vampire as a versatile metaphor for cultural anxieties. The zombie, too, has been afforded an enormous amount of scholarly attention in cultural studies such as Kyle William Bishop's *American Zombie Gothic* (2010) and Roger Luckhurst's *Zombies: A Cultural History* (2015), to name but two examples. Furthermore, Susan Tyler Hitchcock's *Frankenstein: A Cultural History* (2008) reveals the cultural significance of Frankenstein's monster from its literary beginnings to the present, placing particular emphasis on the creature as an evolving metaphor.

The most prolific and enduring horror monsters are all present and accounted for in diverse cultural histories: the alluring vampire; the shambling zombie; Frankenstein's tragic creature. But due to the continued dominance of the beast within, the cultural dimensions of werewolves on screen have been neglected. Psychoanalytical readings have laid the foundation for the study of the werewolf in pop culture, but alternatives are now needed to avoid the perpetuation of a widespread idea that it is a less meaningful or versatile figure than the vampire, zombie or Frankenstein's monster. Furthermore, to accept the beast within as the werewolf's sole symbolic worth is to overlook the specific cultural and historical context of individual films. The werewolf film must be understood not just in terms of the beast within but also the 'beast without': a cultural understanding of the lupine creature as a product of its times.

To present an alternative to the beast within, this study takes a cultural approach to its subject. Over eight roughly chronological chapters, it charts the development of werewolf cinema from its beginnings to the present day, grouping films into thematic cycles in order to understand them in a specific context: their historical, allegorical or cultural 'moment', to borrow phrases from Adam Lowenstein and Brigid Cherry.[46] Like the cultural studies of cinematic vampires, zombies and Frankenstein's monster that have come before it, the book seeks to explore how the werewolf has evolved over a century or more, finding new relevance in shifting social, cultural and political contexts. From the Native American skinwalkers of silent werewolf films to the huge lupine beasts depicted in horror cinema of the 1980s, via the wolf-men and she-wolves common in the first half of the twentieth century, it illustrates that the werewolf myth – which has been in a constant cycle of revision since its inception thousands of years ago – continues to transform through cinema.

The analyses provided here are, in the words of Andrew Tudor, 'particularistic accounts' that investigate the narrative and aesthetic workings of werewolf films in a particular time and place, taking into consideration the historical circumstances surrounding their production and immediate reception.[47] Each film or cycle is analysed alongside a rigorous discussion of its historical context in order to draw clear connections between the thematic content of werewolf films and the wider culture that produced and received them. Importantly, I do not contend that these movies function as 'reflections' or 'mirrors'; rather, I posit that werewolf films – and, in fact, all films – are cultural products, meaning that both their creation and initial consumption are influenced by the ideological debates, social norms and cultural shifts particular to their historical moment.

This study therefore departs from many cultural studies of the horror film in two ways. Firstly, it recognises that a film's meaning is malleable: not rigid, but inscribed. It discusses case studies in socio-political and ideological terms, but allows for a multiplicity of readings even in a film's immediate historical context. As Tudor suggests in his seminal work *Monsters and Mad Scientists: A Cultural History of the Horror Movie* (1989), 'Histories are plainly reconstructions . . . Cultural phenomena only exist in so far as people "read" them, ascribe them meaning; they are constituted as *cultural* in the act of reading.'[48] Thus where a film gives rise to multiple readings in relation to its cultural moment – for example, existing scholarly work on *I Was a Teenage Werewolf* suggests that it can be interpreted from both a conservative and a liberal point of view[49] – this study endeavours to consider the evidence to support each of these potential subtexts, especially where they directly oppose or contradict one another.

Secondly, this study often incorporates the views of filmmakers in its analyses, as evidenced by interviews, commentaries and the wider thematic concerns of their bodies of work. Cultural theorists have long been engaged in a continuing debate as to whether the creators or consumers of popular culture should be privileged as the primary inscribers of its meaning.[50] But filmmakers, the movies they produce and the domestic audiences that consume them all exist within a single culture. As Tudor asserts,

> Film, after all, is more than mere celluloid. It is socially constructed within a three-cornered association between film-makers, film spectators and the film texts themselves, and at every point in that nexus of relationships we encounter negotiation and interaction involving active social beings and institutionalised social practices.[51]

It can thus be extremely revealing to explore a creator's intentions; if nothing else, evidence of authorial intent allows for an examination of how the personal values of a filmmaker might be seen to reinforce or contradict the dominant ideology of the wider society that surrounds them.

The prominence of the beast within in writing on the werewolf film suggests that one of our oldest mythical monsters has been in a form of stasis since the nineteenth century, now only capable of articulating deep-seated psychological anxieties related to repressed masculine aggression and the havoc it might wreak. A cultural approach presents the best opportunity to construct a comprehensive and cohesive history for the werewolf film and its most frequent thematic preoccupations – one that reveals the monster's unbound potential to confront any number of socio-political issues across a century and more. And to give a clear account of the werewolf as a mutating metaphor for the fears and anxieties of its times it is necessary to begin, of course, at the beginning: the cinematic werewolf's first howl in the dark December of 1913.

CHAPTER 1

Wolves at the Door

The First Wolves

The Werewolf (1913) – the first werewolf film on record at the time of writing – is now sadly lost, destroyed in a 1924 fire at Universal Studios.[1] The *Motion Picture News* reveals that it was a two-reel short produced by Bison Motion Pictures (as 101-Bison) and distributed by Universal, while the *New York Clipper* confirms that it was first released on 13 December 1913.[2] Little has been written about the film in modern academic accounts; Jeremy Dyson asserts that *The Werewolf* was based on Native American mythology, while James B. Twitchell notes that the film's plot can loosely be summarised as 'a Navajo [woman] becomes a timber wolf'.[3] It would seem that the only complete cast listing and comprehensive synopsis is contained in a December 1913 issue of *Universal Weekly*. *The Werewolf* starred Phyllis Gordon as Watuma, Clarence Burton as Ezra Vance, Marie Walcamp as a young Kee-On-Ee, Lule Warrenton as Kee-On-Ee in later years and William Clifford as Jack Ford. *Universal Weekly* introduces the film as one 'dealing with the supposed ability of persons who have been turned into wolves',[4] before describing the plot:

> The play opens in pioneer days. 'Kee-On-Ee['], an Indian maiden is married to Ezra Vance, a trail blazer. When her child is five years old, Kee-On-Ee is driven back to her tribe by Ezra's brother, who scorns all squaws. Ezra is killed by an old enemy and Kee-On-Ee, thinking his failure to return to her to be indifference, brings up her child, Watuma, to hate all white men.
>
> When the child is grown, Clifford and a party of prospectors appear. Kee-On-Ee, now a hag, sees her way to be revenged. She sends her daughter to Clifford's camp and he is driven nigh mad by her beauty. Clifford finds her in the arms of a young Indian. She taunts him. Enraged beyond control, Clifford shoots the buck. He flees to the mission. Watuma leads the enraged Indians against the Friars. When one of them raises a cross, Watuma slowly dissolves into a slinking wolf.
>
> A hundred years later, Clifford, how reincarnated in the form of Jack Ford, a miner, receives a visit from his sweetheart, Margaret. Hunting with her he comes upon a wolf which [he] is unable to shoot. The wolf dissolves into the woman of old, and there appears before his puzzled eyes the scene where he slew the Brave. The

'Wolf-woman' would caress him, but he throws her off. She returns again as the wolf and kills his sweetheart. Clifford's punishment for the deed of past life is made complete at the death of the one he loved.[5]

The Werewolf was followed a year later by another short werewolf film, *The White Wolf* (1914), produced by the Nestor Motion Picture Company and distributed by Universal.[6] Unfortunately, *The White Wolf* is also a lost film. However, just as in the case of *The Werewolf*, contemporaneous accounts of its narrative content are obscure but available. This was another film based on Native American mythology. *Moving Picture World* provides a synopsis:

> Swift Wind, a young chief, loves Dancing Fawn. In their ramblings they, too, see white wolves, which is [sic] an object of fear and veneration among the Indians, and return to the village. The two are betrothed by the old chief, but old Red Nose, the medicine man, demands her hand for himself. The chief, fearing his magic powers, considers. Dancing Fawn runs away to her lover. Swift Wind is taught a secret by an old trapper. 'If a trap is baited with an animal's own hair the iron jaws will never fail to catch it.' The Indian decides how he will overthrow his rival. At his instruction Dancing Fawn cuts off a lock of hair from the sleeping medicine man. With it Swift Wind baits the trap. The next day a wolf is caught and as the Indians approach the trap the beast turns into the medicine man. The hand of the great father has proven his love again and Swift Wind and his sweetheart are reunited.[7]

Clearly, it is impossible to analyse either of these films in great detail. However, their surviving story outlines reveal that they can be aligned in many ways with early twentieth-century American werewolf literature, which Stefan Dziemianowicz argues is largely preoccupied with using the werewolf as a xenophobic metaphor to demonise those alien to the white United States.[8] The notion of transformation from human to animal is well known to be deeply ingrained in Native American folklore, and both *The Werewolf* and *The White Wolf* are somewhat unusual in taking their inspiration from Native American mythology – in which men and women who can transform into wolves are traditionally known as skinwalkers – rather than the European tales that would inspire later werewolf films. But that is not to say that either of these films depicted Native Americans in a positive light. In fact, from the existing descriptions of their narrative content, it would seem that they are part of a larger silent-era tradition of negatively portraying America's indigenous peoples, or otherwise using their customs to create a patronising picture of a strange, uncivilised and foreign culture that would shock and excite white Americans. As Angela Aleiss argues, the birth of narrative cinema coincided with a time of great political conflict between white America and the country's indigenous population: 'Recent federal policies (post 1880s) advocating divestment of Indian land, compulsory boarding schools, and the eradication of Indian tradition and lifestyle were attempts to erase cultural differences between Indians and whites and absorb Native Americans into mainstream American society.'[9]

As Aleiss asserts, this was clearly a time in United States history that saw the white establishment attempt systematically to destroy Native American heritage and convert indigenous people into integrated citizens. *The Werewolf* was designed for consumption by white Americans, an apparent dramatisation of the perceived threat that 'uncivilised' Native American culture was seen to pose to the ongoing development of this integrated society led by a Christian patriarchy. This was a film in which a Native American woman with the power to transform into a wild animal uses her occult abilities to attack white America until her rampage is halted by a man of God, who repels her with a crucifix (which, of course, also identifies Native American tradition with heresy). A promotional image printed in *Universal Weekly* would seem to confirm this subtext; it depicts Watuma surrounded by a group of Christian friars (Figure 1.1). And while *Universal Weekly*'s synopsis talks of punishment for white America's past transgressions against the nation's indigenous people, the final scenes merely seem to confirm that the film's Native American monster still poses a threat even after it has seemingly been destroyed.

The Werewolf, then, arises from a culture that deeply feared Native Americans who would cling to their religions, traditions and customs at a time when wider society would have them destroyed, and uses skinwalkers to depict the Native American as an enemy of white America. As Dziemianowicz states, the film was ostensibly the story of 'a Navajo witch woman who assumes the form of a wolf to attack the white men she has been raised to hate'.[10] In this regard, it has a great deal in common with Henry Beaugrand's short story 'The Werwolves' (1898), in which a group of white soldiers recall an encounter with Native American werewolves who actively hunt and kill Christians. In fact, Stephen Jones claims that *The Werewolf* was actually an adaptation of Beaugrand's tale.[11]

From the surviving accounts of its plot, *The White Wolf* did not contain any direct physical or political confrontation between Native and white Americans; rather the film seems to have been a romantic drama set entirely within an indigenous community with an element of the supernatural. However, it does seem to fall into a wider movement in early Hollywood filmmaking which imagined a nostalgic picture of Native American customs in an attempt to depict indigenous society as an exciting and exotic but ultimately extinct culture. As Aleiss states:

Figure 1.1 A still from the lost film *The Werewolf* (1913), originally published in *Universal Weekly*, in which the she-wolf Watuma (Phyllis Gordon) is confronted by men of God.

By the 1890s, [Native Americans] had been herded onto reservations; they were supposed to be 'tame' and their so-called savage attacks belonged to the past. Filmmakers (and other artists) could now concoct romantic fables of presumably lost culture within their own comfortable worlds of nostalgia. What often fascinated these artists and their audiences was the 'exoticism' of [Native Americans] – their adorned clothing and native rituals – which belonged to a race and culture distinctly different from white America.[12]

The Werewolf was certainly sold in this way, with *Universal Weekly* reporting that 'Weird knowledge, gathered in the open West among the Indians and animal life, have prepared the scenes.'[13] *The White Wolf* seems to have been another example of this mode of silent filmmaking, in which a patronising picture is created of a strange society inhabited by individuals with outlandish names and supernatural abilities. And in addition to its romantic 'exoticism', *The White Wolf* appears to have also echoed *The Werewolf* in projecting a negative image of America's indigenous population. After all, beneath the film's romantic drama, the evidence suggests that *The White Wolf* perceived Native American society as a violent culture in which men are willing to embrace dark magic and transform themselves into feral animals in order to kill a love rival. While there was seemingly no direct threat to white Christian patriarchy explicitly communicated in the film, it clearly depicted Native Americans as 'other' for a mainstream American audience: bizarre, 'savage' and, by extension, inferior.

The earliest surviving werewolf film was released eleven years after *The White Wolf*: the independent American production *Wolfblood* (1925). Whether it is a tale of werewolfery or a fictional account of clinical lycanthropy is up for debate, but *Wolfblood* certainly entertains the idea that its protagonist might be a genuine werewolf. The film concerns an American, Dick Bannister (George Chesebro), the foreman for an isolated logging company working in the Canadian wilderness. When one of his men is shot and seriously wounded by an agent working for business rival Jules Deveroux (Roy Watson), Bannister calls for the owner of the company, Edith Ford (Marguerite Clayton), to leave the city and visit the logging camp. She takes her fiancé, surgeon Dr Eugene Horton (Ray Hanford), with her to treat any men who have been wounded. When Ford arrives in the wilderness, she and Bannister immediately begin to fall in love. The first half plays out as a romantic drama that sees Ford questioning her feelings for Horton and spending a great deal of time with Bannister, while a sub-plot sees Bannister have several verbal and physical altercations with Deveroux and a French-Canadian bootlegger named Jacques Lebeq (Milburn Morante).

After a fist fight between Deveroux and Bannister that sees the latter knocked unconscious, Bannister is dumped deep in the forest, where he sees a pack of wolves in what may or may not be a dream sequence. He is found by Horton, who takes him to a nearby cabin which, unfortunately for Bannister, is owned by Lebeq. There, Horton tries to convince Lebeq to donate blood to the dying Bannister, but he refuses, suggesting that Horton transfuse blood from his tame she-wolf instead. Taken by the possibility of scientific fame, Horton goes ahead with the transfusion, which is a success. Despite being sworn to secrecy by the doctor, Lebeq immediately begins to circulate rumours among the loggers that Bannister has wolf blood in his veins, which leads them – and eventually Bannister himself – to believe that the foreman has become a half-animal monster. The stand-out sequence in the film sees Bannister come to the realisation that he might be a genuine werewolf. When Horton tells him the truth about the transfusion that saved his life, Bannister becomes crazed and believes that he can hear wolves calling to him from deep in the forest. He flees his cabin, and runs into the woods. What follows is a haunting sequence in which Bannister runs with a phantom pack of wolves who almost lead him to fall to his death from a cliff top. By the film's conclusion, some doubt has been introduced as to whether Bannister suffered a psychotic break during this sequence – a bout of clinical lycanthropy caused by the accusations of his colleagues and peers – or whether he is truly able to see spirit wolves in the trees.

Wolfblood thus expresses a fear of the America that exists outside the comforting confines of 'civilised' white society. In a strangely jarring sequence, when Bannister calls for Ford's help in the film's first act, we see the decadent life she lives in the city with Horton before both of them leave the comfort of America for the Canadian wilderness. When Bannister's call comes, Ford is throwing a party in her home attended by wealthy, well-dressed men and women who are happily drinking and dancing; cross-cutting emphasises the isolation of the wilderness in comparison to Ford's lavish life in the city. By leaving her urban life behind and venturing into an unsettled North American territory, then, Ford enters an uncivilised world where men are willing to fight and kill each other as a result of the slightest provocation and a phantom pack of wolves – a clear reference to Native American totems – haunt the woods around her company's logging camp. For *Wolfblood*, the urban is the safe, comfortable habitat of the white, Christian American, while the rural – the wilderness that was the traditional home of North America's indigenous peoples – is home to violence, madness and the occult.

The Feral Peril

Silent werewolf films, then, were designed for white, Christian Americans negotiating the sharing of their country with another culture, one which was (and, in many ways, remains) very different from mainstream American society. But the early werewolf film did not just arise from a culture that feared internal threats to the white majority. *Werewolf of London* (1935) – a Universal production and the first werewolf film after the introduction of sound – is easily interpreted as a xenophobic Western vision of the East in the early decades of the twentieth century, amidst mass immigration from East Asia and the establishment of burgeoning East Asian sub-cultures in European and North American nations.

Werewolf of London concerns a botanist, Dr Wilfred Glendon (Henry Hull), who travels to Tibet to retrieve a rare flower that only blooms under moonlight in a secluded valley. He retrieves his prize, but at a cost: he is attacked by a werewolf, bitten, and cursed to become a monster under the full moon. Returning to his native London, Glendon begins to experiment on the flower when he is approached by Dr Yogami (Warner Oland), an academic of unspecified Asian origin who claims to have met Glendon in Tibet. Yogami tells Glendon that he has been cursed with werewolfism and the only treatment is the rare flower that, thus far, has refused to bloom in Glendon's laboratory setting. Yogami also tells him, ominously, that the werewolf is doomed to kill that which he loves most, leading Glendon to become fearful for the safety of his distant wife, Lisa (Valerie Hobson).

Doubling his efforts, Glendon is either unable to force the plant's buds to bloom or finds that its flower has been stolen just when he needs it to halt his transformation. Without the flower to stop him, he begins to butcher victims in his werewolf form. At the film's climax, Glendon rushes to his laboratory to retrieve the flower and stop the onset of his final metamorphosis, only to catch Yogami in the process of stealing it; it is revealed that he was the werewolf Glendon encountered in Tibet, and it is he who has been taking the blooming flowers, the only thing capable of halting or reversing Glendon's monstrous transformations. Glendon transforms and they fight, leaving Yogami dead. Glendon then leaves the laboratory and enters his home, where he lunges for his wife – to kill that which he loves most – only to be shot dead by police sent from Scotland Yard. Glendon offers thanks for the merciful bullet before dying and reverting to his human form.

Werewolf of London has been given some consideration in cultural contexts. Andrew Tudor has pointed out that the film, which concerns a dedicated botanist endangering his life in the pursuit of scientific discovery, might be interpreted as a warning against the destructive potential of science in the same fashion as Universal's *Frankenstein* (1931), *The Invisible Man* (1933) and *Bride of Frankenstein* (1935).[14] Alternatively, Robert Spadoni has argued that *Werewolf of London* creates 'a portrait of a werewolf as a gay man, to represent homosexuality as a form of gender inversion, and to explore the horrors of being a gay man living in a violently repressive society'.[15] In doing so, Spadoni argues that John Colton – the film's screenwriter and an openly gay man – creates a film that 'with deep ambivalence, makes a plea for locating gay men within [the normal and the human] by construing its main character's condition as a natural variation along a continuum that includes us all'.[16]

However viable or well-argued either of these analyses may be, it still seems that a link has been missed – or, at least, not extensively investigated – between *Werewolf of London* and what has come to be termed the 'yellow peril.' Dziemianowicz observes that the film seems to position werewolfism as 'a foreign menace with a primitive or uncivilised origin'[17] and Darryl Jones acknowledges that there is a link to be found between *Werewolf of London* and 1930s fears of East Asian culture.[18] However, neither writer develops their discussion beyond merely pointing out that these are subtexts to be taken from the film. Similarly, Alison Peirse also chooses to concentrate on drawing out a sexual subtext despite acknowledging that Yogami is 'inscribed as monstrous through racial stereotyping'.[19] But an irrational fear of the perceived terrible, unknowable power of Eastern civilisation pervades the text, and in constructing a cultural account of *Werewolf of London* it is an oversight to ignore the xenophobic anxieties surrounding Asian immigration to the West that were rife at the time of the film's production and consumption.

Gina Marchetti suggests that the origin of the 'yellow peril' might be found in centuries-old, medieval paranoia created by Genghis Khan's invasions of Europe, brought back into the Western consciousness amidst mass East Asian immigration to both Europe and North America following the abolition of the slave trade. This created an early-twentieth-century anxiety that immigrants in such large numbers would 'diminish the earning power of white European immigrants' and ultimately led to 'the belief that the West will be overpowered and enveloped by the irresistible, dark, occult forces of the East'.[20] In cinema and other popular media, this xenophobic paranoia led to the development of villainous East Asian characters that are depicted almost wholly negatively. As recognised by Jenny Clegg, this development in narrative fiction toward an irrational fear of Eastern civilisation is personified in Sax Rohmer's literary villain, the infamous Dr Fu Manchu.[21] An Asian criminal mastermind of vicious intelligence, Fu Manchu was given life in the pages of Rohmer's fiction before finding further success in other media, including a series of motion pictures. The most infamous of these cinematic adaptations is one of *Werewolf of London*'s contemporaries: MGM's *The Mask of Fu Manchu* (1932), starring prolific horror actor Boris Karloff. John Soister has suggested that the character of Charlie Chan – a Chinese detective who debuted as the protagonist of ten-chapter serial *The House Without a Key* (1926) and subsequently appeared in features such as *Behind that Curtain* (1929) and *Charlie Chan Carries On* (1931) amongst many others – represents a less malicious incarnation of the 'yellow peril' in cinema.[22]

It is especially surprising that there is only brief commentary to be found on how *Werewolf of London* might be interpreted as a film symptomatic of the 'yellow peril' considering that not only does the film explicitly play on fears of the East to incite its horror, but also co-stars Warner Oland as the film's antagonist. Oland was Swedish by birth, but by 1935 had become well known for his 'yellowface' performances. He had previously appeared in *Shanghai Express* (1932) as Henry Chang, a mysterious Eurasian who is later revealed to be a powerful criminal mastermind and the film's chief villain. Amongst many other Asian characters, he had also been cast as Fu Manchu – in *The Mysterious Dr Fu Manchu* (1929), *The Return of Dr Fu Manchu* (1930) and *Daughter of the Dragon* (1931) – and Charlie Chan before portraying Dr Yogami. Oland was extremely popular in the Charlie Chan role, and is perhaps best remembered today for his portrayals of the character. He starred in six Chan films before he appeared in *Werewolf of London*, and another nine before his death in 1938. Oland, then, had built a career on playing East Asian characters; his success with audiences in the roles of Fu Manchu and Charlie Chan undoubtedly factored into the decision to cast him as *Werewolf of London*'s antagonist.

Werewolf of London opens in Tibet, as Glendon consults with a group of indigenous villagers he hopes will be able to help him find the secluded valley in which the flower he seeks can be found. Some of these supposed 'native' Tibetans are portrayed by white actors in 'yellowface' make-up, although there are a few characters here that are authentically portrayed by East Asian actors. However, their representation betrays underlying xenophobia: the costumes these characters wear are more reminiscent of Genghis Khan's Mongols than Tibetans of the 1930s. Furthermore, they are depicted as an uncivilised and superstitious people; they live in tattered tents and express an irrational fear of a nearby valley that they believe to be occupied by demons.

Ultimately these characters serve no purpose to the wider narrative other than to create a sense of foreboding and to suggest that Eastern culture is inextricable from superstition and the occult. Glendon approaches them for help, but they run in fear from what they believe to be a demon – in fact, a white man who, to further undermine the competence of the locals, provides Glendon with the information and guidance he needs where the Tibetans have failed. The representation of East Asians in this opening sequence seems to typify Marchetti's claim that, in films informed by the 'yellow peril' and interpreted in that context, East Asians are depicted as 'intellectually inferior . . . uncivilised, infantile, and in the need of guidance of White, Anglo-Saxon Protestants'.[23] To further the misunderstanding of East Asian cultures that clearly informed the film's production, the 'Tibetans' in this scene are actually speaking Cantonese, while Henry Hull's replies to them are nonsensical gibberish intended to sound vaguely like an East Asian language.

This opening scene establishes a xenophobic subtext that continues to develop throughout the film: the apparently dangerous nature of immigration from East to West. Glendon enters the valley that the locals fear so intensely, and despite being beleaguered by a supernatural power that impairs his movement, finds the plant he has been searching for. But his discovery comes at a cost: just as he is about to take a sample, he is attacked by a vicious werewolf. During a scuffle with his attacker, Glendon is bitten on the arm. Undeterred, he fights off the werewolf and retrieves his prize. However, Glendon is unaware at this point that he will return to his native Britain a monster, carrying an incurable disease that he is now able to transmit to others. As Yogami warns Glendon, he is infectious, and could cause an 'epidemic that will turn London into a shambles'.

Marchetti's suggestion that the 'yellow peril' contributed to a popular assumption amongst Westerners that 'nonwhite people are . . . disease-ridden, feral, violent'[24] is literalised in Glendon's transformation; in travelling outside of 'civilised' society, Glendon opens himself up to infection by these apparently Eastern characteristics. He returns home cursed to werewolfism: a disease that slowly begins to transform him into a murderous beast and an affliction that the film suggests is wholly of Asian origin. In short, *Werewolf of London*'s deeply problematic conceit is that an 'uncivilised' Eastern disease is brought back into the 'civilised' Western world, where it will shortly threaten to wreak havoc.

At least one contemporary critic recognised that werewolfism functions as a metaphor for a volatile infection in *Werewolf of London*: *Variety*'s review describes Glendon's werewolfery as a 'sickness' and suggests that he spends much of the narrative 'fighting against the awful disease'; the author even goes so far as to coin the term 'werewolfitis' to describe Glendon's ailment.[25] When Glendon returns home infected, a party is thrown for him in the botanical gardens surrounding his estate. One plant on display is carnivorous and is given a frog to digest, much to the disgust of the guests. One particularly sensitive party-goer remarks: 'Fancy bringing a thing like that into Christian England!' This line of dialogue, of course, not only refers to the plant but also to Glendon's newfound affliction. Here, the werewolf's curse is used to embody a literal depiction of the 'yellow peril': the apparently dark, occult power of the East slowly infiltrating and overpowering the West in the form of an infectious disease brought to London by an upstanding citizen who is punished for daring to venture too far from home.

Figure 1.2 The villainous Dr Yogami, as portrayed by Warner Oland in *Werewolf of London* (1935), functions as a xenophobic embodiment of the 'yellow peril'.

The most obvious articulation of the 'yellow peril' in *Werewolf of London*, though, is the character of Dr Yogami (Figure 1.2). Before coming to analyse Yogami's role in the narrative, it is worth observing that the casting of the Swedish Oland to portray an Asian character in this or any other film could be, and has been, interpreted as intrinsically xenophobic. Karla Rae Fuller asserts that there is inherent racism in the 'assumption that the Caucasian face provides the physically normative standard onto which a racial inscription can take place'.[26] And an interesting element of Yogami's character is his distinct lack of national identity or specific country of origin. His name would suggest that the character is Japanese, while he claims to have met Glendon for the first time in Tibet. To confuse matters further, he tells other characters that he is currently employed by the University of Carpathia.

Ultimately, his nationality is never specifically confirmed, and some of the guess-work carried out by contemporary critics in their reviews does a great deal to reveal the film's xenophobic horror. As both Spadoni and Peirse have observed, racially charged language choices made by critics revealed their limited understanding, and even fear, of Eastern civilisation.[27] The review that perhaps most accurately articulates how contemporary audiences may have responded to Yogami appeared in the *Motion Picture Herald*, in which

Oland's character is simply referred to as a 'strange Oriental'.[28] The racism suggested by such a phrase is echoed in the film by the character of Lisa's Aunt Ettie, who repeatedly mispronounces Yogami's name as 'Yokohama' and describes him upon her first meeting with him as an 'interesting-looking' man. Yogami's country of origin and national identity are, I suspect, purpose-fully unspecified. This is a character designed to embody contemporary fears of the East, a perceived evil infinitely more terrifying if its origin is withheld.

However, Yogami's true nature is obscured for much of the film's dura-tion. Initially, he seems to be a benevolent character and, aside from his in-depth knowledge of the occult, does not conform to any negative racial stereotype. Rather he is depicted as well-educated and knowledgeable. He seems to be an altogether helpful presence, determined to aid Glendon in overcoming his curse by making him aware that a treatment is available in the form of the rare flower he risked his life to retrieve: not a cure, but a remedy that can be used to halt transformation. Only keen-eared viewers may have realised that Yogami is not what he seems when he tells Glendon they have previously met in Tibet, following this revelation with a rather cryptic statement: 'it was dark'.

However, it is only as the film progresses that Yogami's depiction begins to take a truly sinister turn when Glendon catches Yogami stealing a freshly blooming flower at the film's climax. Suddenly, all is revealed: not only is Yogami a werewolf, but the same werewolf who bit Glendon, spreading his infection to the film's white protagonist (and later taking away his only hope of salvation). It is in this moment that Yogami con-forms to the early-twentieth-century perception that East Asians were to be treated as 'morally suspect'.[29] In *Werewolf of London*, then, Oland embodies Charlie Chan and Fu Manchu in a single character: at first a seemingly benevolent Asian stereotype who wants nothing more than to aid the film's white, Christian protagonist before he is finally revealed to be a vastly intelligent, calculating criminal with malicious intent.

While the primary effect of this narrative twist is that Yogami is vilified, the secondary effect is that Glendon is exonerated. Following his return to Britain, Glendon stalks the streets of London and kills innocents in his werewolf form. However, in the revelation that Yogami passed his curse on to an upstanding Western citizen, Glendon is rendered an unwitting victim while Yogami is demonised and revealed to be the source of the narrative's horror. All of the film's horrifying acts – physical monstrosity, the threat of epidemic and cold-blooded murder – can be traced back to Yogami's actions and, by association, the East.

Furthermore, while Yogami dies a villain's death at the hands of the film's protagonist, Glendon is ultimately saved by his unwavering commitment to

God. The presence of Christian values within the film is certainly not limited to a disgusted party-goer lamenting the introduction of carnivorous plant life into the white, Christian West; Glendon himself is a staunch Christian, at one point uttering a prayer immediately before a transformation takes place. Having taken refuge at an inn, Glendon seeks divine intervention and pleads: 'Father in Heaven, don't let this happen to me again. If it must happen, keep me here. Keep me away from Lisa. Keep me away from the thing I love.' As the final word leaves his mouth, Glendon begins to go through a metamorphosis by moonlight before crashing from the window of his room and onto the streets below. His prayers go unanswered and shortly afterwards he is seen stalking and killing a young woman at the London Zoo.

Glendon's faith is clearly not shaken by his unanswered prayers. At the film's climax, he succumbs to a final transformation and attacks his wife. After having been shot by officers from Scotland Yard, Glendon lies dying and, with his last words, says: 'Thanks for the bullet. It was the only way. In a few moments now I shall know why all of this had to be.' Glendon clearly still believes that he will be given the chance to meet his maker, a notion confirmed by the film's ending. After Glendon has died and reverted to his human form, the three shots that follow are of skies laden with clouds, the sun beaming through them. To the film's target audience (the white, Christian American), this would certainly have been a clear visual cue that Glendon has made his ascent to Heaven. To reinforce this, immediately before these final moments, Sir Thomas Forsyth of Scotland Yard (Lawrence Grant) – whose fatal bullet puts an end to the werewolf's rampage – tells Glendon's spouse: 'In my report I shall say that I shot him by accident while he was trying to protect his wife.' It seems Glendon's unwavering commitment to Christianity has exonerated him in the eyes of the law. It will be recorded that Glendon died honourably to protect others, presumably from the alien Yogami.

Why, then, do Glendon's prayers go unanswered earlier in the film? It would seem that his werewolfism is a form of divine punishment, retribution for daring to leave Western civilisation and allowing himself to be exposed to the perceived occult power of the East. It is clear that there is a supernatural power present in the valley from which Glendon retrieves his rare and mystical flower; on the trail leading into it, he and his travelling partner are beset by unseen forces that strike them, bind their limbs and slow their movement. Glendon's travelling partner cries: 'I can't move! Something's holding my feet!' Glendon dismisses it as autosuggestion until he too is attacked. Pushed back against a rock, he remarks: 'Something struck me.' Both men experience physical contact from beings that are not visible to human eyes, giving credence to the claims of the indigenous population who say, in Glendon's words: 'the valley we want to visit is filled with demons.' It would seem that here, just as in so much earlier werewolf fiction, the werewolf's curse is Satan's doing. In *Werewolf of London*, however, the Devil and the occult are associated with the East, while God and Christian values are associated with the West. After Glendon is corrupted by the Devil's influence in Tibet and brings it back to the Western world, he can only be saved in death, when he is received into Heaven: 'It was the only way.'

An interesting consideration in this cultural interpretation of *Werewolf of London* is the life and work of screenwriter John Colton, but not necessarily in regard to his sexuality. Colton was born in 1887 in Minneapolis, Minnesota. However, he spent the formative years of his life living with his father, an English diplomat serving in Imperial Japan. Having grown up away from the West, he returned to America in his teens before building a career as a playwright in later life.[30] He specialised in plays that drew on his real-life experiences, often concerning Americans living in far-off lands. A brief survey of Colton's work would suggest that his lasting memory of East Asia was not a positive one. His first Broadway play, *Drifting* (1922), follows the daughter of a Methodist deacon who travels to China to break free of her father's influence. She is coerced into prostitution in Shanghai, and escapes only with the help of a discharged American soldier.

One of Colton's more infamous works is *The Shanghai Gesture* (1918). The play concerns the happenings in and around a brothel in Shanghai managed by the luridly named Madame God Damn: an establishment frequented by diplomats, ambassadors and aristocrats of both Western and Eastern origin. The play expresses a negative view of interracial relationships, depicting them as enormously dysfunctional: a Japanese diplomat is paired with a white, self-confessed nymphomaniac, alcoholic and drug addict in an inevitably doomed union. The play also paints a vicious picture of Chinese culture; at one point in the narrative a vulnerable young woman is auctioned off to an assembly of 'six ferocious, half-naked, pirate-like junkmen'.[31] The play was not well received even in its day; as Amnon Kabatchnik notes, 'Most critics snubbed the play as crude and morally objectionable.'[32] *The Shanghai Gesture* was later adapted into a 1941 film of the same name and directed by Josef von Sternberg, a filmmaker strongly associated with exoticism and who had previously directed Oland in *Shanghai Express*.

Colton's work in Hollywood continued to express negative racial attitudes. Such sentiments are especially evident in *Wild Orchids* (1929), another 'yellow peril' text. A Greta Garbo vehicle, *Wild Orchids* sees a morally corrupt Javanese prince welcome a white couple into his home, only to attempt to seduce Garbo's character away from her Western husband. In

Colton's work, then, the East is often depicted as corrupt and uncivilised, while antagonists are usually of 'foreign' origin; sometimes they may initially appear benevolent, only later to reveal their true nature.

While *Werewolf of London* is a landmark in werewolf cinema – the first feature-length werewolf film since the advent of sound technology – it is also clearly representative of Colton's oeuvre, made up of unashamedly Orientalist texts that derive their drama and horror from negative views of East Asian culture. This is an essential consideration in any cultural interpretation of *Werewolf of London*, and perhaps Colton's sexuality is not as important to understanding this film as is his early life spent in Imperial Japan. Colton's pervading Orientalism and the 'yellow peril' context of *Werewolf of London*'s consumption come together in the film to create an acutely xenophobic subtext in which the werewolf, feral, uncivilised and malicious, becomes a literal manifestation of the perceived dark powers of the East. And, of course, this is why the film's white, Christian protagonist can only find ultimate salvation and forgiveness by affirming his commitment to Christian beliefs and Western ideals.

The Monster Mash

Werewolf of London was not a successful picture at the box office. As Spadoni notes, the film opened within days of Tod Browning's *Mark of the Vampire* (1935) and James Whale's *Bride of Frankenstein*, starring Bela Lugosi and Boris Karloff respectively.[33] The timing of the film's release undoubtedly limited its potential; *Werewolf of London*'s Henry Hull was unlikely to be able to compete with the box-office draw of Lugosi and Karloff, also respective stars of the enormously popular *Dracula* (1931) and *Frankenstein*. Its failure would mean that the werewolf would remain absent from horror cinema for the following six years. The next attempt to produce a werewolf film would once again arise from Universal Pictures: *The Wolf Man* (1941). *The Wolf Man* would prove wildly popular, spawning four sequels – including the horror-comedy *Abbott and Costello Meet Frankenstein* (1948) – and many imitators, including *The Undying Monster* (1942), *The Mad Monster* (1942), *Cry of the Werewolf* (1944) and, perhaps most famously, RKO Radio Pictures' *Cat People* (1942).

Xenophobia is a theme that remains identifiable in a number of these films, but their focus began to shift with the beginning of the Second World War in Europe and particularly after America's entrance into the global conflict in 1941. Of course, anxieties arising from internal racial politics were dwarfed by the horrors of war; all American men of appropriate age – regardless of their racial origins or immigrant status – were united in their conscription to fight the country's aggressors. As Colin Shindler notes, 'For America, one of the biggest single problems of the war was the fusion of its ethnic minorities into a cohesive disciplined united fighting force.'[34] This meant, of course, that vilifying the country's own minorities in popular culture quickly became counterproductive, likely to drive America's people – and its armed forces – further apart at a time when they needed to be unified. However, the werewolf film did continue to express a fear of foreign aggressors, though it was now aimed squarely at antagonists of Germanic, Eastern European or, as many of the films would have it, 'gypsy' descent. In Universal's horror films, these antagonists generally occupy fictional European nations far from American shores.

Despite the prolific nature of werewolf films during the 1940s, Universal's remain the most enduring examples of the decade. The series comprises five films which feature the Wolf Man as chief protagonist: *The Wolf Man*, *Frankenstein Meets the Wolf Man* (1943), *House of Frankenstein* (1944), *House of Dracula* (1945) and *Abbott and Costello Meet Frankenstein*. The series descended into self-conscious parody in the final film, but the four straight horror films before it form a continuous narrative in which an American afflicted with werewolfism is doomed to be perpetually resurrected and continue an ongoing battle against monsters of European origin.

All five of these films star Lon Chaney Jr as Lawrence 'Larry' Talbot, the son of a wealthy British family who has spent his formative years in America before his return to the family home in Llanwelly, Wales, during the opening scenes of the first film. *The Wolf Man* later sees Talbot attacked by Bela – a Romani werewolf played, of course, by Bela Lugosi – after a trip to the elderly fortune teller Maleva (Maria Ouspenskaya), both of whom have arrived in Talbot's home town with a travelling carnival. Talbot spends the majority of *The Wolf Man* trying to understand and control his condition before he is bludgeoned to death with his own silver-topped cane – the handle sculpted into a wolf's head – by his aristocratic father, Sir John Talbot (Claude Rains). In *Frankenstein Meets the Wolf Man*, Talbot is accidentally revived by grave robbers and awakens to a world in which his family and friends have either died or moved on without him, and is forced to come to terms with the fact that he is immortal; even if killed, he can be brought back to life with ease. After he kills more innocents as the Wolf Man, Talbot flees Wales and travels to Europe in search of Dr Ludwig Frankenstein, hoping that the doctor will be able to end his life once and for all. Instead Talbot finds Frankenstein's monster and is forced to continue his search for absolution in the *House* films.

David J. Skal has suggested that 'Talbot's four-film quest to put to rest his wolf-self is, in a strange way, an unconscious parable of the war effort' and summarises the series of films as: 'The Wolf Man's crusade for eternal peace and his frustrated attempts to control irrational, violent, European forces'.[35] Melvin E. Matthews Jr echoes Skal's sentiments, suggesting that 'In many ways, the character was the perfect monster for World War II.'[36] Though neither Skal nor Matthews Jr provides detailed analyses of all four films, it is not difficult to evidence their arguments. Throughout *The Wolf Man* and the 'monster carnival' films the character would appear in thereafter, Talbot is depicted as an American trapped in a dangerous and volatile fictional Europe. As Skal suggests:

> *The Wolf Man*, released in 1941, was yet another Hollywood nightmare of a geographically indeterminate 'Europe' anxiously blurring together elements of America, England, and the Continent, rather as the Great War had done literally, and the new war was in the process of doing all over again. The Europe of American horror movies was a nearly surreal pastiche of accents, architecture and costumes, like the scrambled impressions of a soldier/tourist on a whirlwind tour of duty.[37]

This is a time in American history when home-front solidarity with military personnel stationed overseas is difficult to overestimate. *The Wolf Man* was released only days after the US declared war on the Axis, just as America's fathers, brothers and sons were entering the war in the Pacific Theatre. In *Frankenstein Meets the Wolf Man*, Talbot leaves Wales and travels to 'a monster-haunted Germanic never-neverland called Visaria' in search of Frankenstein.[38] By the time the sequel was released, the American military had mobilised in Europe, their displacement on battlefields far from home paralleling Talbot's disorientating journey into the fictional Visaria. In fact, the stops on Talbot's quest for redemption – from America to Britain and finally a Germanic nation – parallel that of an American soldier's tour of duty, becoming increasingly dangerous as he travels further away from his safe, adopted home in America until he finds himself in mainland Europe. Where in reality the Allies of the Second World War faced an expanse occupied by the Axis powers, Talbot stands against a continent populated by Universal Pictures' catalogue of monsters, including the Hunchback, Frankenstein's monster, Dracula and a host of mad scientists with nefarious intentions.

Three of the Wolf Man films discussed here are works, in part, by writer Curt Siodmak, who wrote the screenplays for *The Wolf Man* and *Frankenstein Meets the Wolf Man*, as well as receiving a story credit for *House of Frankenstein*. Years earlier, Siodmak himself had embarked on a journey remarkably similar to the fictional one he created for Larry Talbot, although his had been in the opposite direction. Siodmak was escaping Europe and travelling towards Hollywood, with several stops on the Continent in between.

By birth, Siodmak was a Jewish German citizen, who had made a promising career for himself writing both screenplays and prose fiction before the rise of the Nazi Party. In 1933, his career came to a premature end as the new Nazi government sought to put an end to the circulation of writing by Jewish authors. Siodmak recalls: 'I received a letter from the National Socialist Chamber of German Writers informing me that I was not going to be permitted to write for any German publisher or motion picture company.' Of course, it was not just Siodmak's career that was in danger, but his life. Remembering 1933, Siodmak remarks: 'When I think back, I wonder how I and my wife survived that time. It is so long ago! But still, it is a nightmare to me.'[39] Sensing the danger they were in, Siodmak and his brother Robert – who would later become a successful director of film noir – fled Germany. As Dennis Fischer notes, 'They gave up their house and cars as a bribe to cross the border, passing through Switzerland, France and England.'[40] Curt Siodmak stayed in Britain for some years and began to carve out a career for himself before moving to America in 1937. Even Siodmak's move to the United States was influenced by a fear of the Nazis catching up to him; he recalls that it was his wife who persuaded him to move to Hollywood, adding: 'I guess she felt the war coming.'[41]

In some respects, then, the Wolf Man saga could be interpreted as Siodmak's immensely personal nightmare, a series of films in which an American citizen is forced to journey into a world the writer himself had left in order to escape financial destitution, persecution and even death. By Siodmak's own admission, he found a life in the United States he could not have dreamed of in Europe: 'I got a job the first week I arrived in Hollywood . . . I rented a house . . . bought a Buick convertible, the usual stuff of Hollywood success.'[42] But he never forgot what he had left behind; the memories of his time in Nazi Germany – and later, the knowledge of what had happened to those who remained there after he left – weighed heavily on his mind: 'We refugees suffer from the past, the Hitler persecution, which we will never be able to absorb completely. We were often so close to death that we are branded for life.'[43] In his screenplays for *The Wolf Man*, *Frankenstein Meets the Wolf Man* and his story treatment for *House of Frankenstein*, Siodmak has his protagonist retrace the writer's steps, from America, to Britain and finally Germanic Europe. These films, then, could convincingly be read as Siodmak's dramatisation of his own fear of going back to Nazi Germany. In this respect, Siodmak clearly empathised with the Allied forces, and particularly with the American military: these were men forced to leave the comfort of Siodmak's newfound home to fight the terror that he had narrowly escaped.

Skal identifies a direct link between the werewolf and the Nazi Party by noting Adolf Hitler's personal fascination with wolves. He continues:

> The wolf is an ancient symbol, deeply linked to militarism and the battlefield, with special meanings in Norse and Teutonic mythology. The ancient warriors called berserkers were said to wear skins of wolves and other animals to increase their ferocity.[44]

This may go some way towards evidencing that *The Wolf Man* is a text intrinsically linked to the horrors of war, and Siodmak had certainly unearthed the connection between militarism and the wolf in his research for the screenplay. He recalls that he discovered that as far back as the Stone Age, 'People wanted to become as strong as the strongest animal they knew of, which was the wolf in Europe.'[45] However, it is doubtful that either Hitler's love of the lupine or the militaristic connotations of the wolf would have been immediately apparent in America.

What would have been at the forefront of the public consciousness, however, was war itself: *The Wolf Man* was released to American cinemas on 12 December 1941. Five days earlier, over 2,000 American citizens had been killed in the attack on Pearl Harbor, a surprise military strike by the Imperial Japanese intended to cripple the US Pacific Fleet. On 8 December, the USA had officially declared war on the Empire of Japan, followed by declarations of war on Germany and Italy on 11 December. Universal's second feature-length werewolf picture began its run at the box office at the end of a momentous week in American history which saw the end of non-interventionist politics and the country's entrance into a global conflict.

The Wolf Man was to be inevitably and unavoidably viewed by domestic audiences in the context of war. American society was profoundly shocked and fearful as a result of the Japanese assault and news of the attack on Pearl Harbor spread within days, causing hysteria in some communities. As Sylvia Whitman notes:

> News of the attack spread quickly, missing only the most remote rural areas, and then for only a day or so. All over the nation, Americans looked to the sky, listening for the drone of enemy airplanes . . . Many cities rigged searchlights and guns on rooftops. Fear gripped the West Coast, the most likely place for a Japanese invasion of the mainland. In Los Angeles, sirens wailed. Antiaircraft gunners fired at random, injuring several people. In downtown San Francisco, crowds tried to enforce a blackout by stoning and smashing movie marquees and streetcar lights.[46]

Even in the cinema, a place commonly associated with fantasy then as now, audiences were confronted with the news of an attack on American soil and imminent war in the form of newsreels, ensuring that their minds would be fixed on these catastrophic global events even before viewing seemingly fantastical genre pictures such as *The Wolf Man*. War was inescapably at the forefront of the media and, in this context, the Eastern European 'gypsies' who arrive in Talbot's idyllic Welsh village become an aggressive invading force. Much like the ill-fated Dr Wilfred Glendon in *Werewolf of London*, they arrive in the Western world and bring violence and the occult with them from foreign lands. After all, Talbot's unwitting induction into an occult world of violence, panic and death following Bela's unprovoked attack parallels America's own entry into the Second World War; until an unannounced act of aggression cost thousands of American lives, the United States had been pursuing a neutral stance. The attack on Pearl Harbor was a profoundly shocking event that brought seemingly distant violence and bloodshed onto home soil.

Following Talbot's infection, *The Wolf Man* is concerned with the protagonist coming to terms with his monstrous condition for the remainder of the film until his death at the hands of his father. As Dziemianowicz notes:

> [*The Wolf Man*] captured the essence of the werewolf's turmoil as the reluctant victim. Talbot experiences no joy in his transformation, which has the look of physical torture. In a scene where his family is attending mass and he finds himself curiously unable to enter the church, there is a sense of deeply conflicted emotions, and inexplicable impulses boiling inside of him. The true horror he feels is the slow and ineluctable revelation that he is the killer in many unsolved crimes that he becomes aware of.[47]

Talbot's pain and enormous sense of guilt have traditionally inspired pyschoanalytic readings. For example, Chantal Bourgault du Coudray interprets his anguish as 'the consequences of failure to "discipline" the "beast within" for male power and identity'.[48] However, in its sociohistorical context, this element of the film's narrative can produce several more specific cultural meanings from the perspective of both creator and consumer.

Before his death in 2000, Siodmak was very open about his experiences in Nazi Germany and how they might have, consciously or unconsciously, influenced his nightmarish work. The writer states that there were 'terrors in my life which might have found an outlet in writing horror stories'.[49] Shortly before his death, Siodmak commented on the connections between the war and *The Wolf Man*, asserting, 'When the moon comes up, the man doesn't want to murder, but he knows he cannot escape it, the Wolf Man destiny.'[50] For Siodmak, then, Talbot personified the changes that occurred in Germany following the rise of the

Nazi Party, and the violence and intolerance they brought with them: his human side the Germany that once was, his bestial incarnation a metaphor for the nation under Nazism. The curse of the werewolf, then, is Siodmak's dramatisation of the transformation of Germany from a republic into a fascist dictatorship. As Matthews Jr notes, in *The Wolf Man* and its sequels, werewolfism could convincingly be read as a metaphor for 'Nazi brutality'.[51]

However, this is an interpretation of the text that is unlikely to have resonated with American audiences. The domestic experience of the Second World War before 1941 had largely consisted of an ongoing debate in Congress between interventionist and non-interventionist camps, which continued until the attack on Pearl Harbor just days before *The Wolf Man*'s release. The American experience thereafter was dominated by the military-controlled war reporting of domestic media over the next four years, which saw the releases of *Frankenstein Meets the Wolf Man* and the *House* films. For America, these films tell the tale of one man defeating European forces that he fights 'so long and hard to vanquish'.[52]

In a domestic context, then, Talbot's situation is more accurately interpreted as analogous to an American soldier's experience of the war, strikingly similar to the plight of men uprooted from their daily lives in a stable society and called upon to fight, in many cases with no previous experience of active warfare. The root cause of Talbot's turmoil is that he is an unwitting and reluctant murderer in his werewolf form. Like Talbot, these ordinary American men were forced to confront a frightening and violent new reality as the United States went to war. As Skal suggests, 'The bestial realities of war came as a shock to untold numbers of servicemen.'[53] However, regardless of whether the Wolf Man's curse is read as a metaphor for the rise of Nazism or the American experience of war, both interpretations are supported by the fictional folkloric poem originally written by Siodmak and recited many times throughout the Wolf Man saga:

> Even a man who is pure in heart
> And says his prayers by night
> May become a wolf when the wolfbane blooms
> And the autumn moon is bright.

The wording of this poem remained constant in *Frankenstein Meets the Wolf Man* and the *House* films, with one minor change. To reflect the development of the notion that Talbot's transformations coincide with the full moon, Siodmak altered the final line to read: 'And the Moon is full and bright.' As is clear without a great deal of analysis, the poem muses that even those 'pure in heart' – essentially 'good' people, as far as such a base judgement of morality can be applied to any person – can commit violent, ethically questionable or 'evil' acts in extraordinary circumstances. Clearly, this is a theme which is equally applicable to the slow transformation of the German people into a fascist society under Nazism as it is to the sudden induction of America's servicemen into a violent and bloody conflict.

While the metaphorical meaning of Talbot's monstrous transformation remains up for debate, he is unwaveringly depicted as being morally upstanding, or 'pure in heart', in his human form, especially in comparison to his European and often Germanic antagonists. Throughout the three sequels to *The Wolf Man*, Talbot comes into contact with several monsters in his search for two things: either a cure for his werewolfery or the eternal peace of death. Regardless of their previous appearances in Universal's horror films, all of Talbot's antagonists are depicted as utterly evil and irredeemable villains, invariably of European origin. For example, the sympathetic monster of *Frankenstein* and *Bride of Frankenstein* as portrayed by Boris Karloff is nowhere to be found in these films. In *Frankenstein Meets the Wolf Man* – in which the monster is one of the chief antagonists – the creature is played by Bela Lugosi before the role passed to Glenn Strange for the *House* pictures. In these three films, the monster is a silent, mindless and hostile creature continually revived by power-hungry scientists: a force that leaves nothing but destruction in its wake.

As Matthews Jr attests, Siodmak had originally written sympathetic dialogue for the creature's appearance in *Frankenstein Meets the Wolf Man*, which was shot but removed by Universal as the studio thought it ridiculous that the monster would speak in Lugosi's Hungarian accent.[54] Regardless of Universal's reasons for cutting Siodmak's dialogue, the monster's silence only adds to its unsympathetic portrayal and, in light of changing times, the sorrowful creature of the 1930s is erased. During wartime, Talbot and his battle with werewolfism become more pertinent to the zeitgeist than the tragic story of Frankenstein's monster. Other than rage, the only emotion the monster shows throughout these three films is lust, and then only once. At the climax of *Frankenstein Meets the Wolf Man*, the monster is restored to full power by the misguided Dr Mannering (Patric Knowles). It aggressively attacks the Wolf Man before picking up the unconscious Baroness Elsa Frankenstein (Ilona Massey) – daughter of the late Dr Ludwig Frankenstein – and attempting to carry her away before Talbot intervenes, illustrating his heroism and virtue (Figure 1.3). Here, then, the creature is reduced from Mary Shelley's sympathetic figure to something truly monstrous: a destructive European hulk, little more than an obstacle on Talbot's path to redemption.

Figure 1.3 The Wolf Man (Lon Chaney Jr) shows his heroism as he prepares to do battle with Frankenstein's creature at the climax of *Frankenstein Meets the Wolf Man* (1943).

After serving as an antagonist in *Frankenstein Meets the Wolf Man*, Frankenstein's monster remains dormant for the majority of the *House* pictures and is revived only in the films' final acts to wreak mindless havoc. In *House of Frankenstein*, the Wolf Man's European rival takes another form: Daniel (J. Carrol Naish) – referred to in the film's marketing material as 'Hunchback' – the physically deformed assistant to disgraced Germanic scientist Dr Gustav Niemann (Boris Karloff). Following their escape from prison and a brief entanglement with Dracula (John Carradine), Niemann and Daniel arrive at Castle Frankenstein in Visaria, discovering the frozen bodies of Frankenstein's monster and Larry Talbot, which have been encased in ice since the flooding of the castle at the climax of *Frankenstein Meets the Wolf Man*. Niemann thaws them out and makes many promises: firstly, to give Daniel a new, beautiful body and secondly to find a cure for Talbot's werewolfery. However, in truth he is more concerned with reviving Frankenstein's monster so that he might use the creature as a weapon against those who have wronged him.

Meanwhile, Daniel and Talbot have become involved in a love triangle with a Romani woman named Ilonka (Elena Verdugo). Daniel is hateful and envious of Talbot, with whom Ilonka has clearly begun to fall in love. Daniel even attempts to dissuade Ilonka from pursuing Talbot by telling her about his werewolfism, which only cements her commitment to him. Talbot and Daniel are actually very similar in some senses – both are labelled 'monsters' in the film's marketing, and both are motivated by seeking a cure for their particular afflictions – but the American Talbot continues to be depicted as a sympathetic hero, while the Germanic Daniel is shown to be a spiteful, scheming coward with no redeeming qualities. This is also reflected in their on-screen deaths: Daniel is unceremoniously thrown from a window by Frankenstein's monster, while Talbot is shot with a silver bullet by Ilonka in a tragic act of love.

The contrast between Talbot and Universal's other monsters continues in *House of Dracula*, in which Talbot's self-sacrificing humanity is juxtaposed with perhaps the quintessential embodiment of occult European evil: Count Dracula. This was the first Wolf Man film for which Siodmak was not credited as a writer, but Edward T. Lowe's script borrows so heavily from Siodmak's contributions to the series that his influence is palpable. It is revealed in the first act that Talbot survived Ilonka's silver bullet, thus denied the peace of death yet again. He arrives in Visaria at the cliff-top castle of Dr Franz Edelmann (Onslow Stevens) – yet another Germanic scientist with an interest in supernatural beings – only to find that Dracula (John Carradine) is already there, using a pseudonym to conceal his identity. Talbot and Dracula have sought out Edelmann for ostensibly the same reason: just as Talbot wishes to be free of the Wolf Man, Dracula is supposedly seeking a cure for his vampirism.

However, while Talbot truly wishes to be cured, Dracula is wholly insincere. Ignoring the warnings of his two female assistants, Mazilia (Martha O'Driscoll) and the hunchbacked Nina (Jane Adams), Edelmann attempts to cure the count by transfusing his own blood into Dracula's body. During the procedure, Dracula hypnotises Edelmann before reversing the flow of blood between himself and the doctor, triggering the slow transformation of Edelmann into a vampiric creature. Before his final metamorphosis, Edelmann kills Dracula and finally cures Talbot once and for all. Just as in *House of Frankenstein*, *House of Dracula* initially draws comparisons between its primary monsters – the Wolf Man and Dracula – only eventually to reveal how different they truly are. Both arrive on Edelmann's doorstep to beg for his help in shedding their curses, but Dracula proves incapable of redemption; while staying in Edelmann's home, he finds Mazilia impossible to resist, wanting desperately to seduce and feed on her. Dracula ultimately proves he is irredeemably evil by turning the doctor's well-meaning experiment against him, fulfilling his urge to see his vampiric curse passed on rather than allowing it to be destroyed.

As has undoubtedly become clear in discussing *Frankenstein Meets the Wolf Man* and the *House* films, present in all three of these narratives is a 'mad scientist' who, regardless of his initial intentions, becomes the chief antagonist by each film's climax. In *Frankenstein Meets the Wolf Man*, this scientist takes the form of the British Dr Mannering, who treats Talbot in a Cardiff hospital following his resurrection. When Talbot flees for Europe, Mannering follows and finds Ludwig Frankenstein's notes in addition to his weakened monster. Mannering quickly loses sight of his logic and morals, becoming obsessed with restoring the creature to full strength. On the next full moon, he misguidedly follows Frankenstein's instructions to unleash the monster's potential; Talbot is transformed just as the procedure is complete. The Wolf Man and the monster fight, but both are consumed by a flood after the townspeople blow up the dam that sits above Castle Frankenstein.

Edelmann is a similar figure; initially he wants nothing more than to help Dracula and the Wolf Man to shed their curses, even if he is motivated by scientific curiosity more than anything else. However, in pursuing his scientific ambitions and conducting strange and unethical experiments, Edelmann becomes corrupted by Dracula's vampiric blood. He becomes a murderous monster, killing his assistant and putting his scientific knowledge to use restoring Frankenstein's monster to full power, seemingly just to witness the destruction it might cause. Conversely, *House of Frankenstein*'s Niemann has always been morally corrupt; the film opens with his escape from prison, and from there he manipulates and deceives every person he comes into contact with, including Count Dracula, whom he resurrects only to use as a weapon against an old enemy.

It becomes clear in these analyses that the only American character in these films, Larry Talbot, is also the only character that is morally incorruptible. He is contrasted against European monsters that possess nothing but negative traits: Frankenstein's monster is a mindlessly aggressive hulk; the hunchbacked Daniel is lustful, spiteful and cowardly; Count Dracula is, as always, cunningly manipulative and irredeemably evil. Talbot, however, is noble, self-sacrificing and, perhaps most importantly, remorseful. The Wolf Man is singularly committed to finding a way to destroy the side of him that might cause pain. Even in his werewolf form, supposedly bestial and unpredictable, Talbot often intervenes to stop his European counterparts – and particularly Frankenstein's monster – from harming others.

The scientists in these narratives serve to valorise him further: Mannering, Niemann and Edelmann are all obsessed with becoming as powerful as the late Dr Frankenstein and, ultimately, they are corrupted by their desire for mastery over life and death. If Gustav Niemann and Franz Edelmann's obviously Germanic names were not enough to link them to Nazism, their desire to play God at any cost certainly is. Mannering, however, is more interesting; he is British by birth and at the beginning of *Frankenstein Meets the Wolf Man* wants nothing more than to help Talbot. However, he loses sight of this noble aim upon arriving in Visaria and is eventually aligned with Niemann and Edelmann when he becomes consumed by the prospect of restoring strength to Frankenstein's monster, as if the land itself has brought about in him a megalomaniacal desire for power. Talbot, however, refuses to be corrupted by his curse, and becomes so dedicated to eliminating his own potential for violence that he is ready and willing to lay down his own life to do so.

The Wolf Man films are exceptionally patriotic, pro-American texts which emphasise an overarching theme of noble sacrifice, a notion that was inestimably important in 1940s America. By the time the war had officially ended in August 1945, the United States military had suffered huge casualties. As Whitman asserts, 'the losses – more than 400,000 troops killed and 670,000 wounded – devastated the home front'.[55] Ultimately, the Wolf Man saga articulates a sense that such an enormous sacrifice is necessary in the pursuit of peace and justice. In *House of Dracula*, Talbot has become so desperate to rid himself of his curse that when Edelmann tells him it is impossible to perform an operation before the next full moon, he attempts – unsuccessfully – to take his own life in the ultimate act of self-sacrifice, jump from a cliff-top rather than live with his guilt.

But Talbot's most noble act occurs when his curse has finally been lifted. Despite knowing that he is no longer immortal, Talbot still feels the need to put an end to the violence and suffering in Visaria. Rather than leaving his Germanic nightmare behind, he chooses to stay and risk his own life by returning to Edelmann's castle with the townspeople. At the film's climax, the demonic Edelmann has revived Frankenstein's monster for the final time. Talbot returns to the doctor's castle knowing that he will have to confront this evil without the Wolf Man's help. He shoots Edelmann dead and subdues Frankenstein's creation, trapping it inside the castle. A fire breaks out and the structure collapses, consuming the monster. A similar ending was written for the unmade *Wolfman vs. Dracula*, a script by Bernard Schubert that was intended to be filmed as a Technicolor sequel to *Frankenstein Meets the Wolf Man* (before Universal dropped it in favour of less expensive projects). In the unproduced screenplay, Talbot confronts and destroys Count Dracula in his human form before allowing himself to be killed with a silver bullet.[56]

After a four-film campaign, then, the American Talbot is the only one of Universal's classic monsters to have survived the series, his antagonists destroyed and his curse finally lifted. Through his humanity, determination and self-sacrifice, he has been cured of his werewolfism, defeated his European enemies and, perhaps most importantly, found redemption. At the time of the film's release in December 1945, just four months after the formal surrender of the Empire of Japan and the end of hostilities, Talbot had finally won his war.

CHAPTER 2

Dogs of War

Foreign Species

The commercial success of *The Wolf Man* (1941) meant that other studios began producing imitations before Universal could even begin work on a sequel. The vast majority borrow heavily from *The Wolf Man* in constructing their narratives, not least in casting foreign aggressors as supernatural monsters during wartime. However, these films generally differ from Universal's in that they depict werewolfism as a hereditary and normally European curse. For example, Twentieth Century Fox's *The Undying Monster* (1942) concerns siblings Helga and Oliver Hammond (Heather Angel and John Howard), the last surviving members of an aristocratic family that has been haunted by a werewolf's curse for centuries. While the exact nature of their affliction is not revealed, the film heavily implies that their ancestor, a medieval knight and crusader, sold his soul to the Devil while travelling between Europe and the Middle East. Upon his death in Palestine, the curse passed to his male heir. Set in an isolated English mansion, *The Undying Monster* has the structure of a mystery and climaxes by revealing that it is Oliver who now carries his family's werewolfery. The hereditary curse – now with a more concrete European origin – recurred in RKO's *Cat People* (1942) and Columbia's *Cry of the Werewolf* (1944), two films which trace a terrible supernatural affliction back to Serbia and Romania respectively.

As Kim Newman suggests, *Cat People* was essentially RKO's response to *The Wolf Man*, designed 'to compete with the Universal hit, on a counterpunching level of following up a Wolf Man with a Cat Woman'.[1] In fact, *Cat People* is essentially a werewolf film, especially as it employs a very familiar narrative device: a dreadful curse with its genesis in Europe that sees a human transformed into an animal. Unlike *The Wolf Man*, however, *Cat People* offers a specific national origin for the protagonist's occult affliction. The film concerns Irena Dubrovna (Simone Simon), a Serbian immigrant living in New York City who believes she is descended from a coven of witches and carries a curse that means she will turn into a murderous panther upon sexual contact with a partner. She meets an American man named Oliver Reed (Kent Smith) while visiting a panther enclosure in a zoo close to her New York apartment. They appear to fall in love and, despite Irena's trepidations, they wed and enter into a sexless marriage.

Tim Snelson suggests that Irena's marriage to Oliver reflects her desire to become 'a nurturing wife and domestic goddess',[2] but there is a sense that her decision to wed is less a path to relinquishing her independence as it is to letting go of her European heritage. Irena seems to want nothing more than to be wholly subsumed into American society, believing that the erasure of her Serbian background will relieve her of her curse. A line of dialogue strongly suggests that only by becoming Americanised will Irena become 'normal'. Shortly before their wedding, Reed tells his wife-to-be: 'You're Irena. You're here in America. You're so normal you're even in love with me, Oliver Reed, a good plain Americano.' However, something stops Irena from accepting the idea that she can be an integrated American citizen; despite the fact that her Serbian ancestry makes her feel abnormal, she clings to it even after attaching herself to Oliver. She tells her husband: 'I want to be Mrs Reed.' When he reminds her of their recent marriage, she replies: 'But I want to be Mrs Reed *really*. I want to be everything that name means to me, and I can't. I can't. Oliver, be kind, be patient. Let me have time. Time to get over that feeling there's something evil in me.' That something evil, of course, is her ancestry – Oliver might be a 'good plain Americano', but Irena is not.

Despite visiting a psychiatrist, Dr Louis Judd (Tom Conway), and continuing to work on her marriage, there is nothing Irena can do to shed her 'evil' Serbian affliction, and she refuses to dispose of items around her apartment that remind her of her Eastern European heritage. Oliver becomes unable to cope with Irena's behaviour and begins to fall in love with his co-worker, Alice Moore (Jane Randolph). Shortly afterwards, he informs Irena that he intends to leave her. In discovering his love for Alice, Reed also realises that while he is strangely drawn to Irena he has never truly been in love with her, suggesting that her curse also provides an occult means of seduction. Incensed by her husband's betrayal, Irena transforms into a panther and attempts unsuccessfully to kill both Alice and Oliver. Following this attack and once again in human form, Irena consults Dr Judd for guidance but he, too, has fallen under her spell and kisses her. She transforms and kills him, but not before he is able to stab her with a sword hidden in his cane. Wounded, forlorn and alone, Irena returns to the zoo where she first met her husband, unleashing a panther from its cage; it immediately attacks her, ending her life.

The apparent American xenophobia towards a Serbian immigrant articulated in *Cat People* is an interesting subtext to interrogate. Before 1941, Serbia was one part of the Kingdom of Yugoslavia, also composed of the modern-day nation states of Slovenia and Croatia, amongst others. Following invasion by Germany and Italy in April 1941, Yugoslavia became Axis-occupied and was annexed into Axis countries or dismantled into smaller, Axis-controlled puppet states such as the Independent State of Croatia. In Serbia, Nazi Germany established a military regime which devolved power to Serbian puppet governments under overall German control. In short, Serbia was far from a willing collaborator with the Axis powers; following the war it would become clear that Serbs living in Croatia had been the victims of genocide.

The Nazi occupation of Serbia was something that Val Lewton, producer of *Cat People*, was acutely aware of and had incorporated into early versions of the film's plot. As Newman notes, the film was 'planned to open with Nazi tanks arriving in Irena's village, and the invader being attacked by night by a population of werecats'.[3] Melvin E. Matthews Jr elaborates:

> The focus of Lewton's original story was a snowed-in Balkan village, the residents of which are now under the yoke of a Nazi Panzer division. During the day the villagers give their captors no trouble but, at night, they transform into predaceous beasts who annihilate the Nazis. In the wake of the massacre, one of the villagers, a girl, escapes, ultimately reaching New York, and falls in love.[4]

Such an opening would have suggested American sympathy towards the Serbian cause by aligning the eponymous cat people with the American war effort, but no such scene appears in the final version of *Cat People*. And while Dubrovna is clearly terrified of her potential to hurt others – particularly her husband – and is desperate to integrate herself into the film's normalised society, she is far from a sympathetic victim. After all, she is seemingly aware of her actions in panther form, as evidenced by her ability to target specific victims for revenge. *Cat People*, then, could be interpreted as a paranoid American vision of Nazi-occupied Yugoslavia, divided into nation states either willing to accept and co-operate with German efforts to defeat the Allied forces or otherwise suffering terribly under Nazi rule. As Newman suggests, there is a connection to be found within *Cat People* between the division of self that is implied by a metamorphosis from human to animal and the 'fracturing of Yugoslavia into a bloody mass of ethnic cleansing . . . and shattered communities'.[5]

Cry of the Werewolf, however, removes all ambiguity; it is not at all forgiving of its werewolf antagonist. Columbia's effort is clearly designed to capitalise on the success of previous transformation narratives, as it combines plot elements from both *The Wolf Man* and *Cat People*. The film concerns a Romanian princess, Celeste (Nina Foch), living in the United States. Like her late mother and generations of women before her, she has the power to turn herself into a wolf at will. She is descended from Marie LaTour, a Romanian immigrant to America and werewolf who is rumoured to have slain her husband in wolf form centuries before.[6] LaTour's hidden final resting place is a sacred secret of Celeste's family that she will do anything to protect. When the secret passageway leading to LaTour's tomb is found inside a New Orleans museum by historian Dr Charles Morris (Fritz Leiber), Celeste embarks on a mission to kill anyone who knows – or attempts to discover – the location of LaTour's body.

The film begins as a group of tourists are arriving for a guided tour around the fictional LaTour Museum, New Orleans. Their tour guide, Peter (John Abbott), promises to show them the history of vampirism, werewolfism and voodoo, beginning with a visit to a reconstruction of a vampire's daytime resting place. Eventually, the tour arrives in the perfectly preserved bedroom of Marie LaTour herself, where the tour guide begins to tell the grisly story of her life. Here, for the first time since the werewolf films of the silent period, an account is given of supernatural beings that are willing and able to transform from human to wolf and maintain their consciousness. Peter's narration tells us that these are not the tortured souls of *Werewolf of London* (1935) or *The Wolf Man*, but intrinsically evil men and women who choose to undergo metamorphosis to commit heinous crimes. As Peter explains:

> The tradition of werewolves and vampires dates back almost to the world's earliest recorded history. Of the two, the werewolf is perhaps the most horrible because the instinct for evil is so strong that they willingly and cunningly assume the shape of a beast in order to kill.

This harrowing description certainly fits Celeste, who is proud of her parentage, embraces her occult past and considers her werewolfery a blessing, not a curse: 'I am the daughter of a werewolf' is a phrase she speaks proudly. She is also remorseless in the use of her occult talents to kill anyone who may endanger her or her followers and throughout the film she willingly commits a number of violent acts to protect their secrets. Her first crime is to lure Dr Morris into LaTour's tomb in order to murder him. She is disturbed during the act by Peter, who follows the sounds of Morris's screams through a secret passageway in LaTour's bedroom exhibit. The sight of Celeste's monstrous visage alone drives Peter temporarily insane, reducing him to a gibbering wreck for much of the rest of the film. The police are summoned and with the help of Morris's son,

Bob (Stephen Crane), and his fiancée, museum worker Elsa (Osa Massen), they begin to investigate the crimes committed within the museum's walls. Celeste's next heinous act is the execution of Jan Spavero (Ivan Triesault), the museum's janitor and an associate of Celeste's, whom she kills for unwittingly leading the police to suspect her of wrongdoing. She then turns her attention to Bob and Elsa, attempting to seduce Elsa's husband-to-be before trying to kill them both at the film's climax.

The xenophobic subtext present in *Cry of the Werewolf* is altogether more straightforward than in *Cat People*. At the beginning of the Second World War, Romania had adopted a neutral stance. However, a fascist regime took control from the country's unpopular democratic government in a 1940 military coup, joining the Axis powers shortly afterwards. Romania continued to collaborate with the Axis until 1944, when the country was invaded by advancing Soviet forces. At the time *Cry of the Werewolf* was produced and released, Romania was an active enemy of the United States, and so it is no surprise that Columbia's film openly demonises the Romanian Celeste and her followers, with Bob referring to them as 'demons', 'devils' and 'devil-worshippers'. He is not the only one to speak of the Romanian characters in such terms. Celeste's followers have a tradition of burying their dead during an annual festival; between death and burial, they are sent to an undertaker in New Orleans who preserves their bodies. Bob visits the undertaker to discuss the werewolf's people with him in the hope of gaining greater insight into their customs; during their conversation, Celeste and her followers arrive, prompting the undertaker to exclaim: 'Speak of the devil!'

Even the Romanian-born Elsa says of Celeste: 'I am as certain that that gypsy girl is evil as I am that I breathe.' It is interesting that Elsa herself is also of Romanian birth; she is the only non-American character in the film to be depicted positively. However, it is only through her willingness to be Americanised that her Eastern European origins are rendered non-threatening. Though he does not investigate the film's xenophobic subtext in detail, Snelson points out that Celeste and Elsa are 'differentiated through their relationship to their European homelands'.[7] Elsa yearns to be accepted, and has no desire to cling to her heritage; she has no relationship to any of the other Romanian characters and enthusiastically accepts Bob's proposal of marriage as an induction into American society. As Snelson suggests, she has 'escaped the irrational belief systems and consequent totalitarian threat of her ancestral home'.[8] In contrast, Celeste is quite openly demonised for being fiercely proud of her ancestry. However, the xenophobia implicit in *Cry of the Werewolf* would not remain relevant to domestic audiences for long, at least beyond the traditional cultural association between folkloric monsters and the Romanian province of Transylvania. On 23 August 1944, only five days after the film was released to first-run theatres, the totalitarian regime in Romania collapsed after four years of fascism. A royal coup executed by Romania's reigning monarch, King Michael I, resulted in the nation's return to democracy and shortly thereafter the country would join the Allied forces for the remainder of the war.

Attack of the She-Wolves

Though the European curse is an important consideration in any discussion of *Cat People* and *Cry of the Werewolf* in their wartime context, there is another significant element of these two films – as well as the post-war *She-Wolf of London* (1946) – that must be interrogated in order to understand them fully: these are the first horror films since 1913's *The Werewolf* to feature female characters undergoing human-to-animal transformation. In large part, as Snelson suggests, this was due to 'wartime contingency rather than auteurial vision'. He continues:

> by the time *Cat People* was released in December 1942 the mobilization of women into wartime employment had made significant changes to many women's lives, in terms of their accepted roles within the workforce as well as more concretely in terms of their financial, social, and geographical positioning in relation to urban leisure activities.[9]

With women entering the workplace in huge numbers and becoming an increasingly important movie-going demographic, it is perhaps not surprising that these films came to concentrate primarily on female characters. However, perhaps it is surprising – considering that they were aimed at a female audience – that they cast women as monsters. In their power to seduce unwitting men and their use of an inherently fatal sexuality as a weapon, these monstrous women are in many ways reminiscent of the dangerous femme fatale common to film noir: cunning women who, according to Frank Krutnik, 'seek to advance themselves by manipulating their sexual allure and controlling its value'.[10] Traditionally, the femme fatale has been interpreted as a conservative reaction to those changes in gender politics that led to women taking much more active roles in American society – and achieving unprecedented levels of independence – during wartime. As Jennifer Fay and Justus Nieland suggest:

> One strand of criticism argues that noir's gender play and the recurrent narrative patterns of the femme fatale's lethal sexuality reflect radical social changes in the US

during and following World War II. As men were drafted and fought in the world's most brutal hostilities, women entered the workforce in unprecedented numbers and achieved a new social and financial independence that upset the traditional gender roles and threatened the structure of the American family. Film noir, some argue, emerges as a response to this shift and offers narratives that help men make sense of this new American woman.[11]

Janey Place argues that there is a specific narrative discourse through which this conservative subtext is delivered, stating: 'The ideological oper-ation of this myth (the absolute necessity of controlling the strong, sexual woman) is thus achieved by first demonstrating her dangerous power and its frightening results, then destroying it.'[12] This is certainly the case in both *Cat People* and *Cry of the Werewolf*, at least in regard to Irena and Celeste. Both are women with a supernatural allure: an occult talent for seduction that will ultimately lead to the destruction of the men who fall for them. In Irena, the notion of fatal sexuality is rendered literal in the suggestion that it is sexual contact that will cause her transformations to take place, at which point she will kill her potential partner regardless of her feelings for him. Irena, the film tells us, is unlovable; Oliver is not truly in love with her, only drawn to her supernatural charm. The fatal conse-quences of her sexuality are laid bare when Dr Judd attempts to initiate a sexual encounter with her, only to watch her transform into a panther before his eyes. In shadow, we see Irena tear him apart before she returns to human form, becomes distraught and commits suicide. Clearly, even Irena feels that her sexuality is so dangerous that she must be destroyed.

As Newman points out, there is another cat-woman glimpsed in the film, one who adds to the horror of female sexuality. After Irena and Reed are married, they have a wedding dinner in a Serbian restaurant, where Irena is briefly approached by a mysterious woman (Elizabeth Russell). The wedding party joke that this woman resembles a cat before she asks Irena 'Moya sestra?' ('My sister?'). Irena does not reply, and the mystery woman walks out of the restaurant and into the snow, her identity an enigma. As Newman notes, this is 'one of the film's eeriest moments' because 'this character is a Cat Person, who has obviously prospered despite (or because of) her curse'.[13] This is a woman who clearly shares Irena's ancestry, and her use of the word 'sister' to describe another of her kin would suggest she is proud of her occult heritage and abilities. It can be assumed, then, that many men have fallen foul of this second cat-woman's draw.

While Celeste's werewolfism is not intrinsically linked to her sexuality in *Cry of the Werewolf*, a connection is formed between the feminine, sex and violence through a flashback sequence at the beginning of the film which recounts the legend of Marie LaTour. In voiceover, Peter tells the assembled visitors to the LaTour museum that many years before, farmers in the area had complained of losing livestock to a wolf. Nobleman George LaTour eventually discovered the truth behind the animal attacks by tracing muddy footprints back to his wife's bedroom, where she lay in wait for him. Peter continues: 'Servants upstairs, hearing screams, rushed up and found their master's mangled body. Over him stood a terrible animal with flaming, dripping jaws; this creature, seeing them, turned and fled through a window. Ladies and gentlemen, that creature – that thing! – was Marie LaTour.'

The wording in this lurid tale clearly equates the female with the monstrous; LaTour's ancestral werewolfery is more important to her than her disposable husband, whom she remorselessly slays in cold blood as soon as he discovers her secrets. LaTour's supernatural abilities are passed down the generations until they reach Celeste's mother and, finally, Celeste herself. Celeste is a woman who believes that her powers allow her to take whatever she wants by force; when she meets Bob Morris, she immediately sets out to seduce him and is willing to use all of her occult abilities in service of that goal. Bob himself is not immune to her charms. He visits her campground and the two engage in a flirtatious exchange. Eventually, Bob realises that his attraction to Celeste has been engineered by supernatural means, and he remains loyal to Elsa. At the film's climax, Celeste attempts to place a curse upon Elsa, to turn her into another monstrous woman. She proclaims:

> I shall teach you a new worship, a new religion. Your first sacrifice upon its altar will be the fate of the man you love. Since I am forbidden to love him, so shall you be. You will learn to live as I must live. Apart – beyond the reach of men and mortals. And for that love that once shone in a man's eyes, loathing will be substituted. You will be feared and hated. When you awaken, you too shall be the daughter of a werewolf!

However, Irena and Celeste are clearly not the only female characters present in these narratives, and there are women in the two films who are depicted in a positive light. In fact, despite being the 'other woman' in Lewton's narrative scenario, Newman attests that Alice is 'the unsung heroine of *Cat People*' and goes on to suggest that Lewton clearly designed her character to subvert the typical Hollywood treatment of a man leaving his wife for another:

> if the 'other woman' in regular film is supposed to be an exotic vamp with a foreign accent (like the wife here), then the *Cat People* 'other woman' will be a bustling, down-to-earth working girl who looks more suited to helpmeet roles than seducing a man away from his wife.[14]

Elsa, too, is a hard-working woman who is engaged to an ambitious, intelligent American man and holds down a humble position working in the LaTour museum. Furthermore, through working with Bob and the police, she comes to play an important part in putting an end to Celeste's murderous rampage.

Clearly, then, these films do not articulate a fear of all women, only a certain type of woman: one who is not actively contributing to society. A more recent academic stance in the study of the femme fatale attests that the dangerous women of the 1940s can, in fact, be said to communicate somewhat progressive political and societal ideals; that they are not designed to demonise sexually liberated, independent women, but parasitic 'slackers' who are unwilling to work hard and assist with the war effort. As Mark Jancovich argues, such femmes fatales were not even exclusive to film noir, but often appeared in 1940s horror films aimed at female audiences.[15] Jancovich claims:

> To the extent that the femme fatale can be said to exist at all, she is far from the independent working woman of wartime. On the contrary, the women identified as classic femme[s] fatales are, almost without exception, examples of the 'kept woman', who had come to signify decadence and corruption in the war years.[16]

In his study of *Cat People* and wartime propaganda, Jon Towlson suggests that Lewton's film subverts America's efforts to encourage its working women by using Irena as a representation of Alice's 'Shadow', or her repressed sexuality. He claims that 'Irena is hidden within the darkness of Alice's psyche, waiting to pounce.'[17] Similarly, Snelson points out that it is common for horror cinema of the 1940s to bifurcate the female experience of wartime into two distinct characters, and that both Irena and Alice come to represent the pressures placed on women during this period in American history. He argues that Alice, 'as a wartime working woman, survives in the all-male world of shipbuilding at the cost of a stable family life', while Irena is a sympathetic character only rendered monstrous because of her 'inability to move beyond the containment and isolation of traditional notions of a woman's role'.[18]

These are both well-evidenced readings, but I would argue that the stark contrast *Cat People* creates between its female leads aligns more with Jancovich's thesis: Irena is openly demonised for her life of leisure, while Alice is valorised for her contributions to society. When Irena first meets Oliver in the zoo, she is holding a sketch pad and tells him that she is a fashion designer, but refuses to let him see what it is that she is drawing. When they walk off together, she leaves behind a sheet of paper on which she has drawn a panther that has been stabbed with a blade; a neat piece of foreshadowing, but not the work of a fashion designer. Irena also possesses a large apartment in New York, but the film does not provide any evidence that she earns the money to maintain it. Unlike Alice – who is routinely pictured in the workplace – Irena is never seen actively working. She spends her screen time either attempting to remain the object of her husband's affections or meditating on her curse.

In contrast, Alice is a hard-working American citizen contributing to society through her employment as a naval draughtswoman – and, as Snelson notes, a line deleted from the script reveals that she is also a civil defence volunteer.[19] Although there is no explicit mention of conflict in the final version of *Cat People*, the fact that Alice is directly involved in the design and construction of warships signals that she is directly contributing to the American war effort. She is also fiercely independent; she openly declares her love for Oliver early in the narrative, but does not show any signs of distress when he begins a relationship with another woman. Rather, she continues with her life as an autonomous, working woman until the point that Irena's occult hold over Reed weakens. To wartime American audiences, then, Alice is rendered a sympathetic character despite embodying an 'other woman' and, as Newman muses, her portrayal is 'guaranteed to seem more unsympathetic to modern audiences than it did at the time'.[20]

Other than sharing a Romanian heritage, *Cry of the Werewolf*'s female leads also represent direct opposites. Snelson explores this idea by aligning the film with his reading of *Cat People*, suggesting *Cry of the Werewolf* is another film that bifurcates the wartime woman into the 'good' (but sexually repressed) Elsa and the 'bad' Celeste, who is 'encoded transgressive both in her predatory pursuit of the engaged Bob' and, as she represents a monster – the werewolf – that is typically thought of as masculine, 'in her blatant adoption of the male role in the proceedings'.[21] He echoes Jancovich's position on the femme fatale by asserting that this division renders explicit a wartime tendency to 'separate women's wartime experiences, bifurcating the office worker by day and sexual adventurer by night into distinct and separate entities – one feminine yet productive, the other sexually aggressive and unproductive'.[22] And Celeste is certainly unproductive; the revered 'princess' of her people, she freely chooses to live outside of normative (i.e. capitalist) American society. The film never reveals how she – or any of her followers – makes enough money to maintain her lifestyle aside from a brief mention of the manufacture and sale of toys and trinkets. She lives in luxury amongst a society of outsiders who fear and adore her, but the film provides no evidence that she has a legitimate source of income. Elsa, on the other hand, has settled in the United States and has found safe employment as well as an American fiancé.

However, Snelson still sees something sympathetic in the she-wolf and suggests that she, like Irena, finds her occult abilities to be a source of suffering; he describes *Cry of the Werewolf* as a film concerned with 'a young Romanian woman attempting to escape a shapeshifting curse' inherited from a sexually aggressive ancestor.[23] But there is no suggestion in the film that Celeste wishes to be free of her werewolfery at all. In fact, what sets *Cry of the Werewolf* apart from *Cat People* is that Celeste does not want to be Americanised; she openly reveres Maria LaTour and is proud to be her descendant, holding nothing but contempt for American culture. And while she seemingly laments that her occult abilities set her 'apart' from wider society, in the same breath she boasts that she is 'beyond the reach of men and mortals'; she revels in the power and respect that her werewolfism affords her. Her aim, then, is to lure Bob into her world – not to become a part of his. *Cry of the Werewolf* is therefore the film in which the xenophobia and gender politics implicit in 1940s werewolf films collide. It compares two female immigrants who have carved out very different lives for themselves in America: Celeste has lived an insular existence with her people and as a result is rendered irredeemably monstrous, demonised for her steadfast refusal to integrate and contribute, while Elsa is depicted positively precisely because she has relinquished her heritage to become a working woman and the wife-to-be of a successful American man.

A critical view of unemployed, 'kept women' is especially apparent in Universal's immediate post-war tale of clinical lycanthropy, *She-Wolf of London*, which lays bare the archaic nature of pre-war gender politics and illustrates Jancovich's notion of the decadent and corrupt woman of leisure. The film concerns a family of three composed entirely of women: Phyllis Allenby (June Lockhart), her aunt, Martha Winthrop (Sara Haden) and cousin, Carol Winthrop (Jan Wiley). All three reside in a stately home in London at the turn of the twentieth century and not one of them is gainfully employed; it becomes apparent early in the narrative that they survive on a fortune left behind by Phyllis's deceased parents. Phyllis is engaged to be married to Barry Lanfield (Don Porter), a wealthy and successful lawyer, until a series of disturbing events lead her to break off the engagement. Several people are attacked or murdered – including a boy of ten years old – in the park and woods next to Phyllis's home, leading her to believe she is suffering under the fabled 'Allenby Curse'. Just as in *The Undying Monster*, *Cat People* and *Cry of the Werewolf*, this curse is rumoured to be one of long-standing, hereditary werewolfism. Day after day, Phyllis awakes to find evidence in her bedroom that she has ventured into the park at night, including muddied shoes and

Figure 2.1 Phyllis Allenby (June Lockhart) fearfully reads up on werewolfery in *She-Wolf of London* (1946), before discovering she is not suffering from the 'Allenby Curse' at all.

bloodstained clothes, and researches the nature of werewolfery (Figure 2.1). Convinced that she is cursed, Phyllis then distances herself from others to keep them from harm.

By the end of the film, it has become clear that Phyllis is not at all responsible for the crimes committed by the film's supposed 'she-wolf'. In fact, there is no werewolf in *She-Wolf of London* at all; rather, Martha has been attacking innocent people – murdering many of them in cold blood – before planting evidence of wrongdoing in Phyllis's bedroom for her to find. Martha's motivations for doing this are largely financial. It is revealed early in the narrative that Martha and Carol are not, in fact, related to Phyllis in any way. Martha was at one time engaged to Reginald Allenby, Phyllis's wealthy father, but chose to marry another man for love and forsake financial stability. She recounts that her husband died when Carol was a small child, leaving her and her young daughter penniless. She was saved from financial destitution by Reginald, who invited her to move into his home as his family's housekeeper. Many years later, Phyllis's parents died, leaving her as the sole beneficiary of their estate. This means, of course, that Martha and Carol stand to inherit nothing.

Martha's plan is to have Phyllis imprisoned or institutionalised in the hope that she will forfeit her inheritance to the Winthrops. She is also hoping that by removing Phyllis from the household, she will be able to engineer a marriage between Carol and Lanfield; on several occasions, she shows disapproval towards Carol's secret meetings with Dwight Severn (Martin Kosleck), a penniless artist with whom she has fallen deeply in love. She hopes that by forcing Carol and Lanfield together, her daughter will have financial security for the rest of her life. Martha, then, holds dear all of the archaic values that were being progressively eroded in 1940s America. She believes that a woman should marry a wealthy man who will provide for her financially; she obviously does not believe that a woman is capable of making her own living or even her own choices. Carol has reached an age where she is beginning to make her own decisions and plan her own life, but her mother is willing to maim and kill to remove those freedoms from her and make sure that she will be forced to conform to an outmoded gender role. Martha's maniacal plot to drive Phyllis insane is, in part, a ploy to control Carol's life by manoeuvring her away from the man she loves and into a marriage of convenience.

Martha's other motivation, of course, is to protect her obscene wealth and maintain her leisurely existence. At the film's climax, she is killed when she falls down the sweeping staircase of the Allenby home, destroyed by the same corrupt lifestyle she would commit murder to maintain. With Martha dead, Phyllis and Carol are free to make their own choices and shape their own lives without her oppressive influence. There is no true werewolf's curse in She-Wolf of London, just a grisly tale concocted by a murderously conservative woman to aid in curbing the progressive ideas of a younger generation. Peter Hutchings argues that the film fails because Martha's physical form – a middle-aged lady of leisure – distances her from the imposing figure of the femme fatale, a woman generally depicted as young and sexually aggressive. He suggests that She-Wolf of London 'struggles to present her as actually dangerous' in cultural or physical terms, 'hence the film's anticlimactic trajectory'.[24] While Hutchings might be correct to assert that Martha does not appear physically dangerous in the same fashion as the traditional femme fatale, she is certainly culturally dangerous. Martha Winthrop is just one of the insidious women of the 1940s who Jancovich suggests 'were clearly presented as selfish, greedy and parasitic, qualities that clearly associated them with the domestic sphere'.[25]

To evidence Jancovich's point further, The Return of the Vampire (1943) actively supports female autonomy during wartime. The film sees a vampire – played by Bela Lugosi, who reprises the role of Dracula in all but name – freed from his tomb when a Luftwaffe bomb destroys his crypt in wartime London. With the help of a werewolf (Matt Willis) – the vampire's unwilling slave, and a character very reminiscent of Larry Talbot in that he is exceptionally uncomfortable with his bestial urges – Lady Jane Ainsley (Frieda Inescort), a female vampire hunter, battles the vampire. Rick Worland asserts that: 'In its portrayal of a strong female protagonist assuming a traditional male role, the movie retooled the vampire tale for wartime propaganda tasks.'[26]

In fact, *The Return of the Vampire* has perhaps the most explicit propagandist subtext of all of the 1940s films discussed here. The German military – in the form of a well-placed Luftwaffe bomb – unleashes an ancient, evil European power in an Allied nation; the vampire immediately enslaves an unwitting werewolf accomplice, alluding to fears of Germanic invasion and occupation of the Allied West. The vampire is then repelled by a physically and mentally strong, autonomous woman – a representation of working women on the home front – and finally killed by his werewolf slave, who finds the courage to revolt against his master in a climactic scene that cries out for occupied nations across the globe to continue their fight against Nazi oppression. The sum of *The Return of the Vampire*'s narrative elements is a horror film that arises from a wartime context and explicitly supports the Allied war effort both at home and abroad with a rare transparency.

Rabid Science

Not all 1940s werewolf films were so supportive of the American war effort. The war brought about a fear of scientific advancement prevalent in horror cinema that would later become a key theme in werewolf films of the 1950s. Tellingly, *The Mad Monster* (1942) – the 1940s werewolf film to tackle this subject most directly – does not articulate a fear of science being misused by the Axis powers, but by a misguided scientist from an Allied nation. Uneasiness with scientific advancement was not a new feature of the horror film, of course. Andrew Tudor suggests that this paranoia had been key to the horror film in general long before the outbreak of war, asserting: 'The belief that science is dangerous is as central to the horror movie as is a belief in the malevolent inclinations of ghosts, ghouls, vampires and zombies.'[27]

Tudor identifies an early expression of such fears in *Werewolf of London*, arguing that 'The price for Glendon's thirst for knowledge . . . is a metamorphosis into a werewolf.'[28] By single-mindedly pursuing his research to the point that he is willing to ignore several warnings that he should not enter a valley possessed by demons, Glendon personifies the idea that striving for scientific knowledge can have disastrous consequences even with the best of intentions. *Frankenstein Meets the Wolf Man* (1943), *House of Frankenstein* (1944) and *House of Dracula* (1945) update this theme for wartime purposes, imagining scientists as easily-corrupted, power-hungry and often Germanic madmen who would use their intellect to unleash the full destructive potential of Frankenstein's monster upon the world. However, as Matthews Jr observes, *The Mad Monster* was unique at the time of its release because 'it boasted America's first *patriotic* mad scientist'.[29]

The Mad Monster is another film that was put into production as a direct result of the success of Universal's *The Wolf Man*, on this occasion by Producers Releasing Corporation, a Poverty Row company. The film, which stars the prolific George Zucco as psychotic scientist Dr Lorenzo Cameron, makes an explicit link between a general fear of scientific advancement and the specific fear of science as a means to wage war. Matthews Jr and Worland are two of only a handful of scholars even to mention the film in academic work, but Worland's brief analysis is interesting chiefly for one understandable but ultimately misguided assumption: he claims that the film concerns 'Nazi scientists labouring to create invulnerable monster-soldiers'.[30]

However, there is actually no evidence in the film's plot to suggest that Cameron is a Nazi (or even German) at all. Rather he is an American scientist who has been cast out of the scientific community and stripped of a university professorship for unethical and outlandish experiments. It quickly becomes apparent that these experiments have seen him transfuse wolf's blood into human beings in the hope of creating werewolf super-soldiers for use by the American military. Furthermore, Cameron is explicitly insane; in the film's opening scene he suffers a psychotic episode in which he imagines hallucinatory manifestations of his former colleagues, lambasting them for not understanding the importance of his work. Cameron's hallucinated colleagues reply with horrified responses: 'You're a madman!' one says, 'Your crazy experiments are a disgrace to science!' cries another. Cameron becomes enraged and screams 'Science! What do you know about science?' before continuing:

You're aware, of course, that this country is at war? That our armed forces are locked in combat with a savage horde who fight with fanatical fury? Well that fanatical fury will avail them nothing when I place my new serum at the disposal of the war department! Just picture, gentlemen, an army of wolf-men: fearless, raging, every man a snarling animal. My serum will make it possible to unloose millions of such animal-men, men who are governed by one collective thought! The animal loves to kill without regard for personal safety. Such an army will be invincible, gentlemen. Such an army will sweep everything before it!

Insinuating that Cameron is in any way affiliated with the Axis suggests that this film articulates a fear of what scientific monstrosities the Nazis may have unleashed upon the world. *The Mad Monster* takes on a very different meaning when it is taken into consideration that it is actually a psychotic American scientist who has been attempting to create weaponised werewolves. Having been stripped of all official titles, Cameron has been continuing his experiments by injecting his wolf's blood serum into his gardener, Petro (Glenn Strange). Petro is a blue-collar worker of low intelligence – Matthews Jr calls him a 'naïve man-child'[31] – who does not understand the nature of Cameron's experiments. Petro believes that the doctor has been anaesthetising him, leading to vivid dreams in which he roams the swamps surrounding Cameron's home, hunting people. In reality, Cameron has been training Petro in werewolf form to do his bidding so that he might use his personal monster to assassinate those who discredited him.

Cameron often claims that his long-term goal is to present his serum to the war department, but he clearly intends to use it first and foremost for revenge. Petro unwittingly kills a small child during his 'training' before Cameron takes him to the city to assassinate his first targeted victim, Professor Blaine (Robert Strange). After Blaine's death, Cameron becomes careless and invites his next victim, Professor Fitzgerald (Gordon DeMain), to his own home before sending Fitzgerald away with Petro. Petro fails to kill the professor, who is brought back to Cameron's house alive but unconscious. Suspicious, Cameron's daughter Lorena (Anne Nagel) and her reporter friend Tom (Johnny Downs) investigate; Lorena finds the transformed Petro locked in a room adjoined to her father's laboratory and unwittingly frees the monster. A fire breaks out and Fitzgerald, Lorena and Tom manage to escape, but monster and creator are trapped inside and consumed by the flames together.

In summarising his brief study of *The Mad Monster*, Matthews Jr states:

> Instead of turning his serum over to the government for the war effort, Cameron unleashes his wolf man creation on those responsible for his ostracism from the scientific community. In this, Cameron resembles Hitler: both are outcasts who seek the destruction of those they felt denied them the realization of their goals.[32]

While this argument is valid, it is somewhat reductive. The film itself does not make any connection between Cameron and the Nazis, explicitly or implicitly. He is fiercely patriotic and, though he first uses his experiment to murder his detractors, his ultimate goal is to be recognised for his ability to end the war with his army of animal-men. *The Mad Monster*, then, arises from far more generalised anxieties.

Firstly, this is a film in which a working-class man finds himself unwittingly manipulated by the warmongering elite. When he wakes up from his first on-screen transformation, Petro recounts his dream of attempted murder and says, forlornly: 'Why should I be trying to kill them? Even in my dreams, I ain't got nothing against nobody.' Later, he laments that he is unable to understand the purpose of Cameron's experiments, saying: 'Gee, it must be great to be educated. I wish I had a lot of book learning so I could understand what this is all about.' Cameron replies, 'Fortunately, you don't need education or intelligence for your part of the experiment – just strength, animal strength.'

Therefore Cameron is chiefly vilified for using a vulnerable man – who does not understand his theories, experiments or even his intentions – as an unwitting assassin with complete disregard for his life. His domination of his test subject is emphasised even in the film's marketing materials; one of the film's lobby cards depicts Cameron aggressively bearing down on Petro (Figure 2.2). In its vilification of a megalomaniacal scientist of considerable intelligence and its acute sympathy for the blue-collar worker

Figure 2.2 A lobby card produced to promote *The Mad Monster* (1942), illustrating the power that Dr Cameron (George Zucco) holds over Petro (Glenn Strange), his test subject. © PRC

forced to do his bidding, *The Mad Monster* laments that wars are ignited by men in positions of considerable wealth, power and influence but are inevitably fought by the working class servicemen who are expected to lay down their lives for their country – a fitting theme for a film produced by a Poverty Row studio. The allegorical transformation of a gentle labourer into a killing machine is summed up in Cameron's grandiose speech to his hallucinated detractors in the film's opening scenes, when he says: 'A few moments ago, Petro was a man – a harmless, good-natured man. Look at him now! He is no longer human. He's a wolf! Snarling, ferocious, lusting for the kill. You're looking at a scientific miracle, gentlemen.'

The Mad Monster also arises from a culture uneasy about the destructive potential of that very same 'scientific miracle': the film expresses a fear of advanced weapons in *any* nation's hands. Cameron is adept at describing how his animal-men could assist the war effort, but he seems to overlook the fact that he is never truly in control of Petro. On two separate occasions, Cameron's monster kills innocent people without any instruction from his master, one of whom is only a child. Cameron does, of course, want to test the abilities of his super-soldier, but other than ensuring that his pre-ferred victim is in close proximity to Petro when he transforms, Cameron has no real control over the monster's actions. As the film progresses, it becomes clear that even if Cameron abandoned his quest for revenge and actually gave his serum to the war department, even the military would not be able to discipline the 'invincible army' Cameron dreams of; in were-wolf form, Petro is a mindless beast who simply cannot be tamed. Fur-thermore, after several transformations induced by Cameron's injections, Petro becomes even more volatile and unpredictable when he develops the ability to transform of his own accord. At this stage, Cameron considers ending his experiment by shooting Petro dead, but his thirst for vengeance overcomes him and he allows the monster to live, a decision that will lead to both of their deaths. *The Mad Monster*, then, is not a product of fears surrounding Axis invasion but rather of science as a means to wage war and its potential misuse by any nation, even the United States.

This fear would not prove to be entirely unfounded. In August 1945, in the first and last usage of nuclear weapons in active warfare, the American military dropped atomic bombs on the Japanese cities of Hiroshima and Nagasaki, killing tens of thousands and effectively ending the Second World War. This action yielded the result the United States intended: it forced the surrender of the Empire of Japan. However, this demonstration of the enor-mous destructive potential of nuclear weapons also had huge, unintended ramifications across the globe for decades to come: this was the beginning of a worldwide fear of the bomb.

Joseph Maddrey asserts that in America 'the threat of an impending atomic war was the ultimate collective nightmare' following the end of the Second World War and throughout the Cold War, and continues:

> Realising that audiences of the day were more afraid of the 'advancements' that haunted the future than of old superstitions, filmmakers updated the monster movie. Most of the monsters in early 1950s American cinema emerged from some new frontier that man had yet to discover or to fully explore.[33]

These monsters appear in films that tread the line between horror and science fiction; pictures that 'represent the nuclear threat by utilizing metaphors that helped American audiences to concretize and tame the unthinkable threat of nuclear war'.[34]

One cycle of films to emerge from this new mode of horror filmmaking in the mid-to-late 1950s is a group of science fiction/horror movies concerning mutant, human-animal hybrids who owe their terrible maladies to misguided scientific experimentation. These are essentially werewolf films for the atomic age that replace superstition, magical curses and the occult with fantastic technology, nuclear energy or untested drugs. Perhaps the most famous example of the cycle is Twentieth Century Fox's *The Fly* (1958), which concerns scientist Andre Delambre (David Hedison) attempting to build a teleportation device that can reduce an object to atoms and reassemble it in another location. Having built two human-sized teleportation chambers, he attempts to test the device on himself, but fails to notice that a housefly has entered the first chamber with him prior to teleportation. Upon reappearance in the second chamber, the scientist emerges as a monstrous hybrid of human and insect, his genetic structure irreversibly bonded with that of the fly.

More mutants would be created with the use of Delambre's teleportation theories in sequels *Return of the Fly* (1959) and *Curse of the Fly* (1965). The popularity of *The Fly* also inspired imitators in *The Alligator People* (1959) and *The Wasp Woman* (1959), the latter an independent picture produced and co-directed by prolific exploitation filmmaker Roger Corman. *The Wasp Woman* concerns Janice Starlin (Susan Cabot), the owner of a large cosmetics company, who agrees to be the test subject for an experimental anti-ageing drug derived from wasp enzymes; perturbed by slow progress, she begins to take increasingly larger doses. As the drug takes effect Starlin appears younger and younger, but in exchange for a second youth she is cursed with a horrible side-effect: periodic transformation into a murderous human-wasp hybrid.

The Alligator People sees unwitting accident victim Paul Webster (Richard Crane) experimented on by Dr Mark Sinclair (George Macready), who injects Webster with a hormone derived from reptiles in the hope that it will aid him in healing wounds and regenerating lost flesh. The unfortunate side-effect of this treatment is that Webster begins to transform into an alligator, an unwanted development that Sinclair attempts to reverse with the use of experimental radiotherapy. However, bombarding Webster with radiation has the opposite of the desired result, and by the film's conclusion he has become more alligator than man. In an allusion to the damage wrought by nuclear fallout, his genetic mutation is only made worse by exposure to intense radiation. It is notable that of all the animal-transformation films of the 1950s that do not explicitly feature a traditional werewolf, *The Alligator People* is perhaps most directly linked to the werewolf film due to the casting of Lon Chaney Jr as its chief antagonist, whose actions directly result in Webster's final metamorphosis.

However, despite the fact that *The Fly* is by far the most highly regarded of these films today, it is not the one with which this small cycle originates. It is pre-dated by Columbia's *The Werewolf* (1956), a B-picture that played on the bottom half of the bill with *Earth vs. the Flying Saucers* (1956). The first werewolf film of the 1950s, *The Werewolf* was also the first picture of the decade to link a transformation from human to animal with the destructive potential of nuclear experimentation and the horror of genetic mutation.

The film concerns Duncan Marsh (Steven Ritch), who finds himself in an isolated town named Mountaincrest with no memory of how he got there. Alone and wandering aimlessly on the town's main street at the film's opening, he visits a bar and orders a drink – inadvertently revealing that he is in possession of a large amount of money in the process – before leaving in confusion and distress. He is followed onto the street by a man who has clearly taken note of the stranger's wealth. After some decidedly aggressive small talk, the local attempts to mug Marsh for his cash. The two men fight in an alleyway before Marsh undergoes an off-screen transformation into a wolf-man, killing his attacker in front of an elderly witness who is later incapable of accurately describing what she has seen. Over the course of the narrative, as people and animals are injured or killed in and around Mountaincrest, the townspeople come to the realisation that they are dealing with a werewolf and begin measures to end the wolf-man's murder spree.

However, as is the case in the vast majority of early werewolf films, Marsh is not in control of his transformations and is himself a tortured victim. As the narrative progresses it is revealed that, before the film's opening,

Marsh was involved in an automobile accident not far from Mountaincrest that left him suffering from amnesia. At some point between the crash and his arrival in the town, Marsh was discovered by two scientists, Dr Emory Forrest (S. John Launer) and Dr Morgan Chambers (George Lynn), who considered him the perfect candidate on which to test an experimental inoculation treatment derived from irradiated wolf's blood. In a cut-away scene to Forrest and Chambers's lab – in which there are several caged wolves, one of which has already died in a radiotherapy chamber – the two scientists discuss the procedure they performed on Marsh and its intended purpose, revealing the atomic horror at the heart of *The Werewolf*. Forrest holds a newspaper and says to his colleague: 'You think this is our man? Newspaper says they found an animal's teeth marks in a dead man's throat. Morgan, what have you done?' Taken aback, Morgan replies:

> Done? Accomplished is a better word, Emory. Someday it will happen: the human race will destroy itself, not quickly but slowly. That wolf-man is the proof. Radiation creates mutants: people who become monsters, no longer human! They'll make the hydrogen bomb more powerful, then more powerful again, enough to change every person on the face of the earth into a crawling inhuman thing through fallout radiation.

At this point, Forrest cuts Chambers off to ask a cleverly worded question, one at the forefront of American culture in 1956: 'Do you really believe it'll happen in our lifetime?' Chambers goes on to confirm the worst:

> The science of destruction always gains on us, Emory. It could happen tomorrow, next day, next week. I don't know. But it won't happen to us . . . the serum we used in that wolf-mutant that died of radiation, that was the answer. By a slow series of inoculations, we can immunise ourselves and a small select group, just as I planned. When the rest of the world has been destroyed, we will be the only normal, thinking persons left. The perfect science, Emory: the one that ends all science.

How exactly Forrest and Chambers have managed to turn Marsh into a werewolf is never fully explained, but Chambers's mention of 'a slow series of inoculations' would suggest that they have perhaps injected Marsh with too high a dosage of their radioactive serum. Far from immunising him against the effect of nuclear fallout, the scientists have mutated his genetic structure and released him back into society with no control over his transformations from human to wolf. This is a werewolf for a culture fascinated by science fiction; superstition has no place in *The Werewolf*, and Marsh is not a man cursed by occult means to transform under the full moon. Rather, the mythical monster thousands of years old is re-imagined for the atomic age and utilised as a metaphor for the genetic abnormalities

Figure 2.3 The atomic mutant as imagined by *The Werewolf* (1956), in which Duncan Marsh (Steven Ritch) becomes a monster after he is injected with irradiated wolf's blood.

that could potentially be caused by radiation exposure – he is, essentially, a lupine mutant (Figure 2.3).

The Werewolf is thus a film less concerned with the initial impact of a nuclear weapon than with the world that would be left behind in its aftermath: a world, it posits, in which those who survive will be transformed from normal, innocent human beings into monsters. And a line of dialogue confirms that the film's horror does not just lie in the werewolf itself but in the idea that any American could become a mutant in the aftermath of a nuclear attack: a nightmare designed to resonate long after Marsh is tragically shot dead at the film's climax, his affliction having proved incurable. After Marsh has been arrested and detained by Mountaincrest's police at the end of the film's second act, the townspeople celebrate in a bar, but the dejected Mack (James Gavin) senses the fear beneath their elation, musing: 'I think I know what they're scared of. They're scared of what Marsh has become, because it could happen to them. It could happen to anyone.'

Another interesting element of *The Werewolf* is that Marsh's transformations are triggered by specific situations. He is seen to transform three times in the film, and on every occasion his metamorphosis is caused by threats against his well-being. As noted, his first transformation follows an attempted mugging, while his other mutations are triggered by Forrest and Chambers's attempts to kill their test subject before he regains his memory and reveals the nature of their experiments to the authorities. The notion that Marsh only has to become angry or feel intimidated to become monstrous and aggressive is an idea exceptionally pertinent to the Cold War culture that produced *The Werewolf*; Marsh is unpredictable, volatile and likely to kill anyone who dares to threaten him, a change in traditional werewolf lore that is symptomatic of a time in American history when a paranoid society told itself that nuclear war could begin without warning. Just as Americans feared that atomic weapons could be launched at any time, supernatural conditions are not required for Marsh's transformations, merely the mildest perception of threat.

A year after the release of *The Werewolf*, the misuse of science and werewolfism would once again be linked in American International Pictures' luridly titled *I Was a Teenage Werewolf* (1957), which concerns a psychiatrist using hypnosis to turn a troubled teenager into a literal monster. However, any fear of scientific advancement in this film is not tied to the Cold War; rather it is an exploitation movie, the product of an American moral panic surrounding juvenile delinquency. Though Britain's *The Curse of the Werewolf* (1961) would soon launch a European cycle lasting into the 1970s, *I Was a Teenage Werewolf* would be the last North American werewolf film for fourteen years.[35] In 1971, a new cycle of independently produced American werewolf films would arise from the enormous social, cultural and political shifts brought about by the Vietnam War, the civil rights movement, the rise of the counterculture and the Watergate scandal.

CHAPTER 3

Pack Mentality

Lupine Delinquency

While it would be the last American werewolf film for over a decade, *I Was a Teenage Werewolf* (1957) is an important milestone in the development of the werewolf film for several reasons. Firstly, it was the first independently produced werewolf movie – a product of American International Pictures – to find widespread commercial success, taking $2 million at the domestic box office. Secondly, AIP's film was the first to use the werewolf as a metaphor for an entirely domestic cultural crisis in America, which would become a key theme in the bleakly pessimistic werewolf films that would come to characterise the werewolf movie from 1971 until 1981. Finally, *I Was a Teenage Werewolf* birthed a concept that would become hugely popular as a recurring theme in cinematic werewolf narratives and remains so even today: the 'teenage werewolf'. Concerning a troubled adolescent who develops werewolfism as a result of being hypnotised by a decidedly untrustworthy psychiatrist, *I Was a Teenage Werewolf* is the first werewolf film produced specifically to exploit the youth market. But, of course, it was not the last horror film of the 1950s aimed at teenagers. In fact, a sudden explosion of adolescent monsters in Hollywood cinema coincided, not surprisingly, with the birth of modern American youth culture.

The 1950s witnessed the stratospheric rise of the teenager, not just as a cultural phenomenon but as an economic force. According to Peter Biskind:

> A number of factors had conspired to create the new youth culture, ranging from World War II, which sent parents off to war or factory jobs, leaving the kids to their own devices; to postwar affluence; the baby boom; the erosion of the authority of the father; and last, but by no means least, the recognition by business that teen-agers would buy everything from records to Clearasil, that they constituted, in short, a market.[1]

Teenagers also, of course, quickly came to constitute a target audience for the Hollywood film industry, and AIP in particular found a lucrative enterprise in producing films aimed directly at teens. Its films were successful largely because of innovative marketing practices designed to capture adolescent minds. As Mark Jancovich has noted, 'the company often designed the advertising campaigns first, tested the campaigns, and then, if these campaigns were successful, hired someone to make the film . . . its success was based on low budget productions, which were clearly directed, through the use of "state of the art" marketing campaigns, at the teenage audience'.[2] AIP found its most distinctive product in a brand of teenage horror in which angst-ridden, adolescent monsters turn on their peers, first producing *I Was a Teenage Werewolf* and, as a direct result of the film's success, *I Was a Teenage Frankenstein* (1957).[3] *I Was a Teenage Werewolf* was so lucrative for AIP that the company replicated its narrative almost entirely – this time with a female protagonist who becomes a vampire – in *Blood of Dracula* (1957), while smaller production companies produced imitations with even lower budgets and lurid titles such as *Teenage Monster* (1957) and *Teenage Zombies* (1959).

But teenagers were not just a growing economic market. They were, to many – not least the American government – a serious social problem that needed to be addressed. As the new youth culture gained prominence, so did the perceived threat of teenagers beyond authoritative and parental control. As the fifties wore on, American society was gripped by a sensationalist moral panic surrounding juvenile delinquency, an apparent epidemic that was said to be sweeping the nation. As James Gilbert asserts:

> By the mid-1950s, growing fear that a whole generation had turned sour overlaid [an] initial bewilderment and curiosity. The frenzied dances, music and ritualised family rebellions fore-warned of a larger and very serious social problem. Stories of mindless gang violence . . . led to the widespread impression that vicious and bored youth turned to murder and mayhem for amusement.[4]

This fear was such that the United States government launched an enquiry into the issue: the Senate Subcommittee on Juvenile Delinquency, headed by Estes Kefauver. Kefauver and his researchers eventually came to the conclusion that the root of juvenile delinquency was in the media and that, 'consequently, parents could no longer impress their value systems on children who were influenced as much by a new peer culture spread by comic books, radio, movies, and television, as by their elders'.[5] The comic book industry particularly suffered; horror comics were essentially outlawed as a result of the Subcommittee's findings. Clearly, these findings were spurious. The conservative backlash that led Kefauver's investigation was created by the establishment's inability to understand or explain the radical changes that had occurred in America's youth in the post-war years; the idea that popular culture was poisoning adolescent minds was

perhaps the most plausible explanation. As Biskind has pointed out, the
juvenile delinquency issue was inflated beyond any basis in reality because
the conservative establishment was afraid of 'an autonomous youth culture, not delinquency *per se*'.[6] The root cause of this panic was not to be
read in comic books, heard on the radio or seen in cinemas but found in
society's fear of independent young people from whom obedience could
no longer be expected.

   I Was a Teenage Werewolf tells the tale of maladjusted teen Tony Rivers
(Michael Landon), whom we first encounter during a fistfight with one of
his best friends. Only Tony refuses to play by the rules; he throws sand in
his friend's eyes and maniacally swings a shovel at him. This is only the
first of Tony's several violent outbursts in the film's first act, which lead
to his father and girlfriend – and local law enforcement – pressuring him
to see a psychiatrist. He eventually relents and goes to see Dr Alfred Brandon (Whit Bissell). However, Brandon is not what he seems. Something of
a mad scientist, the doctor believes that through hypnosis and regression
techniques he will be able to return mankind to its primal state. Tony is
his first test subject, and after a few sessions on Brandon's couch, he transforms from a violent teenager into a vicious werewolf.

   In werewolf form, Tony graduates from hoodlum to murderer and
begins killing off his peers. Panic spreads through the town, leading the
police to instigate a manhunt; Tony hides from the authorities before
finally coming to realise that Brandon is to blame for his condition. He
then returns to the doctor and pleads for help, but Brandon only sees an
opportunity to film Tony's transformation as concrete proof of his own
achievements, his desire for recognition far outweighing any concerns he
might have for his patient's safety. The final metamorphosis complete,
Tony makes the doctor his last victim only moments before the police
arrive at the doctor's office and are forced to shoot him dead.

   AIP's first teen horror is an unusual example of a werewolf film that
has been afforded in-depth investigations of its historical context, notably
by Biskind and Jancovich in their broader considerations of 1950s Hollywood cinema. This is perhaps because the cultural dimension of the film
is explicit – certainly more so than in the werewolf films that had preceded it. During this period in American history, young people had begun
to strive for autonomy and question their parents' values, while their elders
had come to fear this new teenage independence and the violence that they
believed would accompany it; this theme is immediately identifiable in
AIP's picture and the film is inseparable from the social and political situation that surrounded its conception and release. The conundrum *I Was
a Teenage Werewolf* poses, then, seems to be whether the film supports the

plight of teenagers – articulating their frustration and urge for freedom of expression, as would seem appropriate given that adolescents were AIP's target market – or the conservative stance of the establishment, which would stamp out an apparent teenage rebellion.

For Bryan Senn, the very thing that made the film successful was the way it 'addressed . . . issues through the eyes of the average teenager, validating the feelings and actions of this much maligned and ostensibly powerless demographic'[7] and its exploration of '(in a cleverly disguised manner) the individual anguish and alienation that often comes with adolescence'.[8] This view is shared by Jancovich, who interprets Tony as a victim and the film's psychiatrist as a metaphor for an oppressive generation which sought to control the next. He argues that Brandon's experiments in regression function as an allegory for America's obsession with maintaining its paternal power.[9]

I Was a Teenage Werewolf certainly ends by condemning Brandon's work; at the climax, a police officer muses: 'it's not for man to interfere with the ways of God'. However, Jancovich takes issue with the religious basis of this statement, suggesting it 'is not tied to any broader moral or theological positions developed within the film. It is simply tagged on and used to ward off criticism from what is a subversive critique of parental authority and its treatment of youth.'[10] Jancovich's argument is sound, and it would be difficult for any viewer of *I Was a Teenage Werewolf* not to condemn Brandon's actions even in the absence of Christian moralising; he manipulates Tony and transforms him into a monster entirely against the boy's will. However, the film also supports an opposing interpretation, one largely based not on the monster that Tony becomes but in the boy he is before his transformations take place.

After all, Tony is adept at alienating himself from society. The teenager is depicted as maladjusted long before be becomes a werewolf, as prone to attacking his own friends – twice before his first psychiatric consultation – as he is to assaulting strangers over minor grievances; in the film's opening scene, a police officer reminds Tony of a recent occasion on which he has been in danger of arrest for assaulting an employee of a local supermarket. Tony resists adjusting to society, rebelling against his parents and, by extension, the establishment. But the film consistently reminds us that this behaviour puts him at risk of losing everything: his friends, his girlfriend, the respect of his own father and possibly even his freedom. Tony reaches a crossroad in his life after having savagely assaulted one of his peers at a party. At this point in the narrative, he is not portrayed as a victim. Rather, he is a victimiser, the wronged parties being those who feel the wrath of his violent temper. So, immediately before Tony's first transformation into a monster, he has the choice of adjusting to society's conception of acceptable behaviour or embracing insurrection and spiralling out of control. Following his first visit to Brandon, it is clear that conformity is not an option. Shortly after, his first metamorphosis occurs and Tony's friends begin to die.

Jancovich is correct to suggest that Brandon's actions are clearly reprehensible, and an apt metaphor for paternal control in 1950s America. However, it is also important to investigate what the doctor reveals about American society's view of psychiatry during the decade. After all, the film suggests that psychiatric sciences are useless – even damaging – as a means of therapy for troubled adolescents. Brandon's experiments are to blame for worsening Tony's behaviour and pushing him from thug to murderer; Tony might have trouble controlling his anger, but Brandon is little more than a maniac and a charlatan. This is certainly Biskind's view; he argues that the film holds psychiatry and delinquency in equal contempt, asserting that

> Tony becomes dangerous not because therapy has failed but because it has succeeded. Before he sees Brandon, Tony is merely a delinquent; after a few sessions on the couch he leaves a werewolf. The psychiatrist, the pillar of the system of therapeutic control, is simply a mad scientist.[11]

So *I Was a Teenage Werewolf* might express a belief that delinquency is a problem, but one that certainly cannot be cured by science or medicine.

If psychiatry cannot be trusted, then how might Tony's eventual fate have been averted? It is made clear at several points in the film's narrative that Tony was brought up in a motherless environment. This is in stark contrast to his girlfriend, Arlene (Yvonne Lime), who has clearly been raised by affluent and happily married parents. Gathered in their home together while Tony waits outside in his car, they are the quintessential picture of the nuclear family and a representation of everything Tony lacks. Perhaps Tony would never have developed such a violent temper if his widowed father, Charles (Malcolm Atterbury), had re-married. However, a line of dialogue spoken by Charles concludes that his son would not have accepted another woman as a substitute for his mother. In fact, even taking the contrast the film develops between Tony's single-parent upbringing and Arlene's nuclear family into account, it is difficult to read Tony's childhood as an explanation for his actions as a teen. As Biskind attests, 'the point in this film is that his damaged family does *not* account for his strange behaviour. His problems . . . do not come from out there, from the environment. They are not attributable to any psychosocial matrix outside of himself.'[12] Jancovich, too, makes clear that Tony's anger 'is not associated with a dysfunctional family'.[13]

Perhaps peer pressure could be blamed for Tony's outbursts, but while his friends are immersed in youth culture and sneak away from their parents to hold parties with no adult supervision, they lack Tony's violent tendencies and are otherwise well adjusted to society. They are able to indulge in the kind of media – chiefly rock and roll – that Kefauver would have considered dangerous without becoming antisocial. In fact, they are most often the focus of Tony's violent rages before he becomes a werewolf and, other than Brandon, his only victims afterwards. Following his first transformation, Tony ambushes and kills one of his best friends as he walks home alone through secluded woodland. His second victim is fellow high school student Theresa (Dawn Richard), who Tony observes practising alone in the school's gymnasium; his second transformation occurs as he stares at her lustfully, a sexual awakening leading to a savage murder. The fact that we do not ever see Tony attack an adult other than his psychiatrist reveals a great deal; Tony's choice of friends and peers as potential victims further confirms that his problems are his and his alone.

It is clear, then, that Tony's anger is not the result of his upbringing or his social circumstances. As he says himself: 'I say things, I do things. I don't know why.' He is constantly told by parents, teachers and so on that he needs to 'adjust', that he ought just to 'bow to authority', but Tony steadfastly resists conformity. Even Brandon – a maniac – seems to think that Tony is beyond rehabilitation before he begins to experiment on him, telling his reluctant assistant: 'we're probably saving him from the gas chamber'. Furthermore, therapy does nothing but unleash an even darker side of him. But by removing any cause for the teenage werewolf's unbridled rage, the film also provides a stronger point of identification for its target audience. Tony's violent outbursts – in human or werewolf form – are not motivated by any one thing, but by everything: a society that simply doesn't understand him. As Jancovich suggests, 'He is a genuine outsider who only wants people to recognise and respect his difference, a desire which is ultimately frustrated and denied him.'[14] Without a concrete motivation for his fury, then, Tony is either a delinquent who was simply born 'bad' or a vessel for subversive teenage rebellion.

I Was a Teenage Werewolf is an exceptionally interesting cultural product – one that arises from a society simultaneously defined by the birth of the teenager and gripped by a fear of youth – that supports opposing interpretations from either side of the political spectrum. The film's ending continues to assist both readings. For Biskind, Tony's death at the hands of the police is necessary and unavoidable:

> with the therapeutic option in shambles, with psychoanalysis exposed as the work of the devil . . . the only alternative left is the resort to force, which in the case of *Werewolf* means the police . . . the lesson is clear: Delinquents aren't sick, they're evil, and the best thing to do with kids who don't like back slappers is to shoot them.[15]

For Jancovich, Tony is exonerated by the fact that he is controlled and manipulated by Brandon; he argues that Tony only attacks his friends because he fails to recognise his real enemy, his death a tragic result of the doctor's crimes.[16] This is a film, then, that told America's youth that any attempt at insurrection would be stamped out with authoritative discipline – and simultaneously allowed them to live vicariously through a teenage werewolf as he rebelled against the oppressive conservatism of the 1950s.

A new cycle of American werewolf films did not arrive until the early 1970s, and the United States had changed immeasurably in the interim. By the time *Werewolves on Wheels* (1971), *The Boy Who Cried Werewolf* (1973) and *The Werewolf of Washington* (1973) saw theatrical release, a werewolf could not simply be shot dead and its curse would always survive; even the proper authorities had lost any power they had in American horror cinema. The onset of the Vietnam War, the birth of the counterculture and the rapid escalation of the battle for civil rights created one of the most turbulent periods in American history and produced a new kind of bleak, pessimistic and apocalyptic horror film to signal the death of the 'American Dream'. Fourteen years after Tony Rivers was cut down in a hail of bullets on drive-in movie screens, total social breakdown seemed imminent in the United States. The seeds of this crisis had been sown in the 1950s. After all, as Biskind notes in surmising his examination of the film, *I Was a Teenage Werewolf*'s theme of generational conflict was enormously prescient:

> By 1957, when it was made, the signs were in the wind, and conservatives saw them first. The peer group, the youth culture that pluralists had midwived, and then fattened with hamburgers, movies, and [rock and roll], was, like Tony, about to become a monster. With its long hair and wild, unkempt beard, that monster was a hippy.[17]

The Boys Who Cried Wolf

By the early 1970s, America was in turmoil. A cultural, social and political upheaval had been building: as the United States government had escalated military operations in Vietnam, the new youth culture birthed in the 1950s had evolved into the anti-establishment counterculture of the 1960s. Steadfastly opposed to the conservative mainstream, this sizeable section of America's youth formed an ideological movement determined to stand against aggressive foreign policy, resist conformity and champion civil rights. Meanwhile, the authorities began stamping out these protests by any means necessary, even firing on their own citizens. Civil unrest escalated to its peak in 1968, the year the My Lai massacre occurred in Vietnam and the assassinations of Robert Kennedy and Martin Luther King Jr were witnessed on American soil. As Leslie H. Abramson attests:

> During 1968, the actual assumed the status of the harrowing imaginary as history became an unmitigated American nightmare. This traumatic year proceeded with a series of horrific shocks and tumultuous confrontations as establishment and anti-establishment forces clashed on political, cultural, and geographic fields of engagement. Domestic icons, institutions, and policies were attacked, activism climaxed and was suppressed by extremist measures . . . figures and forces of arbitration no longer seemed to exist.[18]

If faith in the establishment had tumbled in 1968, a new low would be found as the 1970s dawned. In 1969, news of the My Lai massacre broke, revealing that American troops had been responsible for the murder of hundreds of unarmed Vietnamese. In 1970, the Ohio National Guard opened fire on anti-war protestors at Kent State University, killing four students and injuring a further nine. Richard Nixon eventually withdrew American troops from Vietnam in 1973, but after '1.3 million Vietnamese deaths and 56,000 American losses, there was little that was honourable about the end of the war in Vietnam'.[19] The Watergate scandal was the final insult; in addition to the numerous horrors that had blighted the preceding decade, by 1973 it became clear to the nation's citizens that they had been lied to by their president; authority was corrupt and self-serving, while society was seemingly on the verge of collapse.

As these events unfolded and a cultural crisis began to develop, in many ways the horror film came to embody the paranoia that was palpable in society. As part of a movement that Jason Zinoman calls 'New Horror',[20] seminal horror films from *Night of the Living Dead* (1968) to *The Hills Have Eyes* (1977) have all been suggested to be 'an indication of an ideological crisis in America'.[21] New Horror broadly describes a body of films released from the late 1960s to the late 1970s, characterised by countercultural themes and typified by the early works of such filmmakers as George A. Romero, Tobe Hooper, Wes Craven, John Carpenter and Bob Clark. With its subversive themes of social, governmental and familial collapse, *Night of the Living Dead* is perhaps the primary progenitor of the cycle. Gregory A. Waller argues that, along with *Rosemary's Baby* (1968), Romero's film 'ushered in the modern era of horror' and established the horror film as a site for social and political debate.[22] This was a new kind of horror film, a product of an era defined by cultural crisis. Kendall R. Phillips argues that this crisis had become so severe by the mid-1970s that the horror films of the period began to depict the complete disintegration of society, an apocalypse to signal the death of the civilised United States. He argues that *The Exorcist* (1973) and *The Texas Chain Saw Massacre* (1974) 'ushered in an increasingly urgent and pessimistic tone . . . [indicating] that the world as we know it is ending and that behind the layers of cultural illusion lies a deep, inner truth about our nature'.[23]

The counterculture, then – and the horrifying social and political events that had created it – birthed a new kind of horror film. Another effect the counterculture had on the American film industry was the proliferation of a new and highly popular exploitation genre: the biker film. *Werewolves on Wheels*, the first American werewolf film since *I Was a Teenage Werewolf*, would be an attempt to marry the biker movie with the New Horror movement. Although the Hells Angels had been established soon after the Second World War,[24] it was as a result of the 1960s counterculture that they and other biker gangs gained notoriety as romanticised outsiders; in 1966, the term 'one-percenter' was popularised as a descriptor for these near-mythical outlaw bikers who refused to conform to mainstream society's laws and moral codes.[25] As John Wood suggests, the perceived but ultimately misguided connection between biker gangs and the counterculture was created, in part, by the American film industry:

> Members of the counterculture, who saw the bikers as being similar to the violent and independent yet goodhearted bikers romanticized in the 1953 movie *The Wild One*, envisioned the Angels as their protectors from the establishment. Sixties popular culture fueled the counterculture's belief in the supposed link between the Angels and themselves with movies such as 1969's *Easy Rider*, which portrayed bikers as little more than motorized hippies.[26]

Of course, an explanation for the interplay between biker gangs, the counterculture and the American film industry during the 1960s and early 1970s is not as simple as Wood suggests. The relationship among the three was cyclical; genre films may have created a popular conception that the Hells Angels and the counterculture were inseparably connected, but it was the rapid expansion of biker gangs and media interest in their violent crimes during times of civil unrest that caused the proliferation of the genre in the first place. As Randall Clark asserts, the biker movie 'was really created in the mid-1960s, when [Hells Angels] and other extremely violent biker gangs were making national headlines'.[27] As Clark observes, *The Wild One* (1953) and *Motorcycle Gang* (1957) were the only biker films produced during the 1950s, while the genre would go on to become hugely prolific in the mid-1960s after the birth of the counterculture and the release of *The Wild Angels* (1966). Produced and directed by Roger Corman, *The Wild Angels* depicted bikers in a wholly negative light and was explicitly designed – in true Corman style – to capitalise on media and public interest in motorcycle gangs and their criminal activities.[28]

Clark suggests that 'The dozens of films that followed [*The Wild Angels*] can largely be broken into two groups: movies in which the bikers are misunderstood rebels, and movies in which the bikers are thoroughly evil.'[29] In other words, the biker films of the period encouraged either a conservative or a liberal interpretation of their subject matter, depicting bikers as a scourge on society or as romanticised outsiders. The genre would remain popular from 1966 until the early 1970s and it was, of course, the latter group of films that the counterculture took to heart.

Werewolves on Wheels was released after the genre's apex, when interest in biker films was waning. As Clark states, it was an attempt to combine a biker narrative with elements of horror, but by this time 'audience fascination with motorcycle gangs had diminished'.[30] The biker movie had fallen into decline partly due to the murder of Meredith Hunter, an eighteen-year-old black man who was stabbed to death by members of the Hells Angels at a Rolling Stones concert which took place at the Altamont Speedway in December 1969. The only member of the gang to be brought to trial for Hunter's murder, Allan Passaro, was not convicted of the crime and, as Wood suggests, 'the Altamont incident signaled the end of the American counterculture's decade-long love affair with the [Hells Angels]'.[31] It was also the incident that put an end to the popularity of the biker film; according to Clark, the genre was 'virtually out of production by 1973'.[32]

Werewolves on Wheels is a rare example of the biker film that ostensibly seems to take neither a liberal nor a conservative stance, perhaps because it was one of the few to be produced and released after the Altamont incident. However, this is more likely a result of its genre hybridity; rather than the biker film, *Werewolves on Wheels* ultimately takes its political cues from New Horror and particularly *Night of the Living Dead*, imagining a desolate America in which two factions – represented by a hedonistic biker gang and the group of satanic monks that curse them to werewolfism – are engaged in an aimless ideological conflict.

Werewolves on Wheels concerns an outlaw gang – the 'Devil's Advocates' – that is travelling through the rural United States. After a violent run-in with

locals at a secluded gas station, Tarot (Gene Shane as Deuce Berry) suggests to the gang's leader, Adam (Stephen Oliver), that they ride on to an
isolated monastery. There, the Devil's Advocates meet a group of faceless
monks dressed in brown hooded robes, led by a high priest known only as
One (Severn Darden). The monks provide the gang with bread and wine,
sustenance which is shortly revealed to be drugged with tranquilisers. As
night falls and with the gang unconscious, the monks begin a satanic ritual in
which they sacrifice a black cat and offer Adam's lover, Helen (Donna Anders
as D. J. Anderson), to the Devil as his bride. Adam and his followers wake
up during the ritual and storm the temple, attacking the monks and rescu-
ing Helen. They leave the monastery, but not before a satanic curse is placed
upon them; in the following days, the Devil's Advocates find themselves lost
in the desert and hunted by an unseen creature.

As in many biker films of the period, from the outset the Devil's Advocates are identified as countercultural. The film's credit sequence – which
sees the gang ride through arid terrain, perform dangerous motorcycle
stunts, smoke cannabis and brawl with locals – is clearly designed to align
the bikers with a contemporaneous popular conception of the counterculture: these are free-spirited, pleasure-seeking drifters who live outside
of normative society. The sequence is also strikingly reminiscent of the
opening of *Easy Rider* (1969), evoking the editing and cinematography of
the earlier film and further strengthening a thematic link between bikers
and hippies. Meanwhile, the gang is actively distanced from notions of
the biker as organised crime figure; the members of the Devil's Advocates
drink heavily, are sexually promiscuous, discuss their indulgence in various drugs and are involved in some minor brawls, but are not seen to par-
ticipate in any truly serious – and certainly not organised – crime. In this
regard they are aligned more with the free-spirited nomads of *Easy Rider*
than with the dangerous criminals of *The Wild Angels*. Crucially, though,
these are not the hippy martyrs of *Easy Rider*; the bikers of *Werewolves on
Wheels* primarily seek personal gratification. They have no interest in the
nobler pursuits of peace and love.

In ideological terms the monks are starkly opposed to the Devil's
Advocates; from the moment they leave their temple, they are mocked
and treated with contempt by the bikers. The monks are the picture of
modesty: they walk barefoot and hide their faces behind hoods; they move
in unison, slowly and methodically, carrying with them archaic symbols
of their dark religion; and they are, aside from fevered chanting, entirely
silent. Their leader is the only member of their party who speaks: a highly
articulate man who enunciates with perfect diction. In many ways, then,
the devil-worshippers are an exaggerated caricature of conservatism.

They are the picture of restraint, uniformity, traditionalism, religious fundamentalism and sexual repression. This is in stark contrast to the Devil's Advocates, who desire the freedoms of sexuality and expression above all else. Both groups are exaggerated metaphors: the conservative monks are repressed traditionalists who are indistinguishable from one another, while the liberal bikers are wild, blithe hedonists, who care for nothing but sex and intoxicants and dress in t-shirts and tattered denim; a striking visual contrast is created between the two groups when they first meet (Figure 3.1). This is further reinforced later as the gang members begin to transform into werewolves; they become, of course, wild in a very literal sense. In short, then, the monks represent a liberal's exaggerated conception of conservatism and vice versa; their crossed paths lead to an occult battle of ideals.

Following the luridly surreal satanic ritual and the bikers' escape from the monks, the Devil's Advocates become stranded in the desert, aimlessly wandering from place to place. They set up camp each night as darkness falls. On the first night, Mouse (Owen Orr) and one of the gang's female followers, Shirley (Anna Lynn Brown), are ripped apart by a werewolf seen only in shadow as they chase each other around, engaging in something between violent sexual foreplay and blasphemy (Shirley repeatedly screams 'Rape me, Satan!'). The next night, Adam orders a member of the gang to be awake at all times to keep watch over the group and an enormous fire is lit in the hope of scaring away predators. Movie (Gray Johnson)

Figure 3.1 The Devil's Advocates meet a group of satanic monks in *Werewolves on Wheels* (1971), creating a striking visual contrast between the bikers and the devil-worshippers.

arrives to take over from Tarot as watchman immediately after having sex with another of the gang's devotees; he is swiftly attacked by the werewolf, mauled and thrown onto the campfire. With no body to bury, the gang moves on. Throughout these harrowing events, the only member of the gang to suspect anything sinister afoot is Tarot, who experiences incessant visions of the monks and believes the group to be suffering under their occult influence. These scenes allegorise a struggle of wills between the counterculture and the establishment; in a line of dialogue that reveals a battle for ideological supremacy between the conservative mainstream and rebellious outsiders, Tarot fearfully remarks to his peers that 'Someone's controlling the vibes.'

Following Movie's death, Adam agrees to take revenge on the monks if only to calm the superstition and terror spreading through the group. The bikers do not make it to the monastery before sundown, however, and are forced to camp in the open. As darkness falls, Adam, Helen and others transform into werewolves and attack the gang before being set alight and apparently killed. Enraged and thirsty for revenge, the remaining bikers storm the monastery with the intention of killing all inside. They freeze when the monks lower their hoods, revealing the stoic faces of the gang's fallen comrades. Adam is now their leader; he offers chunks of bread dipped in fresh blood to the remaining bikers in a form of unholy communion.

This ending could lead to multiple interpretations of the film, all of them linked to its use of the werewolf as a horror monster. From a liberal standpoint, it could be read as a climax in which the bikers have finally been stripped of their individuality and forced to conform to the expectations of an oppressive society. After all, this is a film in which a group of demonic monks – representative of an overbearing conservative establishment – firstly transforms free-spirited nomads into feral monsters, secondly forces them to tear their comrades apart and finally assimilates them into the mainstream. By cursing the bikers to werewolfism, the monks force them to embrace the same bestial, senseless violence that the establishment was using against its own people on city streets and college campuses across America in an effort to suppress peaceful protest. And once they have destroyed dissenters, the bikers are forced to conform to dominant ideology by becoming devil-worshippers themselves.

Contrarily, this climax – and by extension the film's werewolves – could also be interpreted from a conservative point of view. It is notable that, earlier in the film, both Mouse and Movie are attacked and killed immediately after indulging in – or attempting to indulge in – sexual acts, and so their deaths could conceivably be read as retribution for their apparent promiscuity. Moreover, then, their reincarnation as members of the monks' dark congregation – doomed to forever serve the Devil – is suffering earned by giving into their carnal impulses. If the film is read in this way, then as some of the bikers transform into werewolves they not only become instruments through which the other liberals can be punished for their sybaritic lifestyles, they also come to represent a truly monstrous incarnation of the counterculture via a conservative's conception of the hippy: hairy, feral and out of control.

However, to use the climax as evidence that the film is either a right- or left-leaning text would require either the monks or the bikers to be depicted positively throughout the rest of the film. On the contrary, the gang is far from valorised for its wanton behaviour and the monks are, after all, in league with the Devil. Rather, that the bikers have first transformed into monsters and then literally and figuratively become one with the devil-worshippers is symptomatic of an early 1970s paranoia that liberals and conservatives are essentially one and the same. In this regard, *Werewolves on Wheels* is similar to *The Last House on the Left* (1972), in which vengeful middle-class parents do battle with a corrupt family of hippies representative of a 'dark counterculture'.[33] Both films suggest that the two sides are equally contributing to the total degradation of America through an all-consuming ideological war. This is certainly the view taken by Michel Levesque, the film's director; in his commentary on the film's ending he rhetorically asks, 'When evil fights evil, evil's got to win, right?'[34]

Such a subtext is supported by the vision of the United States *Werewolves on Wheels* projects: a sparsely populated, arid wasteland devoid of all civilisation or hope, this America is so empty it could be post-apocalyptic. Aside from its werewolf bikers and demonic monks, there are barely any other characters in the film and certainly no figures of authority, no higher power capable of intervening in the madness and violence. God is absent: a theme common in New Horror.[35] In fact, the film's total disdain for America is revealed during the scene that sees the bikers fight off their werewolf attackers: one member of the gang callously burns the American flag for use as a torch. And so perhaps the film's werewolves are most accurately read not as metaphors for a violent establishment or a monstrous vision of the counterculture; instead, the werewolf's dual nature is used to allegorise the two sides of an ideological conflict that is tearing the nation apart. If the bikers represent the liberal counterculture and the monks stand in for the conservative mainstream, then the werewolf is depicted as the midway point between those warring factions: a contested body in which a battle of ideals is waged. Beyond its exploitative title, then, *Werewolves on Wheels* uses its feral monsters to communicate a very serious message: America is desolate, doomed and, most importantly, divided.

Werewolves on Wheels, then, imagines a collapsing society in which liberals and conservatives are fictionalised respectively as outlaw bikers and demonic monks, the werewolf a metaphor for the conflict raging between them. *The Boy Who Cried Werewolf* followed in 1973, and it too depicts America as a nation torn apart by an ideological war, but the later film uses this political conflict as a backdrop to a much more intimate issue: the collapse of the nuclear family. It employs werewolfism as a metaphor for a broken society and broken homes: an America where the primacy of the family has been eroded, authority has lost its power and America's children are doomed to repeat their parents' mistakes. In fact, New Horror most often levels its criticisms at the family, the most sacred of traditional American institutions. As Phillips observes, 'If broad social structures seemed to have failed, there was little solace to be found in the most intimate structure of social life.'[36]

The 1960s had witnessed the beginning of the sexual revolution and Phillips argues that, as a result, 'the American divorce rate increased dramatically at the same time as birth rates dropped to historic lows. This trend accelerated in the early 1970s as Americans turned away from the traditional models of family life.'[37] There were many reasons for this, primarily continued sexual exploration facilitated by developments in contraceptive technology and the legalisation of abortion.[38] Phillips connects this to the apocalyptic tone present in horror cinema of the era, suggesting that a feeling had arisen from the paranoid zeitgeist to create 'an underlying concern that the next generation might wreak even more cultural destruction'.[39]

However, perhaps the bleak pessimism that pervades these works does not express a fear of America's children so much as it articulates a feeling that the defining political, social and cultural crises of the era are doing irreversible damage to the next generation. In *Night of the Living Dead*, pre-pubescent ghoul Karen Cooper eats her dysfunctional parents; *The Last House on the Left* sees naïve teenager Mari Collingwood tortured, raped and murdered by a family of maniacs, before her own parents commit equally horrific crimes in the name of revenge; and during *The Texas Chain Saw Massacre*, a group of teens are killed and eaten by a family of slaughterhouse workers, leaving the lone survivor laughing hysterically. These films suggest that if America's youth could survive the 1970s at all, they would emerge irreversibly traumatised by their elders. Furthermore, if they were to cause more damage to society in their adulthood, it would be their parents' fault.

The Boy Who Cried Werewolf has identical cultural concerns to these seminal films. Ostensibly the story of a boy on the verge of adolescence who believes his father to be a werewolf, the film encapsulates the horrifying nature of the damage one generation can do to the next. The plot concerns a married couple, Robert and Sandy Bridgestone (Kerwin Mathews and Elaine Devry), who are in the midst of a divorce. Robert has been taking his son, Richie (Scott Sealey), on trips to a cabin in the mountains in order to try and maintain their relationship. During one such trip, Robert is bitten by a werewolf. For the rest of the film, Richie tries desperately to speak out, but no one will believe him: not his mother, not the police and not his psychiatrist, Dr Marderosian (George Gaynes). As a werewolf, Robert menaces Richie and kills several people before taking his wife and son back into the mountains for one last camping trip. There, he transforms and attacks them both, his monstrous aggression aimed firmly at his family (Figure 3.2). He is eventually killed during an encounter with the police, but not before biting Richie, cursing his son to werewolfism only seconds before his death.

Richie's problems begin with his dysfunctional parents. The fact that Robert's bestial rage is primarily directed towards his son is especially telling; his werewolfery is equated with the explosive episodes of an abusive father, and by the film's second act Richie's psychiatrist has become convinced that the child is using a horror story to rationalise parental abuse. Subsequently, Robert kills and mutilates the child's doctor, presumably in a

Figure 3.2 In *The Boy Who Cried Werewolf* (1973), monsters attack their families; here Robert Bridgestone (Kerwin Matthews) looms over his sleeping wife, Sandy (Elaine Devry).

desperate subconscious attempt to conceal his secret from Richie's mother. Nevertheless, they are never able to reconcile their marriage and, just as Sandy begins to rediscover her love for Robert, he attacks his family.

But here society's problems are not the product of one dysfunctional individual. The real cultural issue highlighted in *The Boy Who Cried Werewolf* is reflected in its title. Richie is born to a generation too preoccupied with warring on familial, societal and political battlegrounds to answer his cries for help. Everybody around the Bridgestone family fails to stop Robert from passing the werewolf's curse to his son – and therefore dooming him to a horrifying adolescence – simply by refusing to believe him. It is not only his father's abuse but the failure of his mother and wider society to intervene effectively that blights Richie's future. Like *Werewolves on Wheels*, then, *The Boy Who Cried Werewolf* is a product of the larger cultural crisis of its time and one that also depicts an ideological war between opposing forces – but here a child is trapped between them.

Conservatism is represented by the townspeople and police force local to the Bridgestones' cabin – primarily embodied by their ill-tempered sheriff (Robert J. Wilke) – while liberal counterculture appears in the form of hippies who have made the mountains their home. While Richie's parents fail to reconcile their broken marriage, these two groups stage a political conflict; the hippies attempt to spread a religious message of love and understanding, while the sheriff labels them 'freaks' and does his utmost to run them out of town. Meanwhile, Richie is continually threatened by his werewolf father, forgotten by those who should be coming to his aid. The only person in Richie's life who earnestly attempts to help him is his psychiatrist, but even he fails to stop Robert's abuse. Here, psychiatry is not evil, just futile.

Furthermore, the police are utterly incompetent in their few perfunctory efforts to help Richie, a theme that further aligns *The Boy Who Cried Werewolf* with *The Last House on the Left*, in which the comically bumbling incompetence of the police is juxtaposed with scenes of shocking violence.[40] Their attempts to find the culprit responsible for the deaths occurring around the Bridgestones' cabin amount to scouring the mountains for an animal capable of causing the kind of damage done to the werewolf's victims. The sheriff continues to disregard Richie's story until the film's climax, when he finally sees the wolf-man with his own eyes; but even with the knowledge that Robert truly is cursed, the police are still incapable of putting an end to his rampage. Unlike Tony Rivers, Robert is able to survive a hail of gunfire before he is finally killed in a freak accident, falling backwards onto a wooden stake.

And here not only conservative forces are proven ineffectual. The hippies attempt to rid Robert of his curse by exorcising the demon inside of him with God's love, but this – just as in *Werewolves on Wheels* – is a godless universe. The hippies believe they are successful in curing Robert, but in truth he returns to his human form only because the sun has risen, and later he returns to their commune in a murderous rage, intent to massacre them all. Furthermore, it is ironic that the leader of the commune preaches to his followers that 'God is not dead' in a scene immediately preceding Robert's first transformation; if bullets can't save Richie from his father, divine intervention certainly won't. In the end, the conservatives and liberals can do nothing but stand together and look on in horror as Robert sinks his teeth into his son's arm.

In the seconds before the credits roll at the end of *The Boy Who Cried Werewolf*, it becomes clear that Richie's life will now be filled with horror. A fresh bite wound on his arm, the child stands on the verge of puberty fatherless, destined to become a teenage werewolf, repeat his father's mistakes and live out a life of monstrosity and violence. In a climax that offers no more hope for the future than the pointless death that ends *Night of the Living Dead* or the hollow revenge that concludes *The Last House on the Left*, Richie's only inheritance from his father is the werewolf's curse and the misery that inevitably comes with it. For *The Boy Who Cried Werewolf*, 1970s America is a place where the next generation has been forgotten by a warring society and irreversibly damaged by its distracted and dysfunctional parents.

Animal transformation would also be used as a metaphor for familial breakdown in 1974's *Bat People*, an AIP film which has a strikingly similar plot to *The Boy Who Cried Werewolf*. In *Bat People*, recently married couple Dr John Beck (Stewart Moss) and his wife Cathy (Marianne McAndrew) go caving on their honeymoon. During the expedition, John is bitten by a fruit bat and begins to go through a metamorphosis into a monstrous human–bat hybrid. He unwittingly embarks on a killing spree and infects his wife with the condition before fleeing back to the caves, where Cathy eventually joins him following her own transformation: a truly monstrous marriage befitting of a decade in which the nuclear family was falling apart.

Later in the 1970s, children would become prolific horror monsters and the subject of some of the decade's most enduring examples of New Horror, including *The Exorcist*, *It's Alive* (1974), *Alice, Sweet Alice* (1976) and *Martin* (1977), in which the eponymous, possibly vampiric teenager drugs women before cutting them open and feeding on their blood, believing that he is a creature of the night. These films would all expand on the fear of a disillusioned and potentially dangerous generation of young people birthed by neglect.

A Wolf in Sheep's Clothing

The final werewolf film of the New Horror period is an entirely countercultural picture that uses the monster to criticise the United States
government amidst the Watergate scandal. In fact, *The Werewolf of
Washington* is perhaps the most overtly political werewolf film ever made:
a scathing attack on the establishment that accuses Richard Nixon's
administration of being a self-serving and corrupt institution, one that
can no longer be trusted to serve the American public. This satirical message is so obvious that even the film's theatrical poster referred to its
explicit nature; accompanied by the image of a werewolf dressed as Uncle
Sam, its tagline admits that the film makes its subtext 'perfectly clear'
(Figure 3.3).

The Werewolf of Washington was written and produced during the enquiry
into the burglary of the Democratic National Committee headquarters at
Washington's Watergate complex. Watergate, of course, remains one of the
most significant political scandals in American history and had a huge social
and cultural impact during the Senate Watergate Committee's investigation
into an apparent conspiracy and especially following Nixon's historic resignation in 1974. As Barna William Donovan notes:

> Watergate was a part of popular culture by 1974. The systematic destruction of
> Richard Nixon's image in particular, and a greater faith in politics in general, had
> become the daily fodder for cartoonists and comedians everywhere. Hollywood, in
> turn . . . fashioned some of its most successful thrillers around cynical plots of con-
> spiracy and corruption.[41]

Released in October 1973, *The Werewolf of Washington* is notable for being
the first film to address the Watergate scandal and was seen in theatres
almost a full year before Nixon's eventual resignation and the ignition of
Hollywood's fascination with conspiracy thrillers. In fact, writer-director
Milton Moses Ginsberg had begun to work on the film almost immediately after the Watergate burglary, with no idea at the time how the
situation would eventually unfold. In an interview with Brian Albright,
he recalls:

> I was obsessed with Nixon. There had been this break-in at Watergate, and at
> the time Nixon was trying to push through his Supreme Court nominees. There
> were incredible struggles with the Democrats over the same kind of creeps the
> Republicans put up now for Supreme Court nominees. He was engaged with this
> and arguing with the press. At the same time there was this Watergate break-in in
> the back pages of the newspapers.[42]

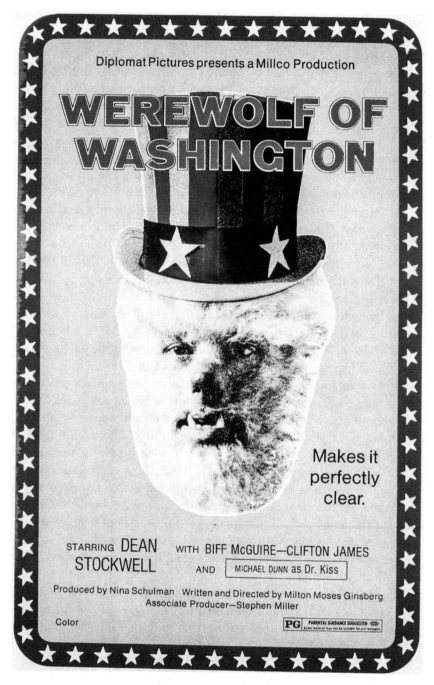

Figure 3.3 An American theatrical poster for *The Werewolf of Washington* (1973), featuring an image and tagline that both belie its obvious political commentary. © Diplomat Pictures

Evidence began to mount against Nixon as Ginsberg was finalising his script and casting his actors. He states that just after he secured Dean Stockwell for the lead role, 'the Watergate story was getting bigger'.[43] Even Ginsberg was unaware of how relevant *The Werewolf of Washington* would be. The film sees Jack Whittier (Stockwell), a reporter stranded in Budapest, bitten by an apparent werewolf. Upon his return to the United States, he becomes both a presidential press aide and a murderous monster. The film thereafter chronicles Whittier's struggle with werewolfism and, more importantly in this instance, the administration's attempts to cover up his crimes and deny any connection between a Nixon-like President (Bill McGuire) and the so-called 'Werewolf of Washington'.

The Werewolf of Washington's first twelve minutes borrow heavily from *The Wolf Man* (1941), to the point that the opening shot sees Whittier being given a silver-topped cane – identical to Larry Talbot's – as a gift by his Hungarian lover Giselle (Katalin Kallay), the handle shaped into the visage of a wolf. Soon after, Jack and Giselle set off for the airport; Whittier is returning to the United States. A car accident leads Whittier into a Romani campground in search of help, but he only finds an elderly woman who does not understand him. Shortly afterwards, Whittier is attacked and bitten by a wolf. In a reference to *The Wolf Man*'s ending, he bludgeons the animal with his cane and is shocked to see it transform into a man.

After a fade, Jack and Giselle are seen talking to a Hungarian inspector, who refuses to believe their story; he claims Whittier was attacked by a wolf and nothing more. Whittier collects himself and asks the inspector: 'What are you trying to cover up – is the White House behind this?' It is at this point that *The Werewolf of Washington* reveals its intention to craft a political allegory by adapting *The Wolf Man*'s central conceits for a Watergate audience; in the age of New Horror, gothic trappings might have seemed old-fashioned, but government conspiracy was all too real. In fact, Jack is so determined that he has been the target of a governmental conspiracy that he asks the inspector how he is able to speak English, suggesting that everything, no matter how minor, is potentially suspect in the post-Watergate world.

This theme continues in the next scene. Outside, the elderly woman is waiting for Jack and Giselle. She reveals that the werewolf Whittier killed was her son, who has now been freed from suffering. But Jack continues to find the explanation of a grand political conspiracy to be much more convincing than an occult curse. To discern the source of his victim's pain, he asks: 'Because of the communists – secret police?' She replies, 'Because of the sign of the pentagram.' This is, of course, a reference to werewolf mythology that has its genesis in *The Wolf Man*: that a werewolf will see a pentagram etched into the palm of his next victim. Jack mishears, and thinks he is beginning to understand; the film continues to update the seminal werewolf text for the paranoid 1970s as Jack replies, 'Ah, the Pentagon is behind all of this.'

Ultimately, the woman tells Whittier that he himself will soon become a werewolf. At this point, an incredulous Jack demands that Giselle – who has been translating Hungarian to English and vice versa – 'Find out who she's working for', refusing to believe that this could simply be an old, superstitious woman with a genuine belief in the occult. This entire exchange is played for overt comedy and, similarly to Jack's ridiculous conversation with the Hungarian inspector, announces the film's intention to twist the werewolf myth into an astute political satire. To Whittier, the idea that he has been cursed to werewolfery is utterly ludicrous. His steadfast determination that a wolf attack was a state-sanctioned attempt on his life mounted by forces within the American government is an even more comically preposterous notion, and in that it is also a clear indication of the growing paranoia of the time.

This paranoia surrounding governmental corruption comes to be a central theme throughout the rest of the film as, on his return to the United States, Whittier becomes involved in a wide-ranging government conspiracy as his bestial side begins to take over. Firstly, he unwittingly becomes the President's personal assassin as, in his werewolf form, he slaughters several people who threaten to bring down the administration. Secondly, he becomes involved in covering up his own crimes and an accessory to systemic oppression by failing to speak out when the Attorney General (Clifton James) decides to use the Black Panthers as a convenient scapegoat for the crimes perpetrated by the 'Werewolf of Washington', arresting a black couple on suspicion of having committed the high-profile murders. Jack then becomes the focus of a shady weapons programme when his affliction is discovered by a corrupt and sinister scientist working at the Pentagon, Dr Kiss (Michael Dunn). Ironically, then, Jack is initially (and falsely) convinced that he has been the target of a government attack, but later becomes embroiled in all manner of corruption and conspiracy himself.

Ultimately, even Jack's death becomes the subject of a conspiracy. After transforming aboard a helicopter carrying both the President and a representative from the Chinese government, Whittier flees to his own apartment (which, of course, is located in the Watergate complex). Throughout the narrative, Jack has been slowly rekindling his relationship with the President's daughter, Marion (Jane House); she is waiting for him when he arrives, and the werewolf attacks. Reluctantly, Marion is forced to shoot him with a gun loaded with silver bullets, given to her by Whittier for protection. When the authorities arrive, the Attorney General immediately plans a cover-up, stating: 'We'll give him a hero's burial – he came between a sniper's bullet and the President's daughter.' In this, the Attorney General concocts a criminal conspiracy, perverts the course of justice and creates *The Werewolf of Washington*'s very own Watergate scandal. An official approaches and says, ominously, 'The President's going to be alright, he just has a little bite on the neck.'

For, during the scuffle in the helicopter, the President is bitten. In the film's infamous final shot, the White House is seen in darkness below a full moon before a wolf begins to howl. Over the film's credits, the President delivers one final speech:

> My fellow Americans, this is your President speaking to you from the White House. First, I want to thank you for your letters and telegrams offering me your best wishes during my recent illness. Secondly, I know I can count on your support as I lash out against the enemies of America. Both in the press, as well as the Senate; Republicans as well as Democrats; white as well as black, who have circulated vicious rumours holding members of my administration responsible for the recent and tragic deaths of just a few of my political opponents. At night, I roam the silent, empty corridors of this great house, wrestling with my conscience, and I've come to this conclusion: if I'm to prevent our enemies to destroy, not me, but the very office of the Presidency, I must have your support. And so, and so . . . And so . . . And so, I . . .

As the President speaks these last few words, his breathing becomes laboured and gives way to high-pitched howls. America's leader has become a werewolf and – in the spirit of New Horror – Jack's curse has not only survived a silver bullet but has been passed on to the President of the United States of America. Just as in *The Boy Who Cried Werewolf*, here the infectious nature of the werewolf curse is used to underline the film's central themes, but *The Werewolf of Washington*'s contagious strain of werewolfism does not just corrupt the family unit but the entire American government, and acts as a metaphor for the criminality that seemed to be spreading through the establishment like a volatile disease in the age of Watergate. In this, the film would prove to be incredibly prescient; just as Jack has passed his awful curse to the most powerful man in the world, soon it would become clear that knowledge of the Watergate robbery reached all the way to the upper echelons of the Nixon administration.

In the same month as *The Werewolf of Washington* was first seen on cinema screens, the 'Saturday Night Massacre' would occur, during which Nixon would either fire or force the resignations of several high-profile members of his administration, and less than a month later he would utter the infamous words, 'Well, I am not a crook' in conversation with members of the Associated Press. Having been found to have actively covered up links between his administration and the Watergate burglary, he would finally resign on national television in August 1974. As Ginsberg suggests, 'One of the problems with the film, aside from its obvious deficiencies, was that when Watergate broke, it was something no fiction could encompass. The reality was just so much bigger than any fiction that my film looked tame.'[44]

Though the film was dwarfed by the scale of the scandal, *The Werewolf of Washington* remains an important cultural document with a very bleak message. That message has been elegantly articulated by S. S. Prawer, who says of *The Werewolf of Washington* and other horror films contemporaneous to his writing in the late 1970s: 'Particularly characteristic of our time are suggestions, in American films of the post-Watergate era . . . that if we want to look for demons, monsters and devil-worshippers, we shall be most likely to find them in the offices of those to whom the destinies of nations have been entrusted.'[45]

I Was a Teenage Werewolf is the last werewolf film of the American film industry's classical period, a film that simultaneously appealed to and demonised a generation popularly believed to be out of control. *Werewolves on Wheels* and *The Boy Who Cried Werewolf* would both dramatise the conflict between liberal and conservative forces in times of cultural change, while *The Werewolf of Washington* would satirise the wholesale loss of faith in authority created by the Watergate scandal. There would be one more countercultural werewolf film of the 1970s: *The Werewolf of Woodstock* (1975), a satirical made-for-television film in which a conservative farmer with a hatred of hippies becomes a werewolf after being electrocuted. Thereafter, he stalks members of the counterculture during electrical storms until the police lure the creature out with loud rock music and eventually shoot him dead. The next prolonged cycle of American werewolf films would begin in 1981, a year which would see the release of three werewolf pictures. Meanwhile, a prolific cycle of werewolf films arose in Europe during the 1960s and 1970s, and used werewolfism as a metaphor through which to explore the consequences of the sexual revolution.

CHAPTER 4

Hounds of Love

Mating for Life

While the werewolf film became largely dormant in North America between 1973 and the beginning of the next decade, it had found a new lease of life in Europe in the 1960s. Between the late 1950s and the end of the 1970s, several European film industries became prolific producers of horror movies. Many of these films embraced gothic aesthetics and drew heavy inspiration from Universal's monster movies of the 1930s and 1940s, albeit with the addition of far more explicit sex and violence than would have been permissible in that period. It was in this context that the werewolf thrived outside of America in the horror cinema of Britain, Italy and Spain.

The year 1957 saw the release of a British horror film that changed the landscape of European cinema: *The Curse of Frankenstein*, Hammer Films' first foray into gothic horror. Hammer had not set out to establish itself as a producer of horror films; this came about by accident. The company had made a habit of adapting BBC radio programmes, and quickly acquired the rights to produce an adaptation of its popular television serial *The Quatermass Experiment* (1953). Hammer's adaptation, retitled *The Quatermass Xperiment*, was released in 1955 to huge commercial success. As Denis Meikle recounts, Hammer surmised that the film's box-office draw was not just due to the popularity of the source material, but also 'the essential humanity of the film's monster'. Accordingly, the company 'began to cast around for subjects of similar appeal'.[1]

It was at this time that Hammer was approached by American film investor Eliot Hyman to finance a new adaptation of Mary Shelley's *Frankenstein* (1818). Already seeking to capitalise on the success of *The Quatermass Xperiment* with *X the Unknown* (1956) and *Quatermass 2* (1957), Hammer agreed to co-finance the project. *The Curse of Frankenstein* was a box-office hit, generating 'brisk business in Britain, the US and then in Europe as well. For an outlay of £64,000, or $270,000, the film made between $7–8 million'.[2]

Having discovered a winning formula, Hammer put a raft of other gothic horror films into production, including *The Revenge of Frankenstein* (1958), *Dracula* (1958), *The Mummy* (1959) and *The Hound of the Baskervilles* (1959).

The year 1957 had also been an important one for Italian genre cinema, as it witnessed the release of the country's first horror picture since the coming of sound: *I Vampiri*.[3] A gothic vampire tale with a contemporary setting, the film was released a month before *The Curse of Frankenstein* and was not a success. But, as Roberto Curti recounts, 'things would soon change in just a couple of years, after the release of a foreign film that dealt with vampirism . . . and which would prove to be an extraordinary success in Italy'. That film was Hammer's *Dracula*.[4] Following the international success of *Dracula*, Italy's film industry took heavy inspiration from Hammer and became a prolific producer of gothic horror, beginning with *Black Sunday* (1960).[5] *Black Sunday* recovered its budget in Italy and, like both *The Curse of Frankenstein* and *Dracula*, went on to be successful in the United States.[6] By the early 1960s, both Britain and Italy had launched into sustained gothic horror cycles; by the end of the decade, gothic chillers were also being produced in several other European nations, including France, Spain, West Germany and even the Soviet Union,[7] while Roger Corman echoed Hammer's style in his series of Edgar Allan Poe adaptations for American International Pictures.

What the European films produced in this period often share in common is a preoccupation with sexualised imagery. As Danny Shipka suggests, 'they relied on shocking and titillating audiences with as much violence and nudity as they could handle'.[8] This was, of course, a sign of changing times. In contrast to the gothic horror produced in the United States during the 1930s and 1940s, the later European cycle found popularity in an era that witnessed rapidly changing attitudes to sex – beginning as it did in the late 1950s, during the early years of the sexual revolution.[9] These films became popular in tandem with rising divorce rates, the availability of antibiotics to combat sexually transmitted infections, the introduction of the contraceptive pill and the increasing sexualisation of popular media.[10] As David Allyn suggests, in the first half of the twentieth century:

> Advertising became more suggestive, avant-garde writers eschewed Victorian proprieties in describing their sexual experiences, magazine publishers began printing sexually titillating images to appeal to their male readers, and young women started to flaunt their 'sex appeal.' To many, these changes were deeply disturbing.[11]

To illustrate resistance to the increasing sexualisation of Western society, Allyn discusses the work of Pitirim Sorokin, a Harvard sociologist, who 'decried the "sex revolution" he saw taking place' as early as 1954.[12]

Just as much evidence for a conservative backlash to the sexual revolution can be found in the critical response to Hammer's early horror films. As Peter Hutchings points out, *Dracula*'s more negative reviews painted it as 'a symptom of a sick society'.[13] He draws particular attention to Peter John Dyer's review for *Films and Filming*, in which the critic laments the sexualisation of Dracula's trio of female companions, here depicted as one 'buxom brunette (no lady, judging by her dishabille)', and implicitly links the film's sex and violence together: 'Blood dripping on Dracula's coffin, trickling down his chin, streaming over Mina's nightie, you get it all over your hands and your neck and your teeth.'[14]

Britain was, at this time, led by a Conservative government under Harold Macmillan. That *Dracula* met with such reactionary critical responses is thus surprising only in that the film is far more in line with its critics than they cared to notice. As Meikle suggests, Hammer's *Dracula* purposely depicted the count as 'a despoiler of female flesh'.[15] And while there is perhaps something progressive in the fact that Dracula's female victims are seen to openly express their sexuality through their desire for the vampire,[16] it remains a socially conservative film in which Christopher Lee's count – a symbol of predatory sexuality – is destroyed by Peter Cushing's morally righteous Van Helsing. This was a film produced by a society in which attitudes to sex were changing – but one that ultimately seeks to maintain the status quo. As Hutchings asserts, for Hammer's early horror films, 'male sexual desire is . . . nearly always seen as either weakening or evil'.[17]

Hammer's first and only werewolf film, *The Curse of the Werewolf* (1961), is similar. A loose adaptation of Guy Endore's *The Werewolf of Paris* (1933), it is set in eighteenth-century Spain and follows Leon Corledo (Oliver Reed), a child of rape who is doomed to become a werewolf after he is born on Christmas Day. His werewolfism develops in adolescence and returns in adulthood, when he falls in love with Cristina (Catherine Feller), the daughter of a wealthy vintner, Don Fernando Gomez (Ewen Solon). Convinced that Cristina will never leave her fiancé (David Conville), Leon visits a brothel, where he transforms under the light of the full moon and kills both his best friend, Jose (Martin Matthews) and a sex worker, Vera (Sheila Brennan). Leon then comes to discover that Cristina does care for him and that her love is a cure for his affliction. But this realisation comes too late: Leon is imprisoned for his crimes, transforms and claims a number of other victims. At the film's climax, he is killed with a silver bullet fired by Don Alfredo Corledo (Clifford Evans), his adoptive father.

The Curse of the Werewolf also received some scathing reviews that drew attention to its sexualised violence. For example, *Monthly Film Bulletin* referred to it as 'a singularly repellent job of slaughter-house horror' and took particular exception to the film's opening, which details the rape of Leon's mother (Yvonne Romaine) – a mute servant to the corrupt Marques Siniestro (Anthony Dawson) – when her master locks her in a dungeon with a beggar (Richard Wordsworth) as punishment for rejecting his sexual advances: 'The prologue's account of the [marques's] sadistic proclivities could hardly be more explicit.'[18] In fact, it could have been far more explicit – but *The Curse of the Werewolf*, like many of Hammer's films in the early 1960s, was subject to censorship by the British Board of Film Censors, which insisted the rape should avoid what BBFC Secretary John Trevelyan referred to as 'bestial nastiness'.[19]

The most popular cultural reading of *The Curse of the Werewolf* suggests that it is a class allegory, in which its werewolf takes revenge against the aristocracy. Jonathan Rigby, for example, suggests that the opening scenes illustrate the 'class struggle according to Hammer horror' by creating sympathy for both Leon's mother and her rapist: 'If treated like animals, the film seems to say, men will eventually turn into animals.'[20] This idea is echoed by Rick Worland, who suggests that 'Hammer's wolf man becomes a driven, class avenger' seeking restitution for his mother's mistreatment by the marques.[21] These readings would convincingly link the film's themes to a class-conscious segment in the British anthology *Dr Terror's House of Horrors* (1965), in which a bloodthirsty aristocratic werewolf, dead for centuries, returns from the grave.

But, as Andrew Tudor suggests, *The Curse of the Werewolf* is far more concerned with sex than class.[22] Despite the worried cries of both its critics and the censors, this is a film – much like *Dracula* – that certainly exploits a public thirst for sex and violence, but simultaneously suggests that sexual freedom has dire consequences. Rigby's assertion that the film deals with class issues rests primarily on the depiction of the beggar who rapes Leon's mother: left to suffer after years of confinement, by the time he carries out this crime he has become feral and animalistic, stripped of his humanity (Figure 4.1). But Rigby's reading ignores two important narrative elements. The first is that the beggar winks suggestively at Leon's mother when she is only a child, a short time after he has been imprisoned – a clear suggestion that he has always had a propensity for sexual violence. The second is that, by the time the beggar has taken on the characteristics of a wolf, the marques has also become monstrous after years of seclusion: thick make-up gives him the appearance of a corpse. The film actively works to create a visual and thematic parallel between the two men.

Tudor points out an unusual element of Hammer's werewolf tale: that Leon is afflicted from birth, his curse inherited rather than transmitted.[23] The genesis of Leon's werewolfery is perhaps the most interesting aspect

Figure 4.1 *The Curse of the Werewolf* (1961) features a beggar (Richard Wordsworth) who takes on the characteristics of a wolf after years of imprisonment.

of the film's narrative. He is a child of rape and therefore his monstrosity is definitively linked, as Hutchings suggests, with 'a male sexual desire that is seen as animal-like and corrupting' and is, importantly, associated with both 'the degenerate beggar who rapes Leon's mother and the syphilitic nobleman who makes advances to her'.[24] The ghoulish marques first attempts to force himself on his servant and then, dismayed that she would dare reject him, leaves her at the mercy of his prisoner. She is certainly mistreated by the ruling class, but there is no escaping the fact that it is a representative of the underclass who rapes her, impregnating her with a child who will grow into a monster. *The Curse of the Werewolf* therefore condemns the behaviour of violent and lustful men – regardless of their status.

Further evidence of this can be found in a scene that sees Leon's adoptive father visit a priest (John Gabriel) in order to discern if his son can be saved. In an extended speech that explicitly articulates the film's Christian values, the priest describes the werewolf's curse as a battle between an evil animalistic spirit and the human soul. He states that if a soul is strong enough it will exorcise the evil spirit at a young age. In Leon's case, however, the priest comments that the soul may be weak: 'an inherited weakness, an accident of birth'. This line of dialogue – spoken, of course, by a man of God for whom lust is cause for damnation – suggests that Leon has inherited his propensity for deviant behaviour from his mother's rapist, and has been condemned to become a monster as a result. His inherent ungodliness is hinted at during his baptism: as the priest christens him, holy water boils in the church font.

The Curse of the Werewolf later comes to definitively link Leon's unholy werewolfery with what the film depicts as sexual deviancy. Having surmised that he can never be with the woman he loves, Leon visits a brothel in search of sexual release (following Jose's promise of 'beautiful girls'). There, under the light of a full moon, he sweats profusely as he stares at the women dancing in front of him – his monstrosity emerging in tandem with his lust. Vera then propositions him upstairs on a garden terrace, and the following scene explicitly connects Leon's transformation with sexual arousal. As patrons drink and embrace each other downstairs, he grabs Vera and begins to kiss her forcefully, pushing her down onto the bed. She rebukes him and breaks free, realising that he has bitten her breast hard enough to draw blood. As she chastises him for his violent behaviour ('If that's what you came for, you came to the wrong place'), she is grabbed by a monstrous hand; shortly afterwards she is dead, her body covered in blood. This scene suggests that Leon loses his ability to control the monster inside of him simply because he gives in to his base desires.

But there is a cure for Leon's werewolfery and, in metaphorical terms, his lust: love. In the film's first half, the majority of which takes place during Leon's childhood, his adoptive father treats him with understanding and affection when his werewolfism develops, quashing his curse until he leaves home as an adult. It is only when separated from his loving parents that his monstrosity comes back to the fore – his transformation in the brothel is his first since he was a boy. The next night, Leon expects to transform again, but a visit from Cristina prevents him from changing. As they embrace in the hours before dawn and agree to marry, Leon casts his eyes upwards and thanks God for salvation ('thank you for sending her to me'). For *The Curse of the Werewolf*, only love and faith can save a monster from damnation; as soon as Leon and Cristina are separated, when the werewolf is arrested on suspicion of having killed both Vera and Jose, he once again transforms and embarks on a final rampage before he is killed by his father at the film's end.

It is ironic that Hammer's tale of werewolfery met with such opposition from both critics and the censors. Thematically, it is itself opposed to the 'sadistic proclivities' highlighted by *Monthly Film Bulletin*'s reviewer, and condemns each and every character that indulges in them. In fact, this is a film that communicates a conservative and patently Christian message. Leon's werewolfism is reactivated when he indulges in casual sex, and the only thing that can save him thereafter is true love. *The Curse of the Werewolf* therefore condemns any sexual activity that occurs outside of a committed relationship, and depicts physical desire as a dreadful transgression. That Leon is eventually destroyed by his father is particularly telling: Alfredo is depicted throughout the film as a loving husband and father, Leon as a lascivious sinner. As Laura Hubner suggests in her discussion of the film in the context of the beast within, it is 'propelled by an overt conflict between untamed primitiveness and the force of Christian purity'.[25] It is a shame that Hubner does not contextualise this argument; *The Curse of the Werewolf* endorses the Christian teachings of monogamy and love precisely because it rejects the burgeoning sexual revolution of the early 1960s, demonising those who would indulge in sins of the flesh.

While Hammer itself did not produce another feature film focused on werewolves, personnel closely associated with the company did work on a number of werewolf-themed projects over the next two decades. The first, an unproduced screenplay titled *The Werewolves of Moravia*, was written in the mid-1960s by Michael Carreras, son of Hammer founder James Carreras and a frequent contributor to the company as a writer, director and producer before he was appointed chairman in 1973. Set in Austria-Hungary at the turn of the twentieth century, it follows Dr Otto Frank – a young physician and, ostensibly, a dedicated family man – as he travels from Prague to Moravia in search of a colleague, Dr Manfred Decker, who dispatches a letter to Frank before he is savagely killed by a pack of werewolves in the opening sequence.[26] Upon arriving in Moravia, however, Frank is seduced by Renata – a beautiful young woman who is later revealed to be the leader of the vicious werewolf pack.

As such a synopsis suggests, *The Werewolves of Moravia* closely echoes the themes of *The Curse of the Werewolf*; it is another Christian morality tale in which a lustful man is punished for his apparent sins. An early scene establishes that Frank is, for the most part, happily married – but sexually dissatisfied. Shortly before leaving his home for Moravia, he laments that his family life stands in the way of his physical relationship with his wife, Gerda: 'The children, the house . . . [Wouldn't] it be nice if just for once, even if only for a few hours . . . we were without them . . . just the two of us . . .'[27] It is Frank's frustration that leads him to give in to temptation and sleep with the 'blonde and beautiful' Renata once he has arrived in Moravia,[28] and to tell her: 'I wish that I were free . . . to be here with you always.' She replies, ominously, 'You mean that your wife and children didn't exist?'[29]

Of course, Frank's wife and children do exist – and they unexpectedly join him in Moravia shortly after the beginning of his affair. Frank's wife forgives him for his transgression – but Carreras does not, and the screenplay's third act is dedicated to punishing the adulterers. First, Renata's innocent façade is stripped away. She attacks Frank and his family in the dead of night with her werewolf followers, and Carreras's description echoes *The Curse of the Werewolf* in aligning the lustful werewolf with the ultimate evil of Christian doctrine; as she transforms into the 'Silver

Wolf', the young doctor watches as 'the devil takes possession of her body in horrified fascination'. A demonic rendering of the 'other woman', she intends to turn Frank into one of her own, take him away from his family and assimilate him into the pack; as she lunges for him, she whispers: 'Be still. It is only your first wish being granted. Soon you will be free.'[30] But Frank ultimately refuses to leave his wife and children; he escapes Renata and kills her shortly afterwards, impaling Carreras's demonic temptress through the heart with a silver lance.

But Carreras does not let Frank go unpunished for his part in the affair, either. Having killed Renata, he naïvely drinks from a pool that is the source of the werewolves' power. Later, after his return to Prague, his wife and children are murdered: 'the ghastly work of some mad creature'.[31] We might assume that this is the revenge of Renata's followers, but the final scene reveals that Frank is responsible for the death of his family: as he weeps over his wife's grave, a full moon rises and the doctor himself transforms. He has become a monster, *The Werewolves of Moravia* suggests, because he violated the sanctity of marriage. By the end of Carreras's script, Frank has paid a high cost for his sexual transgressions. He has lost his wife, his children and his humanity – a 'lonely tortured figure' standing in the moonlight.[32]

The Werewolves of Moravia was never made, but two British werewolf films were later produced in the 1970s. *The Beast Must Die* (1974) – produced by Hammer's main rival, Amicus Productions – is a particular oddity, an attempt by a British studio to marry the werewolf film with the Blaxploitation horror cycle that had become popular in America following the release of *Blacula* (1972) and *Blackenstein* (1973).[33] *Legend of the Werewolf* (1975) is the more pertinent film to this discussion: a thematic reversal of *The Curse of the Werewolf*, in which a violent and controlling man is rendered monstrous for the jealousy and rage he feels towards a woman who spurns him. This is perhaps quite surprising, as the film has several links to the earlier (and far more conservative) film: it is also a loose adaptation of *The Werewolf of Paris*;[34] it shares its screenwriter, Anthony Hinds, with Hammer's film;[35] and it was directed by Freddie Francis, who helmed a number of Hammer productions in the 1960s. However, *Legend of the Werewolf* was released over a decade after *The Curse of the Werewolf*, and Western attitudes to sexual freedom had shifted:

> By the early seventies, the 'sexual revolution' was taking on new meanings with each passing year. It was adopted to describe the showing of hard-core sex films in first-run theatres, not to mention the opening of private clubs for group sex. It was used to capture the new spirit of the swinging singles life, as well as the popularization of open marriage . . . the 'sexual revolution' meant the freedom to have sex when and where one wished.[36]

And as the sexual revolution continued to develop, the 1970s brought about some drastic changes in Britain for women in particular. As Paul Newland notes, 'In some ways, during the 1970s, many more women began to see the freedoms usually associated with the 1960s.' Under Harold Wilson's Labour government:

> The Sex Discrimination Act 1975 was passed, and the Social Security Act 1975 enhanced pension provision and job security for women who sought to leave work to raise families. Moreover, the Domestic Violence and Matrimonial Proceedings Act 1976 responded to fears concerning violence to women being meted out by brutish husbands in an alarming number of British households.

Newland continues: 'Evidence of socio-cultural shifts brought about by the rise of feminism in Britain during this period can be found across film genres.'[37] This includes the horror film, and *Legend of the Werewolf* is a clear example. Set during the nineteenth century, it follows Etoile (David Rintoul), who was raised by wolves in rural France before becoming the 'wild boy' of a travelling circus under the care of its operators, Maestro Pamponi (Hugh Griffiths) and his wife Chou-Chou (Renée Houston). His werewolfism develops in adulthood when, under the light of the full moon, he transforms and kills a follow performer. Distraught, he runs away to Paris, where he falls in love with Christine (Lynn Dalby). But when Etoile discovers that she is a sex worker, he becomes enraged and murders several of her customers in his werewolf form. Eventually, he is shot dead with a silver bullet after an extended investigation by forensic pathologist Professor Paul Cataflanque (Peter Cushing) and Inspector Max Gerard (Stefan Gryff).

Just as in *The Curse of the Werewolf*, here werewolfery is explicitly linked with aggressive male sexuality. The later film makes this conception of werewolfism even more explicit; when Etoile is in his werewolf form, we often see through his eyes via point-of-view shots bathed in a red filter, which associate his monstrosity with masculine rage. As Hubner suggests, these shots establish the werewolf's viewpoint as one 'distinctly masculinized and which, fuelled by fetishized rage, is based upon the sexual desirability of women'.[38] These point-of-view shots recall *Peeping Tom* (1960), an earlier and initially highly controversial British horror film in which a serial killer murders women – including, in its opening scene, a sex worker – while viewing them through the lens of a camera. And, as in *The Curse of the Werewolf*, here a pivotal scene also occurs inside a brothel. Etoile flies into a jealous rage when he discovers Christine entertaining a dignitary (Patrick Holt), crashing through her window and viciously attacking him.

Importantly, though, Etoile carries out this assault in his human form, illustrating that his aggression is not just driven by his curse. It is only later that he transforms, killing two of Christine's regular clients – Etoile the werewolf is simply an exaggeration of Etoile the man.

But here there is no cure for Etoile's werewolfery, and certainly not love. It is interesting that Hubner refers to Christine as Etoile's 'girlfriend',[39] as actually the film provides no evidence that they are engaged in a romantic relationship at all. On the contrary, Christine has no interest in committing to Etoile; she visits him following his intrusion at the brothel, asking him: 'Do you think you own me or something?' When Etoile then proposes to her, she is incredulous: 'Look Etoile, I'm very flattered . . . but marry you?' Christine is not willing to offer Etoile anything but friendship, and it soon becomes clear that he does believe that she is a possession to be owned – a close-up of his wild and reddened eyes reveals that this rejection has filled him with rage, and it is immediately after this scene that he transforms and takes to the streets to slaughter her clients.

Etoile is depicted as a jealous, entitled and controlling man, condemned for his attempts to force Christine into a monogamous relationship. Before he leaves the circus, Etoile's adoptive mother uses tarot cards to read his fortune: 'He will meet a pretty girl and love her until death.' As evidenced by his refusal to believe that his love for Christine is unrequited, he takes these saccharine words to heart. Christine, on the other hand, is shown to enjoy the freedom her profession affords her. Hubner suggests that she rejects Etoile's proposal because she is 'fully aware that societal restrictions prevent her from marrying [him]'.[40] Again, this is not evidenced by the film; she presents her reasons in strictly financial terms: 'What have you got? You've got nothing.' Christine's work gives her a financial independence that she is not willing to surrender.

At the film's climax, Etoile confronts Christine in his werewolf form. As Peter Cushing's pathologist enters the room, he tells her: 'You mustn't reject him!' But unlike *The Curse of the Werewolf*'s Cristina, Christine simply does not love the werewolf. Lynn Dalby's performance reveals that she feels nothing for him but fear; shaking and crying, she is visibly terrified as he lumbers towards her. The terror drains from her face only when he dies and she is finally freed from his control. While they are narratively similar, then, there is a stark thematic contrast between *The Curse of the Werewolf* and *Legend of the Werewolf* that reveals the dramatic social changes that occurred in Britain as the sexual revolution unfolded. While the earlier film preaches the Christian virtues of monogamy and love, *Legend of the Werewolf* celebrates female independence – and makes monsters of men who would use violence to control and subordinate women.

Beasts in Heat

The Italian gothic horror films of the 1960s and 1970s are far more explicit in their depictions of sex and violence than the pictures Britain produced in the same period. This is, perhaps, due to a more relaxed approach to censorship. The script for *Black Sunday*, for example, was the subject of some concern for Italy's Board of Censors when it was submitted for comment prior to the film's production – but the finished film passed uncut with a rating of V.M.16 (meaning it could be viewed by those of sixteen years of age or older).[41] The BBFC, on the other hand, refused to classify the film for British release at all; it remained effectively banned in the United Kingdom until 1968.[42] But Italy's permissive attitude to graphic imagery was itself the result of larger cultural shifts in a nation somewhat more comfortable with the budding sexual revolution under Amintore Fanfani's left-leaning government. As Shipka notes, Italy's early horror films 'basked in a changing social culture in both Italy and certain parts of mainland Europe that were more tolerant of sex and violence, as a result creating a new template for Italian exploitation'.[43]

The nation's first werewolf film, an Italian/Austrian co-production initially titled *Lycanthropus* for its domestic release,[44] was shot in Rome and released in 1961.[45] It is therefore an immediate contemporary of *The Curse of the Werewolf*, but – in line with much of Italy's gothic horror – its concern with sexual violence is more overt. Unlike the majority of British werewolf films produced in the 1960s and 1970s, it employs a contemporary setting: a girls' reformatory, in which sexual exploitation runs rampant. At the beginning, a senior figure at the school, Sir Alfred Whiteman (Maurice Marsac), is being blackmailed by an offender, Mary (Mary McNeeran), whom he has been paying for extramarital sex. Shortly after they meet in dense woodland to discuss their affair, Mary is attacked and killed by a werewolf. Following Mary's death, her close friend Priscilla (Barbara Lass) attempts to uncover the identity of her killer. The suspects include Whiteman and several others: a new science teacher, Dr Julian Olcott (Carl Schell); the school's odious caretaker, Walter (Luciano Pigozzi); and its custodian, Director Swift (Curt Lowens).

Lycanthropus goes to great lengths to explore the sexual exploitation occurring within its reform school, to the point that its werewolf is rendered little more than a sub-plot for a large part of its narrative; it is made strikingly obvious that the reformatory is not a safe place for the young women in its care, regardless of the monster stalking its grounds. Whiteman, for example, is depicted as an insatiable predator. Mary is blackmailing him with letters in which he professes to love her, but shortly after her death he simply starts looking for his next affair; he stares longingly at another student as she crosses the school's courtyard, illustrating that he is driven by lust rather than love. Dialogue later spoken by Sheena (Anna Steinart), Whiteman's wife, confirms that Mary was simply the latest in a long line of girls coerced by her husband. And his corruption is evident throughout the school; Walter bluntly offers money to Priscilla in exchange for sex, and later acts as a liaison for Whiteman when he also sets his sights on sleeping with her.

Both men are punished for their lechery. Walter is killed in the process of attempting to steal Mary's love letters from the girls' dormitory on Whiteman's orders, while Whiteman himself commits suicide when he fears he will be exposed. Whiteman and Walter are therefore depicted as monsters every bit as much as the film's werewolf, who for a large part of the narrative functions primarily as an extension of their animalistic lust. In fact, *Lycanthropus* frames the creature's attacks in a manner that implicitly suggests sexual violence. Its first attack on Mary is effectively a coded rape. The monster tackles her to the ground and then forces itself on top of her, clawing at her neck. As Curti argues, the scene:

> culminates in a point-of-view shot of the female victim, forced to the ground by the monster, which somehow apes the celebrated POV shot of the rape victim in Akira Kurosawa's *Rashomon* (1950), as the camera frames the tops of the trees: then, with a brutal transition [the film] cuts to the wolfman's claws ripping the woman's [blouse] open, partially baring her neck and chest.[46]

The werewolf's other attacks also imply sexual assault. It later attacks Priscilla, and runs its hirsute hand over her cheek in close-up before reaching down to her coat, suggesting that it intends to forcibly undress her before it is attacked by a guard dog and forced to flee. Similarly, its attack on the school's matron, Leonore (Maureen O'Connor), sees it tear open her coat, exposing her neck and shoulders, before biting at her throat. The film's theatrical posters carried similar images, with one depicting bestial hands clasping at a woman's throat under the full moon (Figure 4.2). Even the cause of a werewolf's metamorphosis has a sexual dimension in *Lycanthropus*; as he is explaining his previous experience with werewolves, Dr Olcott reveals that their transformations are caused by an abnormal expansion of the human pituitary gland, which regulates hormones in the body. Here, as Curti suggests, the werewolf's curse is explicitly framed as a 'sexual dysfunction' that must be remedied.[47]

Figure 4.2 An original Italian poster designed to promote *Lycanthropus* (1961), which clearly plays on the film's preoccupation with sexual violence. © Cineriz.

Eventually, the werewolf is revealed to be Director Swift, who is otherwise depicted as an upstanding and morally righteous man throughout the rest of the film. He, like several of his employees, is a violent predator – and, perhaps, a far more sinister one, as he hides his bestial urges behind a veneer of civility. The film therefore depicts its reform school as a hive of corruption and sexual violence, implicating staff at every level – from the vulgar caretaker to the respectable custodian – in the abuse and exploitation of the women in its care. And, like *The Curse of the Werewolf*'s doomed Leon, these men are also condemned for their inability to maintain normative monogamous relationships. Whitemore finds it impossible to resist his urges and stay faithful to his long-suffering wife, while Swift claims to be deeply in love with his colleague Leonore – but his transformations act as a metaphor for his inability to control his violent lust for other women, and he nearly kills his lover once the animal has come to the fore.

Lycanthropus, then, is a product of a nation in which the sexual revolution allowed for a newfound permissiveness in depictions of sex and violence in horror cinema – but one that is uneasy about the potential consequences of a liberated society. It is notable that the film avoids condemning the young and sexually active women of the reformatory; it is suggested in a conversation between Priscilla and Sheena that many of the school's students use sex as a means to obtain money or gain favour with staff, and the film places all blame for any wrongdoing in this arrangement on the men who readily exploit their willingness to do so. The film is therefore not critical of sexual freedoms, but rather expresses a concern that an increasingly sexualised society might serve to embolden predatory men. That fear is further explored in Italy's second werewolf film, *Werewolf Woman*.[48] Released in 1976, it is far more graphic than *Lycanthropus* – or any of the werewolf films produced in Britain during this period – and is another Italian horror picture focused on the consequences of sexual violence.

Werewolf Woman follows Daniela (Annik Borel), a young woman who was raped at the age of fifteen and has been suffering from trauma related to the attack ever since. In adulthood, living at home with her aristocratic father, Corrado (Tino Carraro), she learns that her ancestor – who bore a striking resemblance to her – was accused of werewolfery and executed. She comes to believe that she, too, is a monster, and embarks on a killing spree after she witnesses her sister, Irena (Dagmar Lassander) having passionate sex with her husband, Fabian (Andrea Scotti). She first kills Fabian and then several others, all the while being pursued by the authorities. While on the run, she finds true love with Luca (Howard Ross), but her happiness comes to an end when the house she shares with him is invaded by three criminals (Pietro Torrisi, Salvatore Billa and Vito Domenighini). Daniela is raped for a second time, and is forced to watch as the men murder Luca. She kills her rapists in revenge before the police finally track her down in the forest surrounding her ancestral home.

It must be noted immediately that a literal werewolf appears in *Werewolf Woman* only once – in the opening sequence, a flashback (or, perhaps, a dream) in which Daniela's she-wolf ancestor is hunted and killed. Single shots of the werewolf reappear throughout the film, but Daniela herself never fully transforms; the question of whether she is suffering from werewolfism or clinical lycanthropy is left open to the viewer's interpretation. However, the opening is enormously important, as it establishes *Werewolf Woman*'s thematic preoccupations in a way that has a profound impact on the meaning of the events that unfold across the course of the narrative, regardless of whether Daniela's affliction is ultimately supernatural or psychological.

The film's first shots depict Daniela's ancestor dancing naked in a circle of flame – running her hands over her body in an act of fearless self-expression – before falling to the ground and transforming into a werewolf, forming a visual connection between her unbridled sexuality and her werewolfery (Figure 4.3). A mob then approaches the woodland brandishing torches, searching for her. Importantly, their dialogue reveals that they believe she is in need of rescue, having been kidnapped by a monster they distinctly identify as male. According to their archaic values, it is patently inconceivable that a woman could engage in such subversive behaviour. When they discover that it is the woman herself who is the monster, they burn her at the stake for her transgressions, and a pointed

Figure 4.3 At the opening of *Werewolf Woman* (1976), Daniela (Annik Borel) experiences a vision of her ancestor, who celebrates her sexuality before transforming into a she-wolf.

distinction is made between the writhing, naked she-wolf on the pyre and the repressed women observing her execution from the crowd – all of them wearing puritanical dress, their skin covered and their hair concealed by bonnets. This opening scene, then, depicts a woman being violently punished for daring to bare her flesh and defy a patriarchal society, and thus her werewolfism is not a marker of monstrosity but rather a symbol of liberation and power.

Liberation and power are two things Daniela deeply desires – liberation from the trauma in her past and power over the men who would subject her to further abuse. At the film's beginning, her father tells her psychiatrist (Elio Zamuto) that his daughter has been repelled by the opposite sex since her rape and, as Shipka notes, her deepest psychological problem is that she is initially incapable of seeing 'any man as compassionate'.[49] As a result, her werewolfism emerges as a manifestation of her complicated relationship with her sexuality. Several of her earlier victims are men and women whom she has observed in sexual situations. For example, she spies on Fabian and Irena before killing her sister's husband, and later watches a woman perform oral sex on a man before murdering her. In both cases, Daniela is only able to witness these intimate moments from a physically and psychologically detached position (through a crack in Irena's bedroom door, for example). She is fascinated by the pleasures of sex – but her werewolfism, as a representation of her trauma, prevents her from engaging in these activities herself without harming her sexual partners. The abuse she has suffered causes her to associate intimacy with violence.

But two developments change the course of *Werewolf Woman*'s narrative. One is her meeting with Luca. Her experience of a genuinely loving relationship begins to heal her trauma, and she is able to contain the animal inside of her – for a time. Another is her realisation that she is able to redirect her violent tendencies towards those who would prey upon her – her werewolfery allowing her to take revenge for her suffering at the hands of deviant men. This is evident even in her first attack on Fabian, who is more than willing to submit to Daniela's seduction despite the fact that he is married to her sister. Later, she is picked up by an older man in his car (Pino Mattei), who initially treats her kindly and offers her a place to stay – before squeezing her leg suggestively and attempting to rape her, leading her to kill him. And, of course, the film's final act revolves around Daniela's revenge against her rapists (and Luca's murderers) as the animal takes over. She tracks them down and kills them in cold blood, even setting one of them on fire as he sleeps in his bed.

The metaphorical meaning of Daniela's werewolfery thus shifts as the narrative progresses: at first a representation of the trauma in her past, and then an embodiment of her determination to take power from her abusers and liberate herself from them in the present – an echo of the film's opening scene, in which a she-wolf embraces her werewolfism as a symbol of subversive defiance. It is notable that Daniela begins to believe she is a werewolf after finding a picture of her ancestor and reading her story in a collection of forgotten documents; she is inspired by the tale of a woman determined to express her sexuality without fear, and comes to see werewolfery as a means to destroy her oppressors – regardless of whether her affliction is real or imagined. As director Rino di Silvestri states: 'in her beastly escape, in her fight . . . against a society which is completely adverse to such a personality, every contact with a man brings out her criminal instinct'.[50]

Curti disagrees with Silvestri's interpretation of the film, and suggests that Daniela is an 'embodiment of Italian gothic's deadly dangerous seductresses, who lure the male and kill him: therefore, the sexual humiliations she undergoes are all the more debatable in their cheap exploitation value'.[51] *Werewolf Woman* is undoubtedly an exploitation picture in many regards; it revels in female nudity and could certainly be argued to objectify its star. But it is misleading to suggest that Daniela 'lures' men; this is true of Fabian, perhaps, but every other man she kills throughout the narrative either threatens her with sexual violence or carries it out, and she murders her female victims due to the distorted perception of sex her abusers have caused her to develop. The predators who have subjected Daniela to 'sexual humiliations' are the film's monsters, not the she-wolf.

Werewolf Woman is thus aligned with *Legend of the Werewolf*: an aesthetically problematic but thematically feminist tale for the latter years of the sexual revolution, which makes an earnest plea for women to be able to express their sexuality without fear of violence. Its ending, in fact, laments a society in which such an ideal is not yet possible, as Daniela – wild-eyed and driven mad with grief – is led away by the police in a tragic long shot.

Nights of the Wolfman

Spain's contribution to the European horror boom was somewhat delayed. While Britain and Italy had begun producing gothic horror in the late 1950s, Spain's first horror film of this period – a Spanish/Italian co-production – was *The Awful Dr Orloff* (1962). But unlike *The Curse of Frankenstein* and *Black Sunday*, it did not produce a prolific domestic cycle. Spain did not enter into a period of sustained horror production until after the release of *The Mark of the Wolfman* in 1968, the first of several werewolf films starring prolific writer, director and actor Paul Naschy. Naschy's screenplay for *The Mark of the Wolfman* was inspired in equal parts by the international success of Hammer and his love for Universal's series of monster films. As Nicholas G. Schlegel notes, he was a filmmaker 'enamoured with the films of his youth' and particularly enthralled by the 'monster rally' films Universal had produced in the 1940s.[52]

Both profitable and popular, *The Mark of the Wolfman* spawned a prolonged series of films in which Naschy starred as the wolfman (or 'El Hombre Lobo') Waldemar Daninsky. In fact, he played Daninsky in a total of seven werewolf films between 1968 and 1975, in which his werewolf does battle with a number of other popular monsters: *The Mark of the Wolfman*, *The Monsters of Terror* (1969), *The Fury of the Wolfman* (1970), *Walpurgis Night* (1970), *Dr Jekyll and the Wolfman* (1971), *The Return of Walpurgis* (1973) and *The Curse of the Beast* (1975).[53] All of these films feature Daninsky as a central character, but otherwise continuity between them is limited; for example, the specific origin of Daninsky's curse changes frequently throughout the series, and he is variously depicted as either an aristocrat or a scientist according to the narrative needs of each film.

One element that these films do share with each other, as well as with their British and Italian counterparts, is a preoccupation with sexual politics – but they were produced in a very different context to *The Curse of the Werewolf*, *Legend of the Werewolf*, *Lycanthropus* or *Werewolf Woman*. Following the Spanish Civil War until 1975, Spain was governed by a fascist dictatorship under General Fancisco Franco based on authoritarianism, autarky, nationalism and strict Catholic morality (or 'National

Catholicism'). In fact, Spain's distinct lack of horror cinema until the late 1960s was largely due to censorship in Francoist Spain. As Irene Baena-Cuder notes, it was during the 1960s that Franco was forced to invite foreign investment into the nation's economy after his vision for self-sufficiency faltered; Spain opened up to the world after decades of isolationism and, as 'a consequence of this deep change, censorship relaxed'.[54] But Spain nonetheless remained a conservative state until the demise of Francoism, particularly in its traditionalist conception of gender roles. Upon taking power in 1939, Franco worked to restructure Spanish society according to his vision for the nation, and this included reconfiguring 'both male and female identities into new roles based on . . . Roman [Catholic] principles'.[55]

As Baena-Cuder notes, Franco's ideal man was strong, pious, virile, courageous and disciplined, ready and willing to serve the nation's needs.[56] Women, on the other hand, were figured as little other than wives and mothers, confined to domestic and familial contexts. As Mary Nash recounts, during the early years of the Franco regime:

> Women were politicized through the notion of a common female destiny based on their reproductive capacities. Female sexuality, work and education were regulated in accordance with this social function while motherhood was idealized and considered as a duty to the fatherland . . .
>
> Familialism was another key element in the development of pronatalism and motherhood. Both National Catholicism and the pronatalist drive coincided with the crusade for moral regeneration and the restoration of the family as the primary social unit of Spanish society . . . Furthermore, familialism had specific gender connotations and reinforced the overall conception of the woman as the *angel del hogar* (angel of the home) whose biological and social destiny was motherhood.[57]

Franco's regime thus condemned promiscuity and sex for pleasure, instead endorsing marriage, procreation and family life. Popular attitudes to sex shifted over the decades that followed, though, especially as Spanish citizens were exposed to less oppressive cultures through cinema and tourism;[58] by the 1960s, the Francoist conception of sexuality and gender was increasingly at odds with the Spanish public. The contraceptive pill, for example, became available in 1963. Its sale was strictly regulated but, as Aurora G. Morcillo notes, use of birth control 'increased rapidly regardless of the prohibition from Church and state'.[59] By 1974, Morcillo suggests that Spain's younger generations were deeply opposed to Franco's ideology; they considered sex 'an enriching and positive experience' and 'rejected the traditional morality transmitted through the family, the school, and the Church'.[60] It was in the late 1960s and early 1970s – in the years preceding the nation's transition to democracy following Franco's death in 1975 – that the sexual revolution finally arrived in Spain.

The first seven Waldemar Daninsky films were both produced by and released into this context. Much like *The Curse of the Werewolf*, they are deeply concerned by Spain's burgeoning sexual revolution, demonise sexual promiscuity and endorse monogamous, loving relationships. Perhaps the most obvious indicator of these politics is a recurring narrative element that appears in all seven films produced between 1968 and 1975. Borrowing heavily from Universal's Wolf Man films (1941–5), the Daninsky movies depict their werewolf as a tortured, noble soul forever in search of a release from his curse. However, as Todd Tjersland observes, they contain elements of faux-folklore that are 'quite different from conventional werewolf films . . . having been wholly invented by Naschy'. The most important of these, extrapolated from Larry Talbot's tragic death at the hands of Ilonka in Universal's *House of Frankenstein* (1944), is the werewolf's 'method of destruction requiring a woman's love'.[61]

There is a cure, then, for Daninsky's affliction. In each film, he can be freed from his curse if his heart is pierced by a silver weapon (generally a bullet or a sharpened cross) wielded by a woman who loves him enough to die for him. The Daninsky movies thus consistently revolve around a central romance, and end with the werewolf first finding true love and then the peace of death. This convention is established in *The Mark of the Wolfman*, which ends with the besotted and submissive Janice (Dianik Zurakowska) shooting Daninsky dead to free his soul. The exception is *The Curse of the Beast*, in which Naschy is allowed to survive for the first time in the series. The film sees him cured by a rare Tibetan flower – in an obvious allusion to *Werewolf of London* (1935) – but, in a twist on Naschy's recurrent ending, it can only lift his curse if mixed with the blood of a woman who loves him. At the narrative's end, Daninsky and his love Sylvia (Grace Mills) walk off into the night together after she has cut herself open in order to save him. The driving theme of these films, then, is Daninsky's redemption – something he can only achieve via a woman who is deeply committed to him. They endorse monogamous relationships through their central protagonist and the women who love him.

And the women who love Daninsky become enamoured with him precisely because he is depicted as strong, courageous, heroic and willing to sacrifice himself for the greater good: an exemplar of Francoist masculinity. For example, in *The Mark of the Wolfman*, Daninsky and Janice meet each other at a masquerade ball. Janice is, at the time, in the early stages of a relationship with Rudolph (Manuel Manzaneque). As Antonio Lázaro-Reboll argues, Janice chooses Daninsky over Rudolph because he represents Franco's ideal male, while Rudolph's 'adolescent, well-groomed appearance functions as a counterpoint to Daninsky, the real man'.[62] Even Rudolph submits to the alpha male, later aiding Daninsky in trying to find a cure for the werewolf's affliction – a cure, they hope, can be provided by scientist Dr Janos Mikhelov (Julian Ugarte) and his wife Wandesa (Aurora de Alba).

It is through Janos and Wandesa that *The Mark of the Wolfman* establishes another recurring theme of the Daninsky films: a binary opposition between pure, virtuous love and sinful, monstrous lust. After arriving at Daninsky's estate, the scientist and his wife are shortly revealed to be predatory vampires with no intention of helping the count at all; instead, they force him to do battle with the werewolf that cursed him while they seduce Janice and Rudolph for their own pleasure, using occult hypnotism to turn them into sex slaves. Daninsky eventually dispatches the vampires in his transformed state before Janice is forced to shoot him dead in her final act of love: a conclusion that confirms the film's endorsement of monogamous commitment, as the promiscuous vampires are destroyed and Janice frees Daninsky's soul from torment.

This theme continues in *The Monsters of Terror*, which sees extraterrestrial invaders led by Dr Odo Warnoff (Michael Rennie) enslave a vampire, Janos de Mialhoff (Manuel de Blas), a reanimated Egyptian Mummy (Gene Reyes), Faranksalan's monster (Ferdinando Murolo) – an analogue for Frankenstein's creature – and Paul Naschy's wolf-man with the hope of using the monsters in a plot to destroy the Earth. As in all of the Daninsky films, the werewolf is depicted as a noble and righteous figure. He falls in love with Elonka (Ella Gessler), a woman who has also been enslaved by the extraterrestrials, and together they attempt to escape the aliens. By the end of the film, Daninsky has destroyed the Mummy and Faranksalan's monster, before a mortally wounded Elonka shoots him with a silver bullet; they die together, hand in hand. Just as in *The Mark of the Wolfman*, here tragic love is at the centre of Daninsky's story. The film's vampire, on the other hand, is depicted as a dangerous sexual predator; he attacks Warnoff's assistant Maleva (Karin Dor) as she sleeps, hypnotising her and running his hands over her body. Later in the film, it is heavily implied that he intends to rape Ilsa (Patty Shepard), the lover of a police officer – Inspector Tobermann (Craig Hill) – investigating the aliens' plot. Interestingly, the vampire is not killed by Daninsky. Tobermann runs a stake through his heart as he rescues his beloved Ilsa; here, then, two loving couples stand in direct opposition to the vampire's lust.

Later films in the Daninsky series become far more explicit in their endorsement of traditional values, often casting liberated women as villains to be contrasted with Daninsky's submissive lovers. In *The Fury of the Wolf-man*, for example, Daninsky – here depicted as a scientist and college professor for the first time in the series – is pitted against his colleague, Dr Ilona Ellman (Perla Cristal). Ellman discovers that Daninsky is a werewolf and kidnaps him for use in her mind control experiments. Tellingly, all of Ellman's assistants are women, while the majority of the subjects of her experiments are men whom she keeps locked in the basement rooms beneath her expansive house. Ellman and her followers therefore become a grotesque caricature of feminism; the doctor is demonised for her intellect and her desire for power and, in the conservative world of the Daninsky saga, comes to represent those women who questioned National Catholicism in the latter days of Francoist Spain.

Ellman is, of course, punished for these apparent transgressions and killed – but not before she shoots Daninsky dead. This is an interesting twist, as this is a narrative action that is normally carried out by a woman who has fallen in love with the werewolf across the course of a Daninsky film – in this case Karin (Verónica Luján), Ellman's assistant. And *The Fury of the Wolfman* makes abundantly clear that here – just as in *The Mark of the Wolfman* and *The Monsters of Terror* – Daninsky must be killed by a woman who loves him. Ellman is therefore further undermined by the suggestion that her actions throughout the film have not even been driven by her own ambition or a twisted sense of scientific curiosity, but rather by rage resulting from unrequited love – an idea supported by the fact that, at the film's beginning, Ellman uses her mastery of mind control to coerce Daninsky's wife, Erika (Pilar Zorrilla), into having an affair, leading the werewolf to kill both his spouse and her lover.

Following *The Fury of the Wolfman*, several of the Daninsky films produced in the 1970s followed its lead by casting women as their villains, while returning to the binary opposition between love and lust established in *The Mark of the Wolfman* and *The Monsters of Terror*. For example, *Walpurgis Night* follows two graduate students, Elvira (Gaby Fuchs) and Genevieve (Bárbara Capell), seeking the hidden tomb of a vampire, Countess Wandesa Dárvula de Nadasdy (Patty Shepard). First, however, they find Daninsky living in an isolated mansion. He helps the pair to find Nadasdy's grave, where they accidentally revive the vampire. Genevieve is shortly turned into a vampire, while Elvira falls deeply in love with Daninsky. Nadasdy and Genevieve then become lovers as they seek to consume both Elvira and Daninsky: insatiable, aggressive, sexually liberated and monstrous women completely out of patriarchal control. As Mary T. Harson notes, the two women reject relationships with men and '[prefer] each other's company socially and sexually'. *Walpurgis Night* condemns the sexual revolution, then, by rendering independent women as monstrous, 'their sexuality representing the forces of modernity that threaten' male dominance in the latter years of Francoism.[63] The vampire women are ultimately destroyed by the werewolf, before Elvira's love once again puts him to rest.

The Return of Walpurgis and *The Curse of the Beast* are both similar. In the former, Daninsky is cursed by a group of liberated Romani witches; they send an envoy to seduce him and use an enchanted wolf skull to blight him with werewolfism, thus enacting a centuries-old curse placed upon Daninsky's ancestor by a vampiric woman he executed for heresy. Once cursed by a woman who exploited his lust, he can only be saved – as ever in the Daninsky saga – by love; he is stabbed in the heart with a silver cross by the besotted Kinga (Fabiola Falcón) at the film's conclusion. In *The Curse of the Beast*, Daninsky is cursed by a pair of demonic cannibal women in the Tibetan mountains; they seduce him, stripping naked and writhing with him on the floor of a cave, before he discovers their true nature and destroys them. Daninsky is later forced to do battle with yet another sexually aggressive woman: Wandesa (Silvia Solar), the vicious and sadistic lover of a warlord. Having destroyed not one but three monstrous women that represent a Francoist fear of female sexuality, Daninsky is cured and allowed to survive for the first time in the series.

The later Daninsky films also condemn predatory men, but in most cases this is communicated in a far more subtle fashion than in *The Mark of the Wolfman* or *The Monsters of Terror*. In *The Return of Walpurgis* and *The Curse of the Beast*, for example, Daninsky attacks and kills a number of minor characters in his werewolf form as they harass, sexually assault or attempt to rape women. But the only film in which a predatory man takes a central role after *The Monsters of Terror* is *Dr Jekyll and the Wolfman* – in which the predator is Daninsky himself. Again seeking a cure for his affliction, Daninsky turns to Dr Henry Jekyll (Jack Taylor), who surmises that injecting the werewolf with his infamous serum on the night of a full moon might lift his curse. On the contrary, it causes Daninsky to transform into a particularly vicious Mr Hyde. While Daninsky's wolfman tends to kill indiscriminately throughout the series, his Hyde persona is a lustful monster that rapes and strangles exclusively female victims. Daninsky's Hyde is, then, an exaggerated thematic continuation of the male vampires that appear in *The Mark of the Wolfman* and *The Monsters of Terror*: a deviant corrupted by insatiable sexual urges. Once again, his soul is saved by the love of a woman deeply committed to him: Justine (Shirley Corrigan), who shoots Daninsky with a silver bullet after the Hyde formula wears off and he transforms back into 'El Hombre Lobo'. Fatally wounded by the werewolf's bite, Justine lies by his side; the two lovers die hand in hand in an echo of *The Monsters of Terror*.

It is clear that Paul Naschy's Daninsky movies are heavily influenced by Universal's Wolf Man saga; much like *Frankenstein Meets the Wolf Man* (1943), *House of Frankenstein* and *House of Dracula* (1945), they pit a noble, self-sacrificing werewolf against irredeemably evil monsters. Where in Universal's films those monsters represented anxieties related to war, however, here they embody Francoist Spain's fear of the sexual revolution. Waldemar Daninsky is the embodiment of Franco's perfect man: strong, dominant, heroic and, most importantly, loving and committed to the women who love him in return. Throughout the Daninsky films produced between 1968 and 1975, he is forced to do battle with – and, in *Dr Jekyll and the Wolfman*, even become – monsters associated with promiscuity, lust and debauchery: Francoist conceptions of what Spain might become if it were to embrace the sexual revolution and turn its back on Catholic morality.

The European werewolf films of the 1960s and 1970s are products of societies undergoing dramatic changes as the sexual revolution swept the continent: deeply conflicted films that use the werewolf to explore the potential consequences – both positive and negative – of increasing permissiveness. This cycle came to an end in the 1970s, though Paul Naschy would continue to star in Daninsky films into the 1980s and beyond. However, they became far more sporadic: *Return of the Wolfman* was released in 1980, followed by *The Beast and the Magic Sword* (1983), *Licantropo* (1996) and *Tomb of the Werewolf* (2004). But Naschy's wolf-man would soon become anachronistic; in 1981, just a year after the Spanish release of *Return of the Wolfman*, two American films would usher in the age of the 'new werewolf.'

CHAPTER 5

What Big Teeth You Have

Sick as a Dog

With the exception of television films such as *Scream of the Wolf* (1974) and *Deathmoon* (1978) and the low-budget theatrical effort *Wolfman* (1979), the werewolf fell out of vogue in North America as the 1970s drew to a close, but tales of werewolfery would not be absent from American screens for long. The year 1981 would see the release of three new werewolf films: *The Howling*, *An American Werewolf in London* and *Full Moon High*.[1] The commercial success of *The Howling* and *An American Werewolf in London* in particular would spark a new interest in the werewolf film that continued for the rest of the 1980s. This newfound popularity was bolstered not only by the quality and box-office success of these two films but because they depicted a new kind of werewolf. The 'new werewolf' was distinctly more lupine: all teeth and snout, it was a truly monstrous amalgamation of human and wolf brought to the screen courtesy of pioneering advancements in special-effects technology (Figure 5.1). With the new werewolf came a popular taste for the 'transformation scene', in which those cursed with werewolfism suffer through long, painful and graphic metamorphoses in real time; this addition to the werewolf film's generic qualities replaced the now outdated cross-fade transformations seen in *Werewolf of London* (1935), *The Wolf Man* (1941) and so on. Both films also purposefully eschewed the gothic aesthetics of classic examples of the werewolf movie; their realistic modern-day narratives are slowly invaded by the absurd logic of the supernatural.

The late 1970s and early 1980s saw a shift in the reception of the horror film from audiences, critics and scholars alike. Advancements in special effects – which had been pioneered by artists such as Dick Smith, Rick Baker, Rob Bottin, Chris Walas, Tom Savini and Stan Winston – were such that special make-up effects, creature design, monstrous transformations and gory grotesquery became important conventions of horror. Furthermore, as Steve Neale states, this was the point at which both

Figure 5.1 The monstrous 'new werewolf' as it appears in *The Howling* (1981) – a distinct departure from the wolf-men that had dominated the werewolf film since the 1930s.

audiences and filmmakers became acutely aware of special effects as a narrative device in many genres.[2] By the early 1980s – and certainly by the end of the decade – many horror films were designed around their special-effects sequences and their reception was dominated by evaluations of such scenes over other formal or aesthetic concerns, such as narrative, the quality of performances or overall direction; Ernest Mathijs lists *Scanners* (1981), *The Evil Dead* (1981), *Gremlins* (1984) and *The Fly* (1986) as four such films.[3] Subsequently, special effects, as well as their design and application, became a central point of popular and academic discussions of horror. As Mathijs notes:

> It was in the early 1980s that horror effects in particular were deemed important enough to become a legitimate and respected agent in the critical and academic discourse on the horror film; it was not until these effects proved, almost literally, that they had become 'almost as' important as the stories, which they were supposed to support, that they became an active part of debates on the genre.[4]

This new fascination with special effects undoubtedly contributed to the invention of the new werewolf: huge, lupine and monstrous. However, its birth – and the rise of special effects as an artistic centrepiece in the horror film generally – was not just attributable to industrial factors but cultural factors as well. Pioneering breakthroughs in effects technology rose in tandem with 'body-horror', a sub-genre based on humankind's fear of its own fragile form. These were horror films in which bodily destruction was not just hinted at or discussed, but explicitly shown in extended and unflinchingly graphic sequences designed to shock and disgust as much as scare. The first wave of body-horror was very much in step with developments in American social and political life, particularly as the 1980s dawned. The year 1980 saw Republican candidate Ronald Reagan win the presidential election race that would eject Jimmy Carter from the White House. The Reagan years had begun, and as Susan Jeffords notes:

> The Reagan era was an era of bodies. From the anxieties about Reagan's age and the appearance of cancerous spots on his nose; to the profitable craze in aerobics and exercise; to the molding of a former Mr Universe into the biggest box-office draw of the decade; to the conservative agenda to outlaw abortion; to the identification of 'values' through an emphasis on drug use, sexuality, and child-bearing; to the thematized aggression against persons with AIDS – these articulations of bodies constituted the imaginary of the Reagan agenda and the site of its materialization.[5]

An obsession with the intimate relationship between individuals and their physical forms is clearly identifiable in 1980s horror cinema; to name but three examples, films such as *The Beast Within* (1982), *The Thing* (1982) and *Videodrome* (1983) see helpless protagonists watch their flesh mutate, transform, rot and decay. This shift towards a focus on the body was noted by scholars as early as 1986, when two articles concerning body-horror – in an issue entirely dedicated to the horror genre – were published in *Screen*. In Philip Brophy's 'Horrality – The Textuality of Contemporary Horror Films', the author notes: 'The contemporary Horror film tends to play not so much on the broad fear of Death, but more precisely on the fear of one's own body, of how one controls and relates to it.'[6]

In 'Vile Bodies and Bad Medicine', Pete Boss builds upon Brophy's ideas, asserting:

> What is common is a sense of disaster being visited at the level of the body itself – an intimate apocalypse. The enduring image is of the body irreversibly self-destructing by the actions of inscrutable cellular networks operating in accordance with their own incomprehensible schedules.[7]

According to Brophy, these films are important because they '[incorporate] a mode that both "tells" you the horror and "shows" it. It is this mode of *showing* as opposed to *telling* that is strongly connected to the destruction of the Body.'[8] It is, of course, this idea of 'showing' horror that heavily links with the sudden concentration on the moment of a werewolf's transformation in *The Howling* and *An American Werewolf in London*.

As Jeffords suggests, the American obsession with the body in the 1980s could be interpreted in many ways; she links the rise of a body-obsessed culture with everything from Reagan's anti-abortion rhetoric to the AIDS crisis. Boss asserts that body-horror is primarily linked to advancements in medicine, and points out broad connections to 'Surgery, terminal illness, organ transplants and bio-medical research'.[9] In addition to these concerns, the 1970s and 1980s saw the rise of body-consciousness and a sudden fixation on health and fitness as a means to maintain youth and virility. As Deborah Lupton observes:

> The emphasis placed on youth and beauty as the attributes of a desirable body has generated a huge industry devoted to bodily maintenance. The industries around cosmetics, fashion, fitness, sport, leisure, bodily cleanliness and diet rely upon the discourse which insists that youth and beauty equals normality and social acceptability. The primary message disseminated by this industry is that as long as the correct commodity is purchased and used, the body itself will be a tempting commodity in the market of sexual attraction.[10]

Body-horror, then, does not have its roots in a singular cultural shift but in several interconnected political, social and cultural happenings that resulted in widespread paranoia relating to the relationship between the individual and the body. It is these developments that resulted in the creation of the new werewolf and the lurid transformation scenes that would become common in subsequent werewolf films. Transformations are, and have always been, a key feature of the werewolf narrative. However, until 1981, they had largely been achieved using camera trickery. Cross-fades and clever editing techniques were used to create an apparent metamorphosis. In some films, shots of an actor wearing various stages of make-up were faded together to create the illusion of transformation; in others, the actor's image dissolved into a separate shot of a real wolf. For the first time in cinema history, *The Howling* and *An American Werewolf in London* showed cursed individuals slowly and painfully transforming in real time.

The Howling's central transformation sequence sees Eddie Quist (Robert Picardo) – a werewolf, rapist and serial killer – transform in front of Karen White (Dee Wallace), a reporter visiting a therapeutic commune called 'the Colony' for treatment following another traumatic encounter with Quist in the film's opening scenes. There, she begins to suspect the Colony is a community of werewolves. After pulling a bullet out of his own head ('I want to give you a piece of my mind'), Quist's face begins to transform as his jaw elongates and his eyes glaze over; his fingernails grow into claws before his chest and biceps pulsate and contort, ripping his clothes; his mouth twists into a monstrous smile as a snout begins to protrude from the centre of his face; hair sprouts all over his body as his ears grow into hideous points; finally, after a full three minutes of screen time, a hideous and fully transformed bipedal werewolf stands before Karen.

While Rob Bottin's truly impressive and revolting transformation scene in *The Howling* occurs in relative darkness, Rick Baker was tasked – at the behest of writer-director John Landis – with staging an even more ambitious transformation sequence for *An American Werewolf in London*: one that would take place under fluorescent lighting.[11] David Kessler (David Naughton) is alone in a flat belonging to his girlfriend Alex Price (Jenny Agutter) on the night of the first full moon since he was bitten by a werewolf on the Yorkshire moors. Experiencing a sudden flush of pain, he jumps to his feet and tears off his clothes ('I'm burning up!') before his transformation begins: his hand stretches into a monstrous paw; he drops to the floor as his back arches and his bones begin to snap into new shapes; his teeth grow into points as his spine becomes more pronounced; hair grows all over his body as he screams in pain; and his screams turn into a low-pitched growl as a snout begins to form from his mouth and nose. After an excruciating two-and-a-half minutes, David has become a monstrous quadrupedal werewolf as howling is heard over a shot of the full moon. As Brophy attests, *An American Werewolf in London*'s transformation is 'not unlike being on a tram and somebody has an epileptic fit – you're there right next to the person, you can't get away and you can't do anything'.[12]

Howling at the Moon

Through their focus on the painful and monstrous nature of werewolfism and their invention of the new, distinctly lupine werewolf, both *The Howling* and *An American Werewolf in London* are intrinsically linked to body-horror anxieties; references to the two films in scholarly work typically concentrate primarily on their transformation scenes. However, neither film is just a simple allegory for the destruction of the human form. Rather, they explore the relationship between mind and body, two products of a moment in American history when cultural perceptions of mental and physical illness were shifting dramatically.

As the 1980s dawned, a Western stigma had begun to develop around ageing and disease; the meteoric rise of health and beauty as a consumer industry had turned the ideals of youth, a healthy lifestyle and the pursuit of physical perfection into cultural obsessions. This coincided with efforts to publicise the connections between an unhealthy lifestyle and debilitating disease; the Surgeon General's Office, the National Heart, Lung, and Blood Institute and the National Cancer Institute worked tirelessly in the early 1980s on behalf of the United States government to publicise the connections between diet, heart disease and cancer.[13] By the end of the decade, dieting had become a multi-billion dollar industry.[14] The stigmatisation of disease was compounded by Reagan's reaction to the early years of the AIDS crisis, when the virus was still considered primarily to affect the gay community: he simply ignored the problem.[15]

It is clear, then, that the health and beauty industry and increased awareness of maladies such as heart disease and cancer led to a widespread fear of bodily malfunction and physical sickness in the 1980s. Meanwhile, mental illness was being de-stigmatised from the late 1970s onwards, as psychological afflictions were named, categorised and treated. Therapy became widely available and, as Frank Furedi notes, 'it was in the 1980s that therapeutic culture came to exercise a dominant influence over society. Before the 1980s, terms like syndrome, self-esteem, PTSD, sex addiction and counselling had not yet entered the public vocabulary'.[16]

While those afflicted with serious physical illnesses came to be blamed for their own afflictions – heart disease, cancer and AIDS were all figured as diseases brought on by supposed lifestyle choices of various descriptions, from diet to sexuality – Western society's understanding of, and even fascination with, mental illness was growing. In the late 1970s and early 1980s, there was even a sudden craze for books detailing personal battles with psychological problems, particularly drug and alcohol addiction.[17] In short, this was an exceptionally contradictory decade in regard to public perceptions of health and wellbeing. *An American Werewolf in London* displays these contradictions by having its werewolf attempt to rationalise his werewolfery as a manifestation of psychosis, suggesting that he would prefer to be suffering from serious mental illness rather than a physical malady.

An American Werewolf in London opens as David Kessler and Jack Goodman (Griffin Dunne), two American college students, arrive in Yorkshire during a backpacking holiday around Europe. There, they are attacked by a werewolf on the moors after they are made to feel grossly unwelcome by the proprietors and patrons of an isolated rural pub named The Slaughtered Lamb. Jack is gruesomely mauled to death, while David is bitten and gravely injured before the locals come to rescue them, shooting the monstrous wolf dead; as it dies, the werewolf transforms into a bloodied human corpse. Three weeks later, David wakes up in a London hospital, where he meets Nurse Alex Price – with whom he begins to fall in love – and Dr Hirsch (John Woodvine), who will later come to suspect something is seriously wrong with David. Shortly after being discharged from hospital, David experiences his first transformation and is responsible for the deaths of several people before he is finally gunned down by police in a back alley adjacent to Piccadilly Circus.

The original idea for *An American Werewolf in London* came to Landis when he was working as a production assistant on the set of *Kelly's Heroes* (1970) in Yugoslavia. He recalls witnessing the traditional Romani burial of a criminal, who was buried in a vertical grave and wrapped in canvas, rosaries and garlic to avoid his return as a member of the undead.[18] As an educated American witnessing the sacred ritual of a deeply traditional European people, Landis found their superstition baffling:

> I just found the whole thing completely insane. And then I thought, as I was being driven along, if it was nighttime, and the camera moved in on the crux of the crossroads, and I saw the earth start to be disturbed, the fingers crawling their way to the surface, and the guy dug his way out like Peter Cushing, how would I deal with that? Because when you have a certain amount of education, you know these things are not true. So I thought, that's a good idea for a movie. When you know the supernatural does not exist, how do you deal with it when it's standing in front of you?[19]

From the moment he wakes up in his London hospital bed, David begins to experience recurrent supernatural phenomena, including vivid fever dreams. First, David dreams that he is running through woodland naked, before pouncing on a deer and tearing into its flesh with his teeth. His second dream sees him standing in the same wood, this time wearing the clothes he wore when he was attacked on the moors. From a distance, he sees himself lying in a hospital bed; Nurse Alex is tending to him when his face suddenly becomes monstrous and animalistic.

His third dream – and perhaps the film's most unsettling sequence aside from its transformation scene – sees David's family sitting at home watching an episode of *The Muppet Show* (1976–81) when someone knocks at the door.[20] David's father answers it to find a group of demons wearing Nazi uniforms standing on the other side; after a short pause, they slaughter the family with knives and automatic weapons before setting the house alight. In a further dream-within-a-dream, David believes he has woken up in his hospital bed, but when Nurse Price opens the curtains another Nazi demon jumps from the windowsill and graphically stabs her to death. When David tries to explain some of these dreams to Dr Hirsch, the doctor ends the conversation by questioning David's mental state: 'Please, remain sane. At least until you're no longer our responsibility.'

Most disturbing to David, though, are inexplicable waking episodes in which he sees the rotting corpse of his best friend Jack. Essentially a ghost, Jack claims that he – and others David will murder during his lunar activities – will be cursed to walk the Earth as members of the undead until the werewolf who killed them is destroyed. Jack's ultimate mission is to convince David to kill himself before the werewolf claims any further victims. David's reaction to his first encounter with the phantom is logical and entirely understandable: 'I'm going completely crazy.' He will come to question his sanity again and again during his encounters with the ghostly Jack and, before the film's final set piece in Piccadilly Circus, the mauled corpses of his other undead victims in a darkened adult movie theatre.

After all, Landis intended for his characters to react realistically when faced with the impossible. But David's reaction also has a deeper function: it is telling that the early symptoms of his werewolfism – before he experiences a physical transformation – have more in common with the signs of mental than physical illness. His nightmares reflect psychological trauma rather than a physical malady, while his encounters with Jack fit with the symptoms of severe psychosis rather than disease. What is important here is that, because his experiences bear a resemblance to a psychotic break, David wants to convince himself that he is losing his grip on reality. Of course, he does not want to be insane, but he finds the idea more plausible than – and, importantly, preferable to – the suggestion that he is truly able to see ghosts, or that he will actually transform into a werewolf on the night of the next full moon, or that he has contracted a dangerous and potentially fatal disease.

An American Werewolf in London clearly frames werewolfism as a disease: it is – as in many werewolf films – an affliction that is passed on by a bite from a carrier. A more concrete connection between werewolfery and disease is also created by the fact that David spends much of the film's first act confined to a hospital bed: he is in a medical environment, being cared for by medical professionals. Landis clearly interprets werewolfism – or at least the version of it most often depicted in cinema – as a form of infection. In a 2013 interview with Adam Savage of YouTube channel 'Tested', he suggests the idea of werewolfery as a disease can be traced to Curt Siodmak's screenplay for *The Wolf Man* (1941):

> Curt Siodmak's innovation – which is really radical – is that he made Larry Talbot not a vicious, mean monster but a victim of the curse. I mean, he took the idea of lycanthropy as one disease: a bite. Not a curse, not a magic trick, but a bite. So it's like AIDS . . . The idea of, 'it's a disease that's not your fault.' When you get cancer, it's not because you're a bad guy. You get cancer, you get a disease. So what he did was, is he made Larry Talbot the victim and separate from the beast . . . It's not Jekyll and Hyde . . . the thing with Jekyll and Hyde is that they're essentially the same guy. It's the other side of him. It's about psychopharmacology and schizophrenia and stuff . . .

Anyway, so Siodmak's big innovation was he made the Wolf Man a victim . . .
So in mine, taking that idea that he's a victim, I wanted to take something ridiculous
and try to make it real. So if you take these two young men who are smart – fairly
sophisticated, educated guys – well, how do you deal with something that's not real?[21]

Landis's answer to this – in addressing a question about the film's elements of comedy – is that 'You laugh at it. I mean, well, that's what most intelligent people do.'[22] David does make light of the situation; on first seeing Jack he asks, with a hefty dose of irony, 'Does it occur to you that it might be unsettling to see you rise from the grave to visit me?' But beyond his nervous humour, David's primary instinct is that he is losing his mind, something that is clearly a better prognosis in his eyes than having contracted the disease Landis describes. It is interesting that Landis compares werewolfism to AIDS and cancer specifically; while the AIDS crisis was yet to begin when *An American Werewolf in London* was released, it would come to be associated with inevitable death and was the source of great fear only a few years later. Cancer was also perceived – and, to a lesser extent, is still seen today – as invariably fatal. And, of course, it is a mutation of human cells that often manifests as a malignant tumour disease.

Like cancer, David's werewolfery threatens to cause his body to change against his will. The grotesque transformation sequence at the centre of the film is a potent allegory for the potential of such diseases to mutate the human form. Once he has been bitten, David has two choices: he can commit suicide or allow himself to experience a painful and drawn out metamorphosis that will render him a grotesque monster (Figure 5.2). Clearly, both choices are unpleasant and, further to align the film's werewolfism with terminal illness, either choice will ultimately prove fatal: having chosen not to take his life, David dies at the film's conclusion regardless. In line with the widespread scaremongering surrounding serious physical disease and with society's growing understanding of mental illness in the 1980s, David finds the suggestion that he is experiencing psychotic symptoms – symptoms that could potentially be treated and controlled – comforting in comparison to the idea that he has been infected with a volatile and likely fatal supernatural infection.

Inspired by his experience in Yugoslavia, Landis wrote the script for *An American Werewolf in London* in 1969. He recalls that there were 'very few changes between that script and the film I made many years later'.[23] However, Landis could not find funding for the film at this time; he recalls that producers disliked the film's genre hybridity ('It was either "this is too scary to be funny" or "this is too funny to be scary"') and it was only when he had obtained a reputation for producing financially successful pictures that he managed to secure funding.[24]

Figure 5.2 David Kessler (David Naughton) experiences extreme pain and suffering as he transforms in *An American Werewolf in London* (1981).

Had Landis been able to make his werewolf film earlier, it might have offered a realistic, modern depiction of a traditionally gothic monster before George A. Romero's *Martin* (1977) performed a similar service for the vampire. However, the film would not have had such strong cultural resonance. It is unlikely – and in the case of the AIDS virus, impossible – that the connection between werewolfism and disease occurred to Landis in 1969. *An American Werewolf in London*'s eventual release, then, came at the perfect time to transform Landis's story about logical men confronting the absurdity of the supernatural into a meditation on cultural perceptions of physical and psychological illness. David is given the choice to believe he is either psychotic or a werewolf. He would rather assume he is psychotic and – considering the violent, repulsive and agonising nature of the film's infamous transformation scene – it is difficult to disagree.

The Howling also creates a connection between physical transformation, mental illness and monstrosity. At the beginning of the film, investigative reporter Karen White is taking part in a police sting operation designed to catch serial killer Eddie Quist, who has been stalking her. She meets him in a private viewing booth in a sex shop, where he forces her to watch a violent porn film depicting rape while, behind her, he transforms into a werewolf. Quist manages to escape before the police arrive, and afterwards Karen begins to suffer from symptoms consistent with amnesia and post-traumatic stress disorder; she struggles to remember the exact details of her experience, but suffers momentary flashbacks to fragments of the event that she finds greatly distressing.

Her therapist, Dr George Waggner (Patrick Macnee) – named for the director of *The Wolf Man* – suggests that Karen visit the Colony, a private therapeutic commune dedicated to treating patients suffering from psychological trauma. However, none of the patients receiving treatment at the Colony are suffering from any traditional mental illness: they are cursed with werewolfism and have sought out Waggner in the hope of finding a cure. Even Waggner himself is a werewolf, and believes that others of his kind need to repress their animalistic desires through psychotherapy. However, other members of the group – notably Eddie Quist and his nymphomaniac sister Marsha (Elizabeth Brooks) – disagree, and would like to embrace their lupine attributes.

While the Quists are the film's central antagonists, they are as much victims as they are monsters. These are Waggner's patients, and therefore their violent behaviour is a clear suggestion that his brand of therapy has done nothing but amplify any deviant desires. At first Eddie and Marsha Quist were werewolves. After treatment from Waggner, Eddie becomes a rapist and serial killer while Marsha becomes an insatiable sexual predator; his care for the mind has done nothing but push them to embrace their physical monstrosity. It is important to note here that *The Howling*'s werewolves are able to transform by choice, and their werewolfery is in no way linked to the lunar cycle. They can choose to become a werewolf at any time; conversely they can also choose to ignore their animalistic instincts entirely. Waggner's brand of therapy consists of teaching his patients to suppress the lupine instincts that come with their affliction; he would have them live their lives in denial of their true nature. Here, then, werewolfism becomes a metaphor for any behaviour considered unsavoury by mainstream society, and psychotherapy a form of oppression and control. At the film's climax, it becomes clear that Eddie and Marsha are not the only members of the Colony who feel uncomfortable with wholly suppressing the wolf; when Karen's friends and colleagues Terri Fisher (Bellinda Balaski) and Chris Halloran (Dennis Dugan) arrive and threaten to expose the Colony's true nature, the vast majority of Waggner's patients are immediately prepared to transform and kill them without remorse.

The Howling's screenplay was penned by screenwriter John Sayles (who made many changes to the plot of Gary Brandner's 1977 source novel, chiefly transferring its action from a small American town to Waggner's Colony). In his work on Sayles, Mark Bould links the film to Robin Wood's work on the horror genre.[25] He produces a psychoanalytical reading of the film and suggests that its principal concern is precisely with the dangerous nature of cultures that encourage the repression of natural urges. Bould draws attention to the film's opening scene, which sees Waggner on television discussing the dangers of repression, before adding:

> In *The Howling*, the main source of the horror is the family – the Quist siblings – and the Colony of which they are part and, despite Waggner's words quoted above, it is clear that he created this community by encouraging repression, by convincing its members to abandon the old ways so that they can pass unnoticed in human society.[26]

Bould's reading of the film is sound, but it is possible to detach it from the apparatus of psychoanalysis. After all, this theme is not an abstract notion but one very relevant to its cultural moment; where *An American Werewolf in London* frames mental illness as a fate preferable to physical mutation, *The Howling* expresses a severe distrust of psychotherapy. Like David Cronenberg's *The Brood* (1979) – in which another psychotherapist, Hal Raglan (Oliver Reed), offers experimental treatments to victims of trauma that result in the development of malignant tumours and terminal diagnoses – *The Howling* articulates a distrust of psychiatry as a business. As John Kenneth Muir attests, the film is 'a parody of pop psychology and self-help'.[27] Psychotherapy grew enormously as an industry from the late 1970s onwards and both *The Brood* and *The Howling* lament this growing commoditisation of mental health treatment. These are films in which doctors become media sensations for their experimental techniques, only for it to become clear that they – like Dr Brandon in *I Was a Teenage Werewolf* (1957) – are charlatans and their methods either do not work or result in hideous side effects. Both Raglan and Waggner are demonised for their willingness to exploit the vulnerable to further their own careers. At the film's climax, having been bitten and infected during her time at the Colony, Karen chooses to transform – and be killed with a silver bullet – during a news bulletin on live television to expose Waggner and prove the existence of werewolves to the world.

Such a countercultural subtext is not uncommon in Sayles's early genre screenplays, written before he became a respected writer-director in later years. In addition to *The Howling*, Sayles was also the writer of *Piranha* (1978) and *Alligator* (1980), two other monster movies that have been noted for their subversive subtexts. *Piranha* sees mutated fish released from an abandoned army compound, where they had been developed as a potential weapon. They go on to wreak havoc at a summer camp, killing several people. Bould reads *Piranha* as an indictment of big business and the military-industrial complex, in which society's apathy towards the ills of capitalist modernity ends in death.[28] *Alligator* is a retelling of the popular 'Alligators in the Sewers' urban legend, which renders its eponymous reptile as a metaphor for the American underclass and uses the cyclical nature of urban legends as an allegory for cycles of societal oppression and revolt.[29] And, of course, *The Howling* was helmed by Joe Dante, the director of *Piranha* and a number of similarly subversive films such as *Gremlins*, *The 'Burbs* (1989), *Gremlins 2: The New Batch* (1990), *The Second Civil War* (1997) and *Small Soldiers* (1998). In *The Howling*, Sayles and Dante lament the immorality of modern capitalism by alluding to the corruption inherent in monetising mental health and the dangers endemic in encouraging an entire society to become dependent on psychotherapy to find peace of mind.

Wolf Blood

While the reading above would suggest that *The Howling* warns against the suppression of desire, sexual and otherwise, it is not the only possible reading of the film. Separated from the larger concerns of its narrative, much of the body-horror imagery in *The Howling* could be seen to form a link between sexuality and monstrous transformation. Of course, such images would become all too relevant only a few years after its theatrical release, at the height of the AIDS crisis. Before Karen even arrives at the sex shop where she will encounter Quist for the first time, she has already been mistaken for a sex worker and has been framed walking down a neon-lit street dominated by the sex industry, where Karen's fearful expression is juxtaposed against shots of adult bookstores and massage parlours; sexuality itself is made the subject of fear. These opening scenes potentially create a link between horror and sex that is compounded during Karen's traumatic experience in the peep-show booth, where Quist transforms while she is forced to watch violent sexual imagery.

Later, at the Colony, it becomes clear that Karen and her husband Bill Neill (Christopher Stone) are the only two guests staying at the retreat who are not werewolves. But this does not last for long. Karen has found herself psychologically unable to have sex with her husband as a result of the violent trauma she suffered at the film's opening. Meanwhile, Marsha has set her sights on Bill. After he is attacked by an unseen creature in the forest surrounding his cabin, Bill and Marsha give in to their desires and have sex in open woodland. During their encounter, they begin to transform into werewolves, biting and scratching at each other, tearing flesh and opening wounds. By the end of the scene, they have both fully transformed and, in a long shot, they are framed in the act of coitus with lupine heads. Here, *The Howling* depicts horrifying transformation as occurring during the actual act of copulation, creating imagery that explicitly links sexuality with monstrosity. Though a werewolf is created in *The Howling* in much the same way as in *An American Werewolf in London* – through a bite – this scene gives the impression of werewolfism as a sexually transmitted infection.

The Howling's grotesque sexual imagery would come to dominate a great many werewolf films as the 1980s wore on, including several of its own sequels. Two early examples saw release in 1982: *Cat People* (1982) – a loose remake of the 1942 film of the same name – compounds *The Howling*'s sexual themes into a frightening depiction of sex as the trigger for a hideous metamorphosis, while *The Beast Within*, in which a child of rape grows into a monstrous human–insect hybrid, was marketed on an apparent similarity to *The Howling* and *An American Werewolf in London*. It is tempting to read these films retrospectively in the context of AIDS, but in truth the discovery of what would come to be known as the Acquired Immune Deficiency Syndrome was in its early stages when *The Howling* was released, and medical professionals had yet to decide on a definitive name for the virus when *Cat People* and *The Beast Within* began their theatrical runs.

The term AIDS was not coined until mid-1982 and, until later that year, the virus was popularly thought to be a disease that could only affect gay men and intravenous drug users. In December, the media destroyed this perception when they reported that the disease had been identified in twenty children.[30] The panic caused by this news was compounded in May 1983, when it was falsely reported that AIDS could be transmitted through everyday household contact.[31] So, while a connection between sex and monstrosity may have been apparent at the points of these films' immediate consumption, it is exceptionally unlikely that they were read in the context of AIDS – though such interpretations would become more likely when the films became available on home-video formats later in the decade.

But, of course, any reading of these films that links their body-horror imagery to a monstrous depiction of sexuality need not be directly linked to the AIDS crisis. Politically and socially, American perceptions of sexuality – and what was considered by the conservative mainstream to be 'deviant' behaviour – had been changing since Reagan entered office in 1981. Reagan was a staunch anti-abortionist and espoused the need for America to return to family values. As Michael Schaller asserts, his administration was representative of a movement in American politics termed the 'New Right', traditional conservatives made up of:

A loose coalition of religious fundamentalists, computerized fund raisers, members of Congress, unorthodox economists and political action committees . . .

Whether they had a religious, secular, or congressional background, New Right activists believed that environmentalism, arms control, gun control, abortion rights, gay rights, feminism, welfare, affirmative action, pornography, and the Equal Rights Amendment all fostered a destructive 'permissiveness' that undermined the value of family, church and state.[32]

The New Right represented Americans who railed against the progressive social and political attitudes of the 1960s and the 1970s, and sought a return to a more traditional society built on the foundations of conservative values: the nuclear family, patriarchy, Christian worship and community. It is not surprising that Reagan enjoyed particular support from religious fundamentalists, who 'expressed outrage over the greater acceptance of divorce, abortion, pre-marital sex, homosexuality, and feminism'.[33] Sandra Scanlon points out that the practical importance of the Religious Right to Reagan's presidential campaign has been contested; she suggests it was primarily the ongoing Iranian hostage crisis, Jimmy Carter's apparent economic failings and Reagan's promise to lower inflation that secured his presidency.[34] Furthermore, Reagan's drive for Christian values was somewhat hypocritical: in adulthood he rarely attended church and was the first American president to have been divorced.[35] However, while the Christian morality he was eager to project may not have secured his election, Reagan clearly worked to appeal to the Religious Right; he claimed to identify as a Christian, spoke highly of traditional family values and endorsed traditional gender roles. The staunch moral and religious values he was keen to promote came to be strongly associated with his presidency.

Reagan's stance on one issue in particular appealed to the Religious Right more than any other: sexual health. As discussed above, his administration took a steadfastly pro-life stance on abortion and framed unwanted pregnancy as an issue entirely for female consideration:

[Reagan] persuaded Congress to bar most public funding for birth control and stop Medicare from funding abortions for poor women. An administration measure provided funding for religiously orientated 'chastity clinics' where counselors advised teenage girls and women to 'just say no' to avoid pregnancy.[36]

His opposition to abortion was a major element of his election campaign; following his win in 1980, attacks on abortion clinics and their employees by pro-life activists rose by 450 per cent.[37]

Reagan's political rhetoric demonised sexuality years before the outbreak of the AIDS panic and his administration framed sex as an activity that should occur only within the sanctity of marriage. When the realities of

AIDS became common knowledge, the epidemic proved a double-edged sword for Reagan; at first an uncomfortable topic, later a useful tool in furthering his own agenda. In the early years – when the virus was discovered, named and initial studies began – he was keen to dismiss it entirely: 'The president appeared to find the entire subject distasteful and felt that anything he said expressing a sympathetic attitude towards its victims might upset religious conservatives who called the illness divine punishment for sinners.'[38] This policy of ignorance did not last. The year 1985 saw the death of actor Rock Hudson from an AIDS-related illness, an event that brought the realities of AIDS to the forefront of the public consciousness and led to a dramatic increase in media coverage.[39] But even after Hudson's death, Reagan's administration did not offer a sympathetic view of AIDS. Rather, it used the epidemic as an excuse to reinforce the underpinning concerns of its sexual health policies. A report from the Surgeon General in 1986 suggested only three measures to prevent contraction of the AIDS virus: abstinence, monogamy and condoms. Even then, high-profile conservatives such as the Secretary of Education, William Bennett, criticised the report for mentioning prophylactics and thereby encouraging sexual promiscuity.[40]

Politically, the AIDS crisis became just another tool for Reagan's administration to utilise in its attempts to reframe sex in America: 'Reagan, like many conservatives, pursued the goal of recoupling sex and reproduction, two activities which since the 1960s had been decoupled. Women's access to abortion and contraception, like gay sex, defied the linkage of sex, reproduction and marriage.'[41] In summary, then, Reagan's administration was keen to reinforce its religious leanings by framing sex as an act that should be confined to committed heterosexual relationships and preferably in the pursuit of planned pregnancy. Any other sexual activity was considered deviant, immoral and against the wills of both God and government. So, any link between sex and monstrosity in 1980s horror cinema does not need to be interpreted in the context of AIDS. As David J. Skal asserts, AIDS would certainly have an impact after 1983: 'Prosperous America of the 1980s denied the reality of AIDS, locking its doors against the victims of the plague, while monstrous images popped up everywhere in its collective dreams.'[42] But while the theme of monstrous sexuality would proliferate as public awareness of the virus and its mode of transmission increased, Reagan had been working hard to demonise sex since he announced his candidacy in 1979.

The Beast Within is an early example of a horror film closely linked to werewolf narratives that creates a connection between sex and monstrosity. Although *The Beast Within* is not specifically a werewolf film, its title alone is clearly designed to invite comparisons with *The Howling* and *An*

American Werewolf in London. Furthermore, the film's opening shot is of a full moon, while its trailer purposely obscures the nature of the film's monster and attempts to align itself with the new werewolf by selling the film based on its transformation scenes ('WARNING: This preview cannot show all of the terrifying and grotesque transformation sequences from the last thirty minutes of *The Beast Within*'). In fact, the film's protagonist turns into a hybrid of human and cicada, an insect that develops into an adult over a period of time; some species take a full seventeen years to reach maturity. This is the life cycle mimicked in the film, as Michael MacCleary (Paul Clemens) begins to transform into an insect around the time of his seventeenth birthday.

The Beast Within focuses closely on deviant sexual behaviour. The opening scene takes place seventeen years before the rest of the narrative. Michael's parents are forced to seek help near an isolated Mississippi town when their car breaks down during their honeymoon. Their dog runs off, prompting Michael's mother to chase it into the woods. There, she is confronted by a hideous monster that has broken free from its imprisonment in the cellar of a decrepit house. In a shocking scene, it tears off her clothes and rapes her.

As the narrative jumps to the present day, we soon learn that Michael was conceived as a result of the rape and his mother's rapist – his biological father, Billy Connors – is being reborn as the monstrous insect growing inside of his body. In the film's pivotal transformation sequence, the giant cicada bursts out of Michael's skin in what Kim Newman calls a 'riot of protracted bladder effects and hydrocephalic queasiness'.[43] In the build-up to this climactic scene, much of the film concentrates on Michael's inability to control his lust for a local girl who has become the object of his desires, Amanda Platt (Katherine Moffat). First, he violently kisses her during a walk with her to an isolated swamp. Later, he visits her house with the sole purpose of convincing her to leave before he is physically unable to stop himself from assaulting her; Michael is forced to throw himself from a window when his urges become unmanageable.

By the end of *The Beast Within*, both Billy and Michael have become monstrous as a result of their inability to control their urges: fully transformed, Michael inevitably rapes Amanda and perpetuates the cicada's lifecycle. In the context of Reagan's politics, the film becomes a morality tale that clearly outlines the apparent consequences of failing to repress desire. In fact, it is disclosed that the very reason Michael's father mutated into a monster is because he was imprisoned in a dilapidated basement, having been caught sleeping with a married woman. Her husband, an undertaker, killed his wife and locked her lover in his cellar, feeding him the corpses brought to his mortuary for burial; Billy's metamorphosis is revealed to have been the direct result of consuming human flesh. Billy, then, is demonised for two distinct acts of apparently deviant sexual behaviour: seducing one married woman and raping another. Reynold Humphries suggests that because Michael's lustful violence is the result of Billy's influence both figuratively and literally growing inside him, he is 'a character afflicted through no fault of his own'.[44] But in this, Reagan's pleas for the return of traditional family values are affirmed: Michael is a side effect of sexual deviancy and is therefore monstrous.

Apparent perversion is also central to *Cat People*. This is a film, as Muir notes, in which 'A lonely woman played by [Nastassja] Kinski feared that she would "transform" into a murderous wildcat if she were to attain orgasm with a lover, showcasing . . . the decade's fear of sex and disease.'[45] Like the 1942 original, the 1982 version of *Cat People* is designed to capitalise on the popularity of werewolf films, only in this case it is *The Howling* and *An American Werewolf in London* that serve as inspiration rather than *The Wolf Man*.

Remakes are an interesting indicator of cultural change, and it is the differences between the 1942 and 1982 versions of *Cat People* that reveal the latter's grounding in Reagan's America. Where the protagonist of the 1940s version is – aside from one brief encounter with another cursed individual – the sole 'cat person' in that film's narrative, the 1982 version features a brother and sister, Paul (Malcom McDowell) and Irena Gallier (Nastassja Kinski), both of whom are, according to Paul, unable to engage in sexual activity with anybody but each other without triggering a transformation into a black panther. In another change, Paul also reveals to Irena that it has only been through incest that their bloodline has survived; in this revelation alone the film links unorthodox sexual behaviours with transformation. Through brothers mating with sisters, the cat people have actively proliferated by indulging in taboo sexual behaviour rather than letting their curse die out.

The addition of McDowell's character to the narrative serves further to strengthen a theme of lethal sexuality. In order to satisfy his sexual desires, Paul routinely sleeps with sex workers and then murders them following his transformation; in order to return to human form, he has to kill again. Because Paul is employed by a Christian organisation, there is some suggestion that he kills his victims out of a sense of religious guilt – he is referred to as a 'religious fanatic' at the scene of one of his crimes – but in truth this idea is not adequately explored. By the film's climax it is equally likely that Paul is using his supposed faith to hide his true nature and divert suspicion. Conversely, Irena is a virgin. She is determined that she will not give in to her sexual desires as Paul does, even when she meets a man she is immediately attracted to: zoologist Oliver Yates (John Heard).

When Oliver meets Irena he is already in a committed relationship, here with a zookeeper named Alice Perrin (Annette O'Toole). After a sexless courtship, Irena and Oliver finally succumb to their desires at the film's climax. Even this union is not traditionally hetero-normative; as Muir suggests, Irena and Oliver's singular sexual encounter is aligned with 'bondage and domination'.[46] When they do finally decide to sleep together, Oliver ties Irena to his bed before having sex with her. Immediately afterwards, Irena suffers through a horrifying transformation reminiscent of those seen in *An American Werewolf in London*, *The Howling* and *The Beast Within*, in which a black panther bursts through her skin, tearing her body apart. At the film's climax, Oliver and Alice return to the relationship they had before Irena entered their lives, while Irena becomes an exhibit in their zoo, trapped forever in the body of a cat as punishment for her transgressions. As Tudor suggests, *Cat People* frames 'the disordering impulse in sexual terms'.[47]

The AIDS crisis had begun by the mid-1980s and a rise in awareness of the virus occurred in tandem with a further proliferation of the werewolf film. *The Company of Wolves* (1984) and *Monster Dog* (1984), two European productions aimed at achieving success at the American box office, would play on fears of AIDS by explicitly linking the notions of sexuality, disease and transformation. *The Company of Wolves* – a UK production from writer-director Neil Jordan – is a surreal reimagining of the 'Little Red Riding Hood' fairytale, in which mysterious men seduce young women before wolves burst forth from their mouths in showers of blood. The Italian *Monster Dog*, an exploitation film starring American rock star Alice Cooper, concentrates on werewolfism as a disease. At the film's climax, *Monster Dog*'s protagonist, Vince (Cooper), has been infected and pleads with his girlfriend, Sandra (Victoria Vera), to shoot him before his transformation can take hold; he would rather be dead than live his life as a werewolf. After a sanguinary and, by this time, obligatory transformation sequence, she complies.

In America, 1985 would see the release of *The Howling*'s first sequel, *Howling II: Your Sister is a Werewolf* (or *Howling II: Stirba – Werewolf Bitch*). As the title suggests, *Howling II* would abandon any semblance of the first film's subversive subtext and concentrate solely on the expression of female sexuality as the source of horror in a film that combines Reagan's moralistic rhetoric with fears regarding sexually transmitted infections. The plot focuses on Karen White's brother Ben (Reb Brown), who is attending his sister's funeral following her televised death at the end of *The Howling*. There he meets one of Karen's colleagues, Jenny Templeton (Annie McEnroe), and a werewolf hunter, Stefan Crosscoe (Christopher Lee). Crosscoe informs Ben and Jenny that Karen had discovered the existence of werewolves and convinces them to travel with him to Transylvania. There, Crosscoe intends to confront and destroy Stirba (Sybil Danning), a 'werewolf queen' so powerful that she can only be destroyed with titanium; meanwhile, Stirba intends to unleash her cult of loyal werewolf followers upon the Earth. After several encounters with her minions, Crosscoe leads an assault on Stirba's castle, where she is finally destroyed.

Stirba's werewolf cult is entirely framed in a sexual context. The first scene in which she appears sees her followers bring her ageing body to an altar, where they transfer her soul into the body of a nubile young woman. Except for the elderly, all of Stirba's disciples are pictured here in various stages of undress and wear costumes that align them more with sadomasochism than with the occult. The women wear tight leather undergarments adorned with buckles and chains, cut to expose navels, legs and breasts, while men are routinely shirtless. Some of their chests are wrapped in leather straps, while others wear helmets and masks to obscure their faces: Stirba's dehumanised sexual possessions. Shortly after her rebirth, Stirba has group sex with two of her followers: one male and one female, a new initiate to the werewolf cult. In an elongated scene of sexual body-horror, all three participants slowly transform into werewolves while writhing in ecstasy on an ornate bed (Figure 5.3). In fact, unorthodox sexual behaviour defines the cult even more than their werewolfery; they are most often depicted indulging in pleasures of the flesh in their human forms. Throughout the rest of the film, Stirba is often seen being worshipped by her male bodyguards, while at the climax she is watching her followers engage in mass sex when she is informed that Crosscoe has arrived at the gates of her secluded fortress.

Despite its relatively explicit sexual content, *Howling II* actually eschews the modern settings embraced by *The Howling* and *An American Werewolf in London* and adopts a more gothic aesthetic, typified by its Transylvanian setting. Stirba's castle lair is positively medieval in appearance, while the casting of Christopher Lee creates an intertextual connection to gothic horror in the Hammer Films style. Of course, Lee has been consistently associated with Hammer largely because of his recurring role as Dracula. Crosscoe's character embodies the religious moralising that was often the central theme of Hammer's horror films; the company infamously cast righteous men of faith and nobility as heroes and sexually liberated women as their demonic aggressors in films including *The Brides of Dracula* (1960), *The Vampire Lovers* (1970), *Countess Dracula* (1971) and *Blood from the Mummy's Tomb* (1971).

Figure 5.3 In *Howling II: Your Sister is a Werewolf* (1985), werewolfery is associated with sexual deviancy; here, Stirba (Sybil Danning) has group sex with two of her followers.

As discussed in Chapter 4, even the company's solitary werewolf film, *The Curse of the Werewolf* (1961), depicts werewolfism as the result of a mute woman's rape by a feral beggar. In *Howling II*, Lee comes to represent similar religious values for the Reagan years. When he finally kills Stirba with a titanium blade, he does it 'in the name of God', before praying that she will 'rest in peace'. Stirba is demonic not only because she is a werewolf but because she is a nymphomaniac who spreads her infection through bizarre sexual rituals. Crosscoe's staunchly religious werewolf hunter is the only man who can kill her: a hero representative of the conservative Christian values that Reagan desperately wanted to impress on the American public.

Howling II was followed by the American-Australian co-production *Howling III: The Marsupials* (1987), in which a new marsupial breed of werewolf – descended from the extinct thylacine – is discovered in Australia. Some elements of *Howling III* are strangely subversive considering its predecessor's conservatism; the film satirises the then ongoing Cold War by imagining a world in which the Russian and American governments enter into a supernatural arms race after they both discover the existence of werewolves, while there is also some suggestion that the film ultimately seeks to lament humankind's unfortunate habit of hunting animals to extinction. However, both of these themes are underdeveloped and *Howling III*'s body-horror once again ultimately creates a link between sex and werewolfism. The film's protagonist, a young woman who refers to herself only as Jerboa (Imogen Annesley), is a marsupial werewolf and the step-daughter of Thylo (Max Fairchild), the leader of Australia's thylacine werewolf pack. Just as in *Cat People*, *Howling III*'s pack indulges in incest; Jerboa runs away from her tribe to avoid sexual abuse at the hands of her step-father, a practice endorsed by her people.

Jerboa arrives in Sydney, where she meets Donny Martin (Leigh Biolos), a young American working on a film set. In another strange tonal shift, the film he is working on is a low-budget horror picture helmed by a blatant caricature of Alfred Hitchcock. Donny is immediately infatuated with Jerboa, and convinces her to audition for the film's female lead. They fall in love and begin sleeping together. Shortly before they are to have sex for the second time, Jerboa viciously bites at Donny's neck, creating another connection between her curse and her sexuality. Afterwards, Donny becomes suspicious as to why Jerboa refused to remove her top. As she sleeps, he sees that her stomach is covered in a fine fur and she has a long, thin opening across her stomach: a marsupial pouch.

Jerboa shortly learns that she has fallen pregnant with Donny's child. While the stand-out body-horror sequence in the vast majority of 1980s werewolf films is the transformation scene, *Howling III* chooses to concentrate on the moment Jerboa gives birth to her baby. In a sequence designed to evoke disgust, Jerboa births a partially formed werewolf foetus, before using her saliva to flatten the fur on her stomach, creating a path for her child to transition from her vagina to her marsupial pouch. Even when Jerboa's child is fully developed, he is depicted as a monstrous infant: a grotesque mixture of human and lupine characteristics who has resulted from a bloodline maintained by incestuous relations. At the film's climax – set many years after the central narrative – Jerboa, Donny and their son have found peace away from the werewolf community. Jerboa and Donny have chosen new names; she is now a famed actor, while he is a respected director. However, in a repeat of *The Howling*'s climax, Jerboa transforms into a werewolf on live television when a metamorphosis is triggered by flashbulbs at an awards show; like *The Beast Within*'s Michael MacCleary, Jerboa and her son are the results of unorthodox sexual behaviour and must be exposed.

The next *Howling* sequel – *Howling IV: The Original Nightmare* (1988) – also contains body-horror imagery that could be considered to support Reagan's views on sexual health and the worsening AIDS crisis. As a loose remake of the original film, *Howling IV* contains a character reminiscent of nymphomaniac Marsha Quist: Eleanor (Lamya Derval), a werewolf who sets her sights on seducing Richard (Michael T. Weiss), a married man, from the moment he arrives in her isolated rural town. After an initial sexual encounter, Eleanor lures Richard into the woods and bites him, infecting him with her werewolfery. In one of the finest transformation sequences in all of the *Howling* series, at the film's climax Richard goes through a metamorphosis that clearly depicts werewolfism as a wasting disease; the early stages see his flesh, muscle and sinew melt away, leaving only a skeleton drenched in showers of infected blood. Richard's bones then descend into viscera and resurface as a monstrous werewolf. However, outside of Richard's affair with Eleanor and its impressive transformation sequence, *Howling IV*'s larger narrative has less in common with body-horror narratives than it does with a cycle of satirical werewolf films that criticise Reagan's policies. While films such as *The Beast Within*, *Cat People* and the first two *Howling* sequels condemn sexual liberation and play on fears of sexually transmitted infection, this second group of 1980s werewolf films would critique the social, political and economic changes that took place during Reagan's years in office, beginning with 1985's *Silver Bullet*.

CHAPTER 6

The Better to Eat You With

White Fangs

The mid-to-late 1980s witnessed the birth of an American horror cycle centred on an aversion to conservative family values and religious morals; a series of films that depict evil lurking beneath the surface of idyllic white Christian communities. For example, *Poltergeist* (1982) sees a white middle-class family haunted by the ghosts of the forgotten souls buried beneath their new home in suburbia; the original *A Nightmare on Elm Street* series (1984–91) sees successive groups of middle-class teenagers forced to do battle with Freddy Krueger, a supernatural monster of their parents' creation; *Fright Night* (1985) pits a teenager against the yuppie vampire – posing as a property developer – who moves in next door; and in *The Stepfather* (1987), a man committed to conservative principles marries into a small-town American family. A real estate agent, he claims to 'sell the American dream'. Of course, he is not what he seems; a volatile psychopath, he murdered his previous family in cold blood and intends to do the same again.

Blue Velvet (1986), *The 'Burbs* (1989), *Society* (1989), *Parents* (1989) and *Meet the Applegates* (1990) respectively suggest that there could be violent sadists, murderous families, grotesque monsters, cheerful cannibals and even giant, man-eating insects living behind picket fences in American suburbia. While many of these 'community horror' films concentrate on human 'monsters', in some cases this distinct cycle intertwines with the concerns of body-horror by depicting hideous creatures hiding behind the civilised veneers of wealthy Americans. In depicting the rich as a species of highly evolved humans who literally feed on the poor, *Society* undoubtedly provides the most extreme example. But *Society* and others like it do not arise from a fear of the transforming body itself. Rather, where body-horror does appear in this cycle, it does not serve as an allegory for the destruction of the human form but as a countercultural metaphor through which to reveal the ills of political, social and moral conservatism. These films tell us that seemingly harmonious communities hide terrible secrets.

In counterpoint to the moralising of films such as *Cat People* (1982) and *Howling II: Your Sister is a Werewolf* (1985), this sub-genre is considered by Reynold Humphries to be a countercultural product of several social and cultural changes in 1980s America, and particularly the traditional values impressed on the nation by Ronald Reagan's administration.[1] Because of its shapeshifting nature, the werewolf – a demonic wolf cloaked by human flesh – is an apt metaphor through which to explore the idea of evil disguised by civilised appearances. It is no surprise, then, that several films in this cycle, including *Silver Bullet* (1985), *My Mom's a Werewolf* (1989) and *Mom* (1991), place werewolves in small American communities and can be read as indictments of the Reagan administration's policies, a return to conservative social attitudes and the failings of capitalist modernity. This cycle arises from a culture that changed enormously under Reagan's presidency, and primarily aims its satire at two cultural and political developments. The first is the resurgence of traditional social conservatism, while the second is a widening gap between rich and poor.

As explored in Chapter 5, Reagan was representative of the New Right. With his administration came a reversal of the social, sexual and cultural liberations of the 1960s and 1970s, while his politics were built upon the principles of family, church and community. As Susan Scanlon states, however, undoubtedly the most important change that came with the Reagan administration was the invention and implementation of his economic policies.[2] Reagan was a vocal and dedicated opponent of liberal 'tax and spend' economics, and was committed to the idea that lowering taxes for the wealthy and businesses would reinvigorate an economy still failing to recover from the Carter years. As Schaller recounts, in February 1981 Reagan unveiled his economic plan before Congress:

> The president's tax initiative . . . would cut federal income and business tax rates by 30% over three years . . . reduce taxes on capital gains, lower estate and gift taxes, and allow faster depreciation on business investments.
>
> On the expenditure side of the equation, Reagan sought to cut the inherited Carter budget by $41 billion and to shift many social programs to the states. His spending plan would eliminate numerous welfare programs, trim Social Security, and cut back on parts of the federal bureaucracy that regulated business, the environment and public health.[3]

While Reagan had many working-class supporters, these plans did not improve the fiscal situation for the majority. Rather, as Schaller states, 'the rich got richer and everyone else [trod] water'.[4] During the decade to 1990, the average annual household income of the top 1 per cent of American families increased by \$232,938; the bottom 90 per cent enjoyed only an additional \$1,635 in the same timeframe.[5] Rather than improving quality of life for all Americans, Reagan's economic policies created a culture of greed in which money and status were to be celebrated, but increasing household income was made more difficult for those without considerable assets. Nevertheless, Reagan's administration continued to stress the importance of class mobility, career ambition and the accumulation of wealth; as Schaller asserts, 'Not since the Gilded Age of the late nineteenth century or the Roaring Twenties had the acquisition and flaunting of wealth been so publicly celebrated as during the 1980s. Income became the accepted measure of one's value to society.'[6]

This development was further entrenched by the arrival of what Graham Thompson calls 'Wall Street Mania'. For the stock market, 'the raft of deregulation legislation, together with a steady stock price recovery as high interest rates boosted the dollar on the foreign exchanges, had a profound impact'.[7] Schaller suggests that in Reagan's America, stockbrokers who made obscene fortunes on Wall Street came to be 'celebrated as role models and builders of a better world'.[8] Yuppie culture developed as young men and women structured their lifestyles around financial success; this was a generation of Americans that based its achievements on material wealth and 'plunged joyously into the American mainstream ready to consume'.[9] Meanwhile, cuts to Social Security and Reagan's reluctance to commit spending to welfare schemes impacted heavily on the poor. During the 1980s, one in five American children lived in poverty.[10] And the establishment was largely untroubled by the march of social inequality; as Doug Rossinow notes, 'In the name of freedom, Reaganites declaimed a creed with scant compassion for the disadvantaged. They believed that those lagging in the race of life had no real claim on society and should rely on private acts of beneficence.'[11]

The community horror cycle began in the early 1980s, and continued throughout Reagan's presidency. It critiques the president's social and economic policies by depicting traditional middle-to-upper-class communities as the site for horrific acts of violence committed by figures representative of Reagan's ideal citizen: the wealthy, white Christian conservative. The first werewolf film to belong to this cycle is *Silver Bullet*, which encapsulates the principal themes of community horror. The story of a paraplegic young boy trying to put an end to a series of vicious werewolf attacks in a small rural town, the film concentrates on the failings of familial, social and religious relations in Reagan's America. In this regard, it is not surprising that the film was written by Stephen King, a screenplay based on his own short novel *Cycle of the Werewolf* (1983): a rare example of the writer adapting his own work.[12] As Tony Magistrale asserts:

> [King] is interested in probing some of our darkest and primal collective cultural fears: that the government we have installed through the democratic process is not only corrupt but actively pursuing our destruction . . . and that our fundamental social institutions – school, marriage, the workplace and the church – have, beneath their veneers of respectability, evolved into perverse manifestations of narcissism, greed and violence. The particular horrors of King's novels are aligned with, and often emerge from, culturally specific disturbances; throughout his fiction are signs that traditional concepts of social solidarity are fraying or have dissolved.[13]

Silver Bullet is closely aligned with King's staple themes: it attacks the nuclear family, traditional American community and the Christian Church with aplomb. Marty Coslaw (Corey Haim) is a pre-teen paraplegic living with his white middle-class family: mother Nan (Robin Groves), father Bob (Leon Russom) and sister Jane (Megan Follows). They live in Tarker's Mills, a green, peaceful town in rural Maine that becomes the hunting ground for a werewolf. However, before the monster intrudes on Marty's life – and by the end of the film he will become the werewolf's chief target for destruction – all is not right in Marty's family. Marty's closest familial relationship is with an uncle on his mother's side, Red (Gary Busey). Something of a 'black sheep', Red is a middle-aged alcoholic; at the film's opening he is finalising his third divorce. However, he has a very warm relationship with his nephew. He regularly visits the Coslaw household and has built several motorised wheelchairs for Marty, not just to improve his quality of life but to bring him joy. One of these vehicles, the 'Silver Bullet', provides the film's title.

In contrast, Marty's parents are distant and treat his disability as a series of chores. Early in the narrative, Red visits Marty and drinks heavily while playing cards and telling jokes; shortly after she has sent her son to bed, Marty's mother confronts Red and asks him not to drink in front of her children. Red becomes incensed and openly suggests that Nan sees her son as little more than a burden, exclaiming: 'You know, you think your only responsibility is getting his butt out of the chair and into the tub and out of the chair and onto the toilet. And you ought to realise there's more to Marty than him not being able to walk.'

In *Cycle of the Werewolf*, Marty's father is emotionally stunted and embarrassed by his son's disability. In *Silver Bullet*, Bob is barely characterised at all. In his study of King's films, Michael R. Collings suggests that the film sidelines Marty's father 'to the detriment of the character'.[14] However, *Silver Bullet* creates an equally damning picture of Bob Coslaw through this absenteeism; while the novel depicts Bob as a distant but emotionally complex father, the film depicts an almost entirely absent one. Both Marty's mother and father illustrate the truth behind the façade of the 1980s nuclear family in their failings to protect their children. Ironically, they are concerned that Red is a bad influence on their son but fail to realise that he is in very real danger from another source.

Marty's relationship with his parents is such that when he begins to suspect the identity of the werewolf stalking Tarker's Mills, he chooses not to share this information with either his mother or father. After all, as Collings asserts, *Silver Bullet* has already created the impression of a mother 'most likely unwilling to believe her son's story'.[15] Tellingly, Marty does not even approach his parents after the werewolf has made several attempts on his life. Instead, he pleads for help first from his sister and then from Red. It is they who aid Marty in revealing the werewolf's identity and finding a way to rid Tarker's Mills of its murderous presence. Red is reluctant to accept the children's fantastic story that the murders in the town are the work of a werewolf, but he is willing to listen and help in any way he can. It is he who contacts the local sheriff and tries to convince him to investigate Marty's claims; takes the children's silver necklaces to a gunsmith to be turned into a silver bullet; and sits up with them in the Coslaw household on the night they suspect the werewolf will launch its final attack.

In fact, Marty's parents are so ineffectual that Red arranges for them to be on vacation during the film's final full moon so that he can ensure the children's protection. At the climax, it is Red, Marty and Jane who lie exhausted in the Coslaw house, satisfied that they have finally destroyed the werewolf of Tarker's Mills; the film ends before Nan and Bob Coslaw return. In this, *Silver Bullet* rejects the Reagan era's conception of the nuclear family by eschewing the traditional conservative image of happily married, hardworking parents fostering and protecting their children. Instead, this notion is replaced with a mother, father and child who fundamentally lack the ability to trust, understand or communicate with each other. Although Red is introduced as a drunkard incapable of maintaining a lasting relationship, by the film's end he is the closest thing Marty has to a guardian. As Collings asserts, *Silver Bullet* expands Red's character from his literary counterpart in *Cycle of the Werewolf* and emphasises 'the depth of his love for Marty'.[16] In doing so, *Silver Bullet* simultaneously questions the devotion of his parents.

Silver Bullet also reveals the fundamental failings of Reagan's vision of community. Tarker's Mills is a small, Christian town in which citizens cheerfully interact with each other at church and social events. However, some of them guard terrible secrets. The werewolf's first victim is an alcoholic railroad worker, Arnie Westrum (James Gammon), who is drinking on the job. Its second is a young woman, Stella Randolph (Wendy Walker), who has become pregnant outside of wedlock; she is attacked and savagely killed on the night she intends to commit suicide after the father of her baby has rejected her at a community event. At that same event, the town's religious figurehead, Reverend Lester Lowe (Everett McGill), addresses the township and tells them that Tarker's Mills 'seems to me to be the very definition of community'. But while their families, friends and neighbours might seem superficially friendly and understanding, the prevalence of strict Christian values in their society means that the most vulnerable individuals in the community feel unable to share their afflictions or misfortunes for fear of prejudice, shame and religious judgement; Stella would rather end her own life than admit to engaging in pre-marital sex. The first signs of a killer in Tarker's Mills only make matters worse, and reveal the barely concealed cracks in the town's community spirit.

In his book on cinematic adaptations of King's work, Mark Browning identifies *Silver Bullet*'s second social dimension; he points out that as soon as the townspeople suspect a murderer is at work, they descend into pack mentality as gun store owner Andy Fairton (Bill Smitrovich) attempts to form a posse to hunt the killer. As Browning asserts, the town's Sheriff, Joe Haller (Terry O'Quinn),

> imposes a curfew but seems powerless to do much to catch the monster and unwilling to call for outside help. He loses the battle to prevent mob rule, signified by a stream of cars, guns and dogs out into the woods.[17]

As the vigilantes spread out into the trees, they are quickly and easily dispatched by the werewolf. In a scene atmospheric and amusing, many of their number are dragged down into dense fog and torn to shreds. Browning goes on to express some confusion over the depiction of the mob and their demise, suggesting that they are 'figures of slapstick comedy rather than horror' because of their swift and unceremonious deaths.[18]

This is an unfair criticism. Here – in contrast to *Night of the Living Dead* (1968), for example – the vigilantes are not designed to elicit a horrified response and their satirical depiction does not change their metaphorical meaning. At the first sign of trouble, the town splits into two opposing camps: those who wish to form a community militia and those who wish to place their trust in the police. Both groups fail to stop the monster and ultimately – in a similar fashion to the earlier countercultural werewolf films *Werewolves on Wheels* (1971) and *The Boy Who Cried Werewolf* (1973) – *Silver Bullet* is less concerned with which group will triumph than it is with the fragile nature of community bonds.

Ultimately, only Marty can put an end to the werewolf's rampage, which corresponds to another of King's key themes: that children and adolescents possess an innocence that allows them to stand apart from mainstream society and must rebel against the conformity inherent in adulthood. As Tom Newhouse suggests, 'King's novels and stories that depict teenage life are profoundly critical of the parental expectations, conservative values, and peer pressures that teenagers must face.'[19] Marty commits himself to unmasking and destroying the werewolf, while the wider community collapses.

This theme is encapsulated by two visual metaphors. The first is a wooden baseball bat that appears several times throughout the film's narrative. At first it is used by the town's barkeeper to keep patrons under control; then it falls into the hands of the werewolf, who uses it to kill one of the vigilantes in the woods; later it is found broken and discarded, a vital clue that reveals the werewolf's identity; and finally, the werewolf uses it to murder Sheriff Haller. A recurring visual motif, it even appears on one of the film's posters, which features a werewolf's hand gripping the bat in front of a terrified Marty (Figure 6.1). Its metaphorical meaning is revealed through an ironic inscription carved into the wood: 'Peacemaker'. That a word associated with calm resolution to conflict is etched onto a weapon used in acts of aggression by the townspeople and the werewolf alike reveals the contradiction at the heart of insular communities like Tarker's Mills. Even in such a seemingly quiet, peaceful and close-knit town, barbarity lies beneath the surface just waiting to emerge: families, friends and neighbours will tear each other apart in times of adversity.

This theme is rendered explicit by the second visual metaphor, which is contained within a dream sequence. Shortly after the vigilantes enter the woods, Reverend Lowe dreams that he is presiding over a mass funeral for victims of the Tarker's Mills werewolf. The dream begins as Lowe stands in front of his congregation, who are swaying from side to side in a dizzying fashion and singing a solemn rendition of 'Amazing Grace' as their friends and family lie dead in front of them. Individual members of the congregation – many being those directly affected by the werewolf's murders – are framed staring intensely at Lowe as they sing. As he begins to deliver his anxious sermon, the townspeople in front of him – including those enclosed in their coffins – begin to transform into werewolves (Figure 6.2). They bite and tear at each other as the church windows smash and the building begins to fall apart. This scene summarises the film's major theme of the fragility and falsity of religious

Figure 6.1 A poster for *Silver Bullet* (1985), depicting the baseball bat that functions as a recurring metaphor throughout the film. © Paramount Pictures.

Figure 6.2 During a dream sequence in *Silver Bullet* (1985), the citizens of Tarker's Mills transform into werewolves during a funeral in an indictment of conservative values.

values and the conservative community. In one moment the townspeople seem to be united in faith and mourning; in the next they literally eat each other. The use of 'Amazing Grace' as a musical accompaniment to the scene only strengthens the metaphor: a Christian hymn often associated with the underpinning values of the United States, it promises sinners redemption and forgiveness in the eyes of God. Here, it becomes the soundtrack to a horrific display of brutality and cannibalism. As he awakes from his nightmare, Lowe prays: 'Let it end, dear God, let it end.'

His words do not just refer to the splintering of his congregation, but to his curse: Reverend Lowe is the Tarker's Mills werewolf. In this, *Silver Bullet* reserves its greatest ire for a single pillar of traditional community: the Church. There are very few academic works that discuss *Silver Bullet* in any detail, but it seems strange that those which do fail to devote any particular attention to the film's anti-religious themes. The fact that *Silver Bullet* casts a Reverend as a werewolf is interesting in itself. *Wolfman* (1979) features a satanic priest who curses the male members of an American family to werewolfism, but *Silver Bullet* is the only film in the history of werewolf cinema to feature a cursed clergyman. And, in contrast to *Wolfman*'s devil-worshipper, Lowe is a genuine man of faith and a staunch believer in God. In fact, towards the film's climax, Lowe implies that his attacks on members of the community have a religious motive. He refers to his victims' apparent sins in order to rationalise his actions: his first victim was an alcoholic; he implies that his third, Milt Sturmfuller (James A. Baffico), was abusive towards his family; he even suggests that Stella's murder was motivated by a desire to kill her before she could take her own life, effectively saving her from the torment of Hell. Browning aligns this element of

Silver Bullet's plot with the thematic concerns of the 'slasher' sub-genre, writing:

> an underlying conservative morality has been linked to slasher narratives, [and] the pattern of the nature of the victims [in *Silver Bullet*] also reinforces the sense of anti-establishment behaviour as the target, i.e. a sententious moral for a teen audience. We have a drunk; a girl, pregnant out of wedlock, attempting suicide; and an abusive, drunk father, showing a lack of respect to the disabled ('Damn cripples always end up on welfare,' he mumbles to himself). Emblematically, in an action that is pure Disney, victim number four, Marty's friend Brady, had pushed a practical joke too far and, in waving a snake at Jane, made her fall back into a puddle.[20]

This is certainly a conservative interpretation of *Silver Bullet*. However, given his thematic preoccupations it seems unlikely that King would have intended such a reading, and in truth it hardly seems correct to align *Silver Bullet* with conservative interpretations of slasher narratives when the film carries such a clear anti-establishment message. Nor does it make sense to compare this werewolf's victims with those of slasher killers; with the exception of the obnoxious Sturmfuller and the posse who die in the woods, all of those slain by Lowe are characterised in such a way that their deaths are clearly designed to elicit sympathy rather than catharsis. The railroad worker, Arnie, is nothing but a harmless drunkard. In his brief screen time he is only seen cheerfully singing to himself before he meets his terrible end. Furthermore, if *Silver Bullet* endorsed his death as punishment for alcoholism it would contradict itself in casting Red, a heavy drinker, as its secondary hero. It is nigh impossible not to feel sympathy for Stella, a woman so oppressed by patriarchal values that she would rather commit suicide than declare her pregnancy. Furthermore, Brady Kincaid (Joe Wright) is only a child. Admittedly, he enjoys tormenting Marty's sister, but it is difficult to read his death as just punishment for such childish antics. *Silver Bullet* does not condemn the werewolf's victims for their questionable choices; it demonises Lowe, the dogmatic religious zealot who tries to suggest his actions are justified by Christian doctrine.

Unlike *Wolfman*'s satanic priest, though, Lowe is not depicted as an inherently evil man, nor is he suggested to be entirely in thrall to the wolf. His actions throughout the film, then, are all the more deplorable for his religious rationalisations. When Marty discovers Lowe's secret, he begins to mail letters to the Reverend suggesting he end his own life. Desperate to conceal his werewolfism, Lowe decides to kill Marty instead. In a harrowing and suspenseful chase sequence, the Reverend attempts to run Marty, riding on the Silver Bullet, off the road with his car in an act of premeditated attempted murder. Hardly adhering to Christian morality, Lowe is willing to murder a child even in full possession of his human faculties.

While he might attempt to justify his earlier murders as God's work, Reverend Lowe's attempt on Marty's life reveals that in truth he is only trying to preserve his reputation and hide his true nature. In this, the film critiques Reagan's religious rhetoric by suggesting that insidious self-interest motivates religious figureheads, so often the leaders of American communities; after all, Lowe's instinct for self-preservation supersedes his Christian morality. At the climax, Lowe attacks Marty, Jane and Red in werewolf form on the night of a full moon and is shot with a silver bullet. In the film's final moments, he reverts to his human form. But Lowe is not quite dead; he lurches forward one more time, striking terror into his killers before slumping back, finally deceased. Browning dismisses this final jolt as a needless shock ending, a 'strangely unwittingly ridiculous element'.[21] On the contrary, that Lowe provides the film's final scare in his human form is confirmation that the Reverend is not just driven by the beast but by his own human selfishness.

Silver Bullet, then, reveals the insidious intent behind Reagan's endorsement of traditional values by attacking the principles of family, community and conservative Christianity. Its particularly scathing attacks on the narcissism of religious belief in the 1980s were not unfounded; after all, Reagan exaggerated his commitment to the Church to secure the support of Christian voters. Furthermore, the Reagan years saw the explosion of televangelism and the transformation of fundamentalist and evangelical Christianity into a lucrative industry. The Religious Right had been vocal supporters of Reagan's presidential campaign and, as Schaller recounts,

> The influence of politically active fundamentalist and evangelical Christians continued well into the Reagan administration. By 1985, the combined take of several hundred electronic ministries totalled well over $1 billion annually . . . [They] promised a place in heaven via generous donations while here on earth.[22]

Silver Bullet's Reverend Lowe, a small-town minister with a vicious wolf hiding beneath his humble veneer, is a metaphor for the transformation of religion into a business; he serves himself before any god, but is always willing to find a religious justification for his self-interest.

Howling IV: The Original Nightmare (1988) is a much less subtle example of community horror under Reagan. A loose remake of *The Howling* (1981) and a much closer adaptation of Gary Brandner's source novel, the film sees Marie Adams (Romy Windsor) and her husband Richard (Michael T. Weiss) retreat to Drago, a small rural town, when Marie begins to experience hallucinations – later proved to be psychic visions of the past and future – involving a mysterious nun and monstrous wolf-like creatures. This is a town frozen in time, unchanged for decades; the buildings, cars and fixtures all make Drago seem like a community unchanged since the 1950s. When she first arrives, Marie comments: 'It's really strange, it's like time stood still.' This theme even carries over into the town's residents; this is a white, Christian community where, according to the local shopkeepers, 'People keep to themselves.' On the surface, it is the quintessential picture of conservative community that Reagan evoked again and again throughout the 1980s.

The film's third act then comes to resemble *Silver Bullet*. Marie finds out that the nun in her visions, Sister Ruth (Megan Kruskal), was murdered for discovering the town's secret: every single resident of Drago is a werewolf, including its sheriff, its trusted physician and even its friendly shopkeepers. So while *Silver Bullet* places a murderous werewolf in small-town America, *Howling IV* imagines an entire rural community as a haven for monsters. The final scene sees Marie lure Drago's fully transformed residents into a disused church on the edge of town and burn them alive: an exceptionally on-the-nose metaphor for destroying damaging moral conservatism inside a building that serves as the most recognisable symbol of its power.

Howling IV's narrative is reversed in *Howling VI: The Freaks* (1991), which sees a single sympathetic werewolf shunned by a Christian community. Set in Canton Bluff – a small town surrounded by arid terrain and another seemingly unaltered since the 1950s – the film follows Ian Richards (Brendan Hughes), a drifter and werewolf seeking shelter and acceptance. In another indictment of the Church, the town's priest is the first to offer him a job, food and shelter, but he is also the first to turn on him when his werewolfery is revealed. His secret out, Ian is kidnapped by Harker (Bruce Martyn Payne), a vampire and the proprietor of a travelling carnival, who forces his newest acquisition to perform in a sideshow alongside other so-called 'freaks': men and women ostracised for their differences. Here, then, the werewolf is representative of groups marginalised by conservative values. With Harker destroyed at the film's climax, Ian refuses to stay in Canton Bluff and chooses to wander into the desert.

She-Wolves of Suburbia

Reagan departed the White House in January 1989, but the effects of his administration's values and policies lingered on. Released in May 1989 – only a few short months after Reagan had been succeeded by his vice-president,

George H. W. Bush – the outrageously satirical horror-comedy *My Mom's a Werewolf* would attack another facet of conservative social rhetoric: the active promotion of traditional gender roles. As Chris Jordan suggests, members of American society in the age of the New Right were expected to be:

> a responsible husband and father or wife and mother, according to a success philosophy that distinguished between the male sphere of public competition and private female sphere of domestic and affective ties. The nuclear family, ordered on the basis of biologically circumscribed gender roles, became a site for the reproduction of values that enabled a middle class of self-governing individuals to reproduce itself from one generation to the next.[23]

My Mom's a Werewolf attacks these values with gusto. The film concentrates on Leslie Shaber (Susan Blakely), a middle-aged housewife and mother who lives with her daughter, Jennifer (Tina Caspary), and working husband, Howard (John Shuck). Ignored by her husband and trapped in her lavish suburban home, Leslie has become bored with her marriage and her mundane middle-class existence. She entertains the idea of an affair with an alluring pet shop owner, imaginatively named Harry Thropen (John Saxon), a man in possession of piercing yellow eyes and unnaturally sharp incisors. He is, of course, a werewolf. When Thropen bites Leslie on the toe during sexual foreplay, she begins to undergo drastic physical and psychological changes; for the rest of the film she experiences a slow transformation before turning into a she-wolf at the climax.

If not for its clever satire, *My Mom's a Werewolf* could be read as a conservative morality play in which an unfaithful wife is punished for daring to stray from her husband. However, its comical and surreal atmosphere – typified by outlandish dialogue (Thropen asks Leslie to be his 'were-wife', she asks if they will live in a 'were-house'), a misplaced pop soundtrack, garish set and costume design and even its title – belie the film's satire and intent to lampoon the lasting effects of Reagan's social and economic vision for America. For example, Leslie visits her doctor when she notices her teeth growing into sharp points; in a bizarre scene in his examination room, Leslie's doctor is draped in all manner of gold jewellery – even wearing comically large, ornate rings over his surgical gloves – suggesting the profiteering inherent in private healthcare at a time when public health was under threat. Similarly, the film contains many scenes involving a caricatured fortune teller (Ruth Buzzi), who seems to have some supernatural ability – she vaguely suggests that Jennifer will 'come into conflict with an animal' – but who is more interested in the relentless pursuit of profit than anything else.

After the surreal visit to her doctor, Leslie hopes that a beautician will be able to tame her hair, which is growing wild and unkempt as her transformation quickens. Much to Leslie's visible horror, her hairdresser replaces her cropped blonde bob with a longer conservative hairstyle much more befitting of a suburban housewife and far more terrifying to Leslie than her budding werewolfism. Most damning of all, perhaps, is the presence of a teenager wearing what appears to be a crude Ronald Reagan mask at Jennifer's Halloween party, suggesting that the one-time President of the United States belongs amongst monsters. These comical and subversive minor details clarify that the film's true focus, Leslie's transformation into a she-wolf, is to be taken as a satire of the staunchly restrictive behaviour, moral values and aesthetic appearance demanded of women by a patriarchal society.

Echoing Jordan's thoughts on gender politics in the 1980s, Schaller suggests that Reagan 'urged pre-marital chastity and championed the "traditional" family of husband as breadwinner, wife as mother and homemaker'.[24] Leslie, Howard and Jennifer Shaber begin, then, as Reagan's archetypal nuclear family: Howard works hard while Leslie stays at home, caring for their teenage daughter and pet dog. But like *Silver Bullet*, *My Mom's a Werewolf* rails against the concept of the nuclear family, and Leslie is clearly not enamoured with her life. She abhors the loneliness of a housewife's existence and is frustrated when her husband comes home from work only immediately to fall asleep in an armchair, or suggests that she should bring him beer while he watches sports. It is her boredom and restlessness with her sexless, one-sided marriage that leads her to succumb to Thorpen's advances. *My Mom's a Werewolf* plays out Reagan's ideal domestic setting only to highlight its failings and illustrate how unfulfilling such a traditional lifestyle can be. Leslie's marriage oppresses her desires and ambitions, reducing her to nothing other than a homemaker. In a comical parody of conservative attitudes, her first and only flirtation with escape is punished by her transformation into a monster.

Not that the effects of Leslie's werewolfery are entirely negative. The first sign of her transformation is an increased sex drive and sudden attraction to her husband: a satirical suggestion that their marriage had previously been characteristic not just of societal oppression but sexual repression. However, her transformation largely takes the form of physical changes. In a link to the decade's preoccupation with body-horror, Leslie finds that werewolfism begins to impede her ability to adhere to societal expectations of a woman's aesthetic appearance.

As her transformation takes hold, Leslie slowly begins to take on a subtly bestial visage before her full transformation occurs: she grows fangs, loses the ability to control her hairstyle and begins to sprout body hair that, in one of the film's central comedic set pieces, she attempts to shave only for it to grow back moments later. The image of a hand attempting to shave a slender, furry leg with a bathroom razor would become the defining image of the film's marketing campaign, combined with a tagline reading: 'Jennifer's mother is having an identity crisis.' To parody 1980s fixations on traditional family values and body image, *My Mom's a Werewolf* comically punishes a marital transgression with the embarrassing annoyances of imperfect teeth and untameable leg hair. And, of course, her hirsute appearance is in itself a transgression; as Jazmina Cininas suggests, 'the hairy female body has . . . been viewed as a manifestation of animalistic lust since at least the Renaissance'.[25]

Howard is so characteristically oblivious to these changes that he does not even notice anything different about his wife, aside, of course, from her increased sex drive. Tellingly, it is Leslie's daughter who is most committed to ridding her mother of the werewolf's curse. With the help of her horror-obsessed friend Stacey (Diana Barrows), Jennifer discovers her mother's relationship with Thropen and is disgusted with her behaviour. She is even more horrified to discover that her mother is a werewolf after witnessing the physical changes Leslie is going through. Unlike *Silver Bullet*, however, here the film's minors are not fighting against a conservative force, but for it: in helping to lift Leslie's curse – by killing Thropen with a silver meat fork tied to a wooden broom handle, a preposterous weapon with thoroughly domestic connotations – Jennifer forces her mother to return to her middle-class suburban existence, thus ensuring that the nuclear family will be restored and its values will be passed down to the next generation.

In this, *My Mom's a Werewolf* laments the unwavering grip of patriarchy on familial relationships. Jennifer is utterly committed to the idea that her mother must remain faithful to her father and that curing her of her werewolfery is the only way to preserve their family unit and ensure a swift transition back to their previous life. However, the film takes some time to reflect ironically on the fact that Jennifer must save Leslie's life because Howard is comically inept and incapable of doing so himself; he fails to break down the door to the bedroom where Leslie is being attacked by Thropen, and then leaves in abject terror after seeing the two werewolves locked in battle. By casting Leslie's daughter as the cure for her subversive werewolfism, the film also alludes to the cyclical nature of female subservience; in her choice of weapon, it implies that Jennifer will live a life identical to Leslie's. However, the film subverts this notion in its final moments. Following the Shabers' reconciliation, Stacey discovers evidence – in an issue of horror magazine *Fangoria* – that unless an exorcism is performed on a deceased werewolf, its killer will themselves transform. It seems that, like her mother, Jennifer is soon to test the boundaries of patriarchal society.

Mom also features a mother who becomes an animalistic monster; unlike the satirical *My Mom's a Werewolf*, however, it strikes a sombre tone. Furthermore, *Mom* does not specifically focus on the familial ills of Reagan's legacy but on economic horror. The film sees an elderly resident of suburban Los Angeles, Emily Dwyer (Jeanne Bates), take in a mysterious lodger named Nestor (Brion James). In a similar narrative progression to *My Mom's a Werewolf*, Nestor bites Emily when she attempts to feed him a home-cooked meal and thus begins her transformation. It is worth noting here that the nature of *Mom*'s monsters is ambiguous; Nestor refers to himself as a 'flesh-eater' and muses that vampires, werewolves and ghouls are 'all the same'. However, the opening scene – in which Nestor murders a young pregnant woman under the stars – is accompanied by the sounds of lupine howling, while Nestor's visage in his monstrous form resembles *The Howling*'s partially transformed Eddie Quist. This is a werewolf film despite a lack of concrete exposition for its monsters, and one with a powerful subtext drawn from grisly images of an elderly middle-class woman literally feeding on those less fortunate than herself.

For Nestor soon teaches Emily that as a flesh-eater she must prey on humans, and the homeless serve as their easiest targets. On their first hunt, Nestor takes Emily away from the safety and comfort of the suburbs and into the city. The film takes some time to establish the differences between its urban and suburban settings. Emily's home is surrounded by large detached houses, picket fences and lush greenery, while the city streets are grey, cold and dark, scrawled with graffiti and home to those left broken by the capitalist system. One of the film's most shocking moments arises when Emily reveals her conservative attitudes to social justice. She is horrified to hear from her son, Clay (Mark Thomas Miller), that in her animal form she may have injured a police officer. When Clay asks her in dismay if she thinks it is acceptable in comparison to hunt, kill and eat a homeless person, she replies, almost as if asking for confirmation: 'It's better?' Her reply reveals a capitalist reasoning to her choice of victims beyond their base vulnerability: that a person's material wealth determines their human worth. It is later revealed that she has attacked any number of homeless people, their partially eaten corpses now buried in her meticulously tended garden. In *Mom*, the only hope the poor have for social mobility is to be buried in a middle-class back yard.

Despite his dismay at his mother's actions, Clay eventually comes around to Nestor's way of thinking. Having discovered his mother's yearning for human flesh, he locks her in her bedroom. Distressed and hungry,

Emily pleads with her son to let her out to hunt, or at least to bring her something to eat. When Clay finally relents, he adopts the same attitude to choosing a victim as both Nestor and Emily, revealing that he, too, is influenced by his privileged social status. Clay travels into the city – as if to suggest that the suburbs could not possibly offer a person worthless enough to be eaten alive – and enters a seedy bar. There, he approaches a sex worker (Stella Stevens) and takes her back to the suburbs, where he attempts to trick her into entering Emily's bedroom. He has a last-minute change of heart, but he is too late to stop his mother from consuming her.

Mom, then, demonises both Emily and her son for believing that the poor are the most suitable members of society to be reduced to meat. At the film's climax, Emily commits suicide by setting herself on fire, an action that is as cathartic as it is tragic: the guilt she feels for literally feeding off society's victims has finally consumed her. Conversely, the earlier *Howling V: The Rebirth* (1989) sees a werewolf literally 'eat the rich'. Its plot sees a group of wealthy and prosperous yuppie caricatures – including an actor, a tennis player, a writer, a photographer and a retired rock star – invited to a Hungarian castle by a mysterious Count Istvan (Philip Davis). There, they discover that they are all descended from a family of fifteenth-century werewolves who once occupied the castle, but only one of them is cursed. With most of the cohort murdered, the quiet Marylou Summers (Elizabeth Shé) – a waitress and the only member of the group without considerable wealth – is revealed as the werewolf.

Growing Pains

In 1981, the emergence of body-horror rendered werewolves physically monstrous in a way their earlier counterparts could not match. Meanwhile, from the mid-1980s to the early 1990s, a distinct cycle of werewolf films is preoccupied with the ills of the Reagan administration and its social legacy. A third and final cycle of werewolf films would arise during the 1980s: 'teen wolf' films, typified by *Teen Wolf* (1985) and its sequel *Teen Wolf Too* (1987). Like *My Mom's a Werewolf*, these two films are a product of America's shifting gender politics under Reagan, combining a less overtly repulsive form of body-horror with cleverly crafted satire that critiques the return of traditional gender roles in the 1980s.

Teen Wolf and *Teen Wolf Too* concern male adolescent werewolves – respectively cousins Scott and Todd Howard (Michael J. Fox and Jason Bateman) – who discover they have inherited familial werewolfism. They are able to transform into 'The Wolf', a flamboyant and extroverted werewolf alter ego. Ostensibly, their ability to transform into wolf-men seems like a blessing, amplifying their masculine traits: in werewolf form, they enjoy increased sporting prowess, greater physical strength, a sudden popularity with their male peers and an apparent sexual magnetism. But both Scott and Todd come to realise that their werewolfery is really a curse, one that allows them to conform to an aggressive male stereotype but ultimately serves to alienate those they care about most.

Teen Wolf and its sequel are indebted for inspiration to *I Was a Teenage Werewolf* (1957), the first werewolf film to turn a high-school student into a monster. But *Teen Wolf* was not the first werewolf movie of the 1980s to pay homage to AIP's picture. *Full Moon High* (1981) is responsible for reviving the teenage werewolf four years earlier, and would even provide one of the principal narrative elements of *Teen Wolf* and *Teen Wolf Too*: the idea of an adolescent werewolf as a high-school sports star. In *Full Moon High*, Tony Walker (Adam Arkin) – named for *I Was a Teenage Werewolf*'s Tony Rivers – is a promising American football player before his transformation. Werewolfism renders him ageless, and he attempts to re-join his high-school team decades later. *Teen Wolf* and *Teen Wolf Too* see Scott and Todd Howard use their werewolfery to enhance their abilities as a basketball player and boxer respectively.

However, the similarities between the three films do not stretch much further than the borrowing of minor narrative elements. While *Teen Wolf* and its sequel are teen comedies with elements of fantasy and horror, *Full Moon High* is more of a broad parody in the Mel Brooks tradition. Less interested in constructing a cohesive narrative, it takes the form of a series of comedic vignettes designed to satirise the generic tropes of the werewolf film. This is not to say that because it is a parody it does not have any social relevance. *Full Moon High* was written, directed and produced by Larry Cohen, a filmmaker often associated with radical views; Tony Williams suggests that these themes only intensify in the director's 1980s works, during the considerable surge in social conservatism that accompanied Reagan's election campaign and his years in office.[26]

In fact, *Full Moon High* is thematically very similar to the community horror cycle. *I Was a Teenage Werewolf* could be read as either a liberal or a conservative reaction to the juvenile delinquency moral panic of the 1950s, but regardless of the film's political leanings it undoubtedly arose from an era of dominant conservatism. As Joseph Maddrey suggests, *Full Moon High* 'transplants the 1950s monster onto the similarly conservative 1980s'.[27] Here, however, there is no question as to the film's politics: in common with much of Cohen's work, *Full Moon High* is a thoroughly countercultural text.

The film begins in 1960, when high-school football star Tony is living with his CIA agent father, Colonel William Walker (Ed McMahon).

Tony's father is an outrageous caricature of a 1950s conservative, one whose home is fitted with a nuclear fallout shelter complete with a hanging portrait of Joseph McCarthy. Colonel Walker takes his son with him on a diplomatic mission to Romania, where Tony is bitten by a werewolf. Upon his return home, Tony serves as a minor nuisance to the community as his transformations begin. His werewolf activities are limited to menacing townspeople with minor bites. But his behaviour causes greatest concern to his father, who sees Tony's animalistic traits as insubordination ('I will not tolerate growling in this house!'). As Williams suggests, Tony's werewolfism is a comic metaphor for the rise of counterculture and the sexual revolution of the 1960s, as his 'werewolf infection results in his transgression of civilized and sexual boundaries'.[28]

Then Tony commits his first murder: the teenage werewolf kills his conservative father in an act of countercultural revolt. After an eventful funeral in which Colonel Walker's coffin is eventually crushed by a falling tree branch, Tony decides to remove himself from society and travel the world. A montage marks the passage of time between Tony's departure and his return; images of his travels around the globe are interspersed with shots of presidential portraits being hung and taken down. One half of this montage is designed for no other purpose than comedy. For example, outrageous newspaper headlines from various countries describe Tony's international escapades (e.g. 'Australian Tourist Bitten Down Under'). The other half, however, is politically charged. Tellingly, while the portraits of John F. Kennedy, Lyndon B. Johnson and Jimmy Carter survive unscathed, Richard Nixon's is smashed with a rock while Gerald Ford's is dropped to the floor before it can even be hung.[29] Clearly, *Full Moon High* does not hold Republican presidents in high esteem.

Tony quickly realises that his werewolfery has halted his ageing process and rendered him immortal. He finally chooses to return to his home town in 1980, masquerading as his own son. He has not changed, but his town, once a prospering community, has: homes and businesses are now derelict, while the front steps of Tony's former high school are home to crowds of drifters and homeless people. Meanwhile, Tony's high-school friends Jane (Roz Kelly) and Jack (Bill Kirchenbauer) are now middle-class conservatives, (unhappily) married and living together in a house full of brand new furniture, modern conveniences and garish ornaments.

The subtext here is clear: in the time that Tony has spent separated from his community, the counterculture has come and gone and his father's politics have been revived. While Tony is still young in body and mind, his friends have aged and become passive supporters of oppressive politics. Interestingly, the crowds of displaced, homeless and financially destitute people who sleep on the streets of Tony's crumbling home town are barely mentioned in dialogue, but they are satirically juxtaposed with the materialistic lifestyle of Tony's middle-aged peers. In *Full Moon High*, the rich simply ignore the poor and, in the twenty years since his departure, Tony's friends have turned into his father. In this, *Full Moon High* laments that the political rebellion of the counterculture was so short-lived and reveals the insidious nature of the New Right.

Full Moon High also takes aim at the sexual politics of the 1980s, implying that the sexual revolution died with the counterculture. Although she is now married to Tony's best friend, Jane has been obsessed with Tony since their teenage years and begins pursuing him as soon as he returns, suggesting that her marriage is financially sensible but sexually unfulfilling. However, Tony ultimately finds himself in a relationship with a teacher at Full Moon High, Miss Montgomery (Elizabeth Hartman). Montgomery is introduced as a conservatively dressed, sexually repressed young woman who baulks at any talk of lewd behaviour; she describes having suffered six sexual assaults while in the employ of previous schools. However, at the film's climax she finally transgresses by sleeping with Tony: the final shot shows Tony and Montgomery in a framed photograph with their werewolf children. As Williams asserts, 'Tony re-awakens her repressed sexuality, leading her to break rigid social taboos by sleeping with one of her own students before she becomes a werewolf herself.'[30] The family portrait might suggest that in forming a nuclear family, Tony and Montgomery's transgression has led them to adhere to Reagan's conservative values. But as Williams notes, their children are overtly monstrous; just as in Cohen's *It's Alive* trilogy (1974–87) – in which successive couples give birth to mutant infants – *Full Moon High* hints at 'the ultimate union of humans and monsters'.[31]

Cohen's vision of the teen-wolf film paints its protagonist – a satirical re-imagining of *I Was a Teenage Werewolf*'s juvenile delinquent – as the last remaining relic of the countercultural sixties, an immortal werewolf who will forever be a free-spirited teenager in an increasingly conservative world. The film itself endorses Tony's countercultural spirit; after all, *Full Moon High* was produced in the build-up to the election race between Reagan and Carter. Clearly unsatisfied with either choice, Cohen has Jimmy Carter's portrait replaced with America's first – and, of course, fictional – black female president at the end of the montage that marks the passing of time. In reality, Reagan would be in office by the time the film saw release in October 1981, boosting its political relevance. Ultimately, *Full Moon High* not only parodies the generic conventions of the werewolf film but also the oppressive nature of social and sexual conservatism. It is also an extremely prescient film that presages the concerns of *Silver Bullet*, *My Mom's a Werewolf* and *Mom*.

Teen Wolf uses werewolfism as a metaphor for a related social problem: a dramatic shift in the popular cinematic depiction of masculinity that arose in parallel with Reagan's presidency. The 1980s marked the popular peak of the action film, and the rise of muscle-bound action stars such as Sylvester Stallone, Arnold Schwarzenegger, Jean-Claude Van Damme and Dolph Lundgren. As the respective stars of films such as *First Blood* (1982), *Commando* (1985), *Black Eagle* (1988) and *Red Scorpion* (1988), these were film stars of a different breed: rather than the quality of their performances, their box-office draw lay in their physicality, strength and aggression.

If women in Reagan's America were framed as subordinate homemakers, then men were encouraged to embody traditionally masculine, even overtly aggressive and/or militaristic, roles. As Susan Jeffords notes: 'The depiction of the indefatigable, muscular, and invincible masculine body became the linchpin of the Reagan imaginary . . . these hard bodies came to stand . . . for a type of national character – heroic, aggressive, and determined.'[32] Jeffords argues that this obsession with masculinity in popular culture was a result of the values espoused by Reagan's administration for a re-imagined America – one that pursued conservative values in the domestic sphere and wanted to strengthen its image on the international stage following the embarrassment of the Iranian hostage crisis:

> In contrast to what Reagan's public relations workers characterized as the weakened – some even said 'feminine' – years of the Carter administration, in which the United States government was brought to a standstill by a Third World nation, the Reagan America was to be a strong one, capable of confronting enemies rather than submitting to them, of battling 'evil empires' rather than allowing them to flourish, of using its hardened body – its renewed techno-military network – to impose its will on others rather than allow itself to be dictated to.[33]

The transformation of man into wolf is an apt metaphor for the pitfalls of promoting aggressive masculinity as a societal ideal. Just as *My Mom's a Werewolf* satirises the preferred form of femininity Reagan's administration pressed on America's women through its anti-abortion rhetoric and promotion of traditional family values, *Teen Wolf* and its sequel critique the establishment's view of an ideal masculinity and examine its consequences for impressionable young men. At the opening of *Teen Wolf*, Scott is certainly not representative of the male stereotype promoted by the action films of the era. Rather, he is distinctly average: he plays for his failing high-school basketball team – who lose their first game of the season by some margin in the film's opening scene – and is not overly popular with his peers or the opposite sex.

In *Teen Wolf Too*, Todd is proud that he does not measure his masculinity by his physicality. He arrives at Hamilton University having been offered a mysterious boxing scholarship, but is not at all interested in pursuing the sport. He has a natural aptitude for science, and intends to study to be a veterinarian; it is only later that he realises he was offered a place at the university because Hamilton's sports coach – who, in a minor contrivance, happens to be Scott's former high-school basketball coach, Bobby Finstock (Paul Sand) – suspects that Todd, too, might be a werewolf and wants to exploit his abilities. In both films, it is only when the protagonists choose to embrace their werewolfery that they begin to live up to the politically idealised masculinity promoted by popular cinema in the 1980s.

Catherine Driscoll suggests that the marketing campaigns for *Teen Wolf* 'pushed the idea of puberty as a monstrous transformation'.[34] However, the second acts of both films would seem to suggest that Scott and Todd's transformations ostensibly have a positive effect on their lives. While the initial signs of werewolfism – hair sprouting on his hands, elongated incisors – confuse and baffle Scott, once he comes to embrace his transformations he begins to develop a taste for the seemingly positive attributes that come with being a werewolf. As The Wolf, he is no longer the average teenager: he becomes a wildly popular local celebrity as the star player of his high-school basketball team the Beavers, his academic performance improves and he finds that Pamela Wells (Lorrie Griffin), the girl of his dreams, is suddenly attracted to him.

Todd takes longer to accept his werewolfery; his initial transformation, which takes place while he is dancing with Lisa Goldfluss (Beth Anne Miller) at a formal event for Hamilton alumni, leads to nothing but ridicule from his peers. But their attitudes change when Todd illustrates the strength and agility that comes with being a werewolf; in *Teen Wolf Too*, masculinity is more concretely aligned with sporting success. As soon as Todd transforms during a boxing match and knocks out his opponent, he too finds the respect and adoration of his peers. Todd starts to enjoy his star status when Lisa and her friends begin to pursue his affections and Hamilton's Dean Dunn (John Astin) gives him a sports car as a gift.

However, both Scott and Todd come to realise that their newfound fame and fortune have come as the result of conforming to a shallow, stereotypical conception of masculinity. They have achieved material success, but living their lives as werewolves ultimately does not make them happy. Men are intimidated by them – particularly Scott's team mates, who feel The Wolf is not a team player – while the vacuous women whose attention they have attracted only want to sleep with them due to their celebrity status. While it is heavily implied that Scott and Pamela have sex during a one-night stand, she has no intention of leaving her boyfriend Mick McAllister (Mark Arnold), star player for the Beavers' arch-rivals, the Dragons. Lisa, too, is in a relationship when she begins pursuing Todd. Both protagonists ignore more promising partners in Scott's best friend Boof (Susan Ursitti) and Todd's girlfriend Nicki (Estee Chandler). These are women who are in love with them, rather than The Wolf. Instead, they embrace short-lived, skin-deep relationships with partners who are only attracted to their werewolf alter egos.

Both Scott and Todd also find that werewolfism brings out a selfishness and territorial aggressiveness in their personalities that alienates those closest to them. Much to the dismay of his friends and classmates, Scott transforms and claws Mick during a high-school dance, while Todd is involved in a confrontation with several other men who were previously attached to the girls he has been dating, led by Lisa's boyfriend Gus (Robert Neary). When Gus physically intimidates Todd, the girls go back to their former lovers, illustrating that they are only interested in the strongest, most aggressive suitor: in short, the alpha male. When Todd returns to his dorm room, he finds that his best friends have become so tired of his recent egomania that even they are no longer interested in associating with him. Even Stiles (Stuart Fratkin) – best friend to both Scott and Todd – becomes weary of The Wolf when Todd locks him out of their dorm room so that he can entertain women ('I've created a monster').

In contrast to most of their cinematic contemporaries, when Scott and Todd do transform into werewolves, they take the form of traditional wolf-men rather than the more lupine werewolves associated with body-horror. The intentionally outdated make-up effects used to realise their werewolf alter-egos are designed to allow the actors underneath to move and talk freely as The Wolf. Thematically, though, the two films utilise the old-fashioned wolf-man more common to classic werewolf cinema to produce a less obvious form of body-horror. In their transformed state, Scott and Todd are as simian as they are lupine, giving them the look of early humans (Figure 6.3). No matter the benefits of their ability to transform into wolf-men, in rendering werewolfism as a form of devolution these two films make a connection between The Wolf and a base, uncivilised conception of masculinity based on aggressive behaviour. A satirical link is also formed between werewolfism and Reagan's idealised masculine body, only here the male form devolves into the shaggy visage of a caveman rather than the muscle-bound form of an action hero. In their devolved state, Scott and Todd are only interested in pursuing sex and besting rivals.

Figure 6.3 In a satirical comment on Reaganite masculinity, 'The Wolf' – portrayed here by Michael J. Fox in *Teen Wolf* (1985) – resembles a caveman as much as a wolf-man.

Teen Wolf goes one step further in making light of the hostile, hetero-normative construction of masculinity in Reagan's America by including a scene in which Scott tries to tell Stiles that he is a werewolf. Stiles – himself a would-be womaniser – reveals the pervading 1980s masculine attitude by trying to cut the conversation short just in case Scott is about to come out as gay, using wildly offensive terminology in the process: 'Wait, are you going to tell me you're a fag? If you're going to tell me you're a fag, I don't think I can handle it.' In Reagan's America, masculinity is inseparable from aggressive heterosexuality.

Stiles's conservative attitude to the male societal role is also evident in his rampant capitalist exploitation of both Scott and Todd; in both *Teen Wolf* and *Teen Wolf Too*, he sees their werewolfery as a business opportunity, selling 'Teen Wolf' merchandise at every possible juncture. The *Teen Wolf* films indict the notion of ruthless masculinity embodied by Stiles: the moment when Scott and Todd violently turn against love rivals is the moment when they realise that masculine ruthlessness, physical violence and sexual aggression are not positive attributes. Both teenagers turn to Harold Howard (James Hampton) – father to Scott and uncle to Todd, but parental guardian to both – for help. Also a werewolf, Harold believes he is 'blessed' with werewolfism, but warns against the aggression that can come with it: he implores both Scott and Todd to be wary of their violent urges. Harold's advice suggests that by embracing their lupine character-istics, Scott and Todd are losing their humanity.

Scott and Todd achieve many things traditionally associated with masculine success by embracing The Wolf: money, cars, sex, physical strength and sporting prowess. But they also risk losing their friends and the women who love them. Scott rectifies this by vowing not to live his life in his werewolf guise; he chooses to play the most important basketball game of the season as himself, without the help of The Wolf. Todd refocuses his attention on academia and – like Scott – chooses to fight his big match against Gus without resorting to animal strength.

In this, both films lament the pressure placed on teenagers to conform to grossly irresponsible conceptions of idealised gender roles endorsed by the Reagan administration. As Stefan Dziemianowicz asserts, *Teen Wolf* 'explores the pressures of teenage conformity and its price'.[35] His observation is equally applicable to *Teen Wolf Too*; just before Todd is about to face Gus in the ring, Dean Dunn urges him to fight as The Wolf: 'Fight and win, and I'll take care of the rest: grades, cars, money, women.' Todd is under enormous pressure not only to take on a masculine role but to do it in order to obtain the things that men are supposed to want in return for their efforts; but, as the film has already illustrated by showing how his werewolfism isolates Todd from others, these materialistic rewards are devoid of meaning. Despite pressures to embrace The Wolf, both Scott and Todd resist the urge to use their werewolfery as a crutch.

The Beavers win their basketball game and Scott rejects Pamela for Boof; Todd is losing his boxing match until he sees Nicki mouth 'I love you' from the crowd, granting him a surge of strength that allows him to win by knockout. However, by allowing Scott and Todd to win – essentially measuring their worth by sporting achievements – both *Teen Wolf* and *Teen Wolf Too* undermine their central messages. In a scathing criticism of 'the appalling *Teen Wolf*', Williams notes that it 'bears some derivative resemblances to *Full Moon High*, but departs from it by having its werewolf win the high school championship game'.[36] In *Full Moon High*, Tony's aspirations to re-join his high-school football team just provide another comedic vignette in which the werewolf, out of control, causes so much chaos on the football field that the game is called to a halt. In *Teen Wolf* and *Teen Wolf Too*, the basketball game and boxing match that respectively end the two films provide a misplaced cathartic conclusion.

Despite having learned not to measure their worth by their typical masculine attributes, both Scott and Todd do exactly that. This is particularly true of *Teen Wolf Too*; through boxing, Todd is able to find self-respect by beating Gus inside of the ring rather than out. This final sequence is, in fact, shot in a very similar fashion to the final fights in the original *Rocky* series (1976–90) and is particularly reminiscent of *Rocky IV* (1985), in which Rocky Balboa (Sylvester Stallone) bests his Soviet rival (Dolph Lundgren) in a thinly veiled piece of Cold War propaganda. In this, *Teen Wolf Too* creates an endorsement of aggressive masculinity rather than a critique of it. However, while *Full Moon High* is a fiercely countercultural film, *Teen Wolf* and *Teen Wolf Too* are clearly aimed at more mainstream sensibilities; their confusing and contradictory conclusions are, perhaps, the price paid for commercial viability.

1980s werewolf films, then, are preoccupied with the Reagan years and dwell on a popular obsession with the human body, disease and the relationship between physical and mental well-being; changes in political, social and familial relations caused by a resurgence in popular conservatism; and developments in gender politics as a result of Reagan's promotion of 'ideal' notions of femininity and masculinity. In the 1990s, the werewolf film would become much less prolific than in the 1980s, a golden age for cinematic werewolf narratives boosted by developments in special effects technology and the birth of the new werewolf. However, the werewolf film was far from dead. In fact, 1994's *Wolf* would arise from the very same context that produced *Teen Wolf*, *Teen Wolf Too* and *My Mom's a Werewolf*: the construction of an 'ideal' notion of gender during the Reagan years and a masculine identity crisis created in its aftermath.

CHAPTER 7

Old Dogs and New Tricks

The Alpha Male

By the mid-1990s, audience interest in werewolf films was dwindling. The peak of body-horror had passed and 1995's *Howling: New Moon Rising* would be the last *Howling* film for another sixteen years. The werewolf film needed to evolve. It is no surprise, then, that Hollywood's first werewolf film of the 1990s is a very strange beast in relation to its forebears. In stark contrast to the werewolf films of the 1980s, Columbia's *Wolf* (1994) is not only a prestige picture with a sizeable budget, but has two Oscar winners amongst its cast and crew in star Jack Nicholson and director Mike Nichols. In fact, *Wolf* is just one example of an early-1990s horror cycle designed to retool the genre as a commercially viable subject for high-concept blockbusters. According to Stacey Abbott, *The Silence of the Lambs* (1991) is the cycle's originator: 'It was the success of *The Silence of the Lambs* that specifically renewed Hollywood's interest in the horror genre in the 1990s, with the main studios returning to classic horror tales taken from literature, comics, folklore and film history, but now reinvented through the lens of the high concept movie.'[1]

The Silence of the Lambs would be followed by *Bram Stoker's Dracula* (1992), Columbia's first attempt at turning a classic horror text into a commercial success. Directed by the prestigious Francis Ford Coppola (and starring several celebrated actors, including Gary Oldman and Anthony Hopkins), the film performed well at the box office. As Abbott notes, 'The success of Coppola's film demonstrated the blockbuster potential for classic horror narratives.'[2] The Oscar-winning Robert De Niro was soon cast in *Mary Shelley's Frankenstein* (1994), to be directed by Kenneth Branagh. Columbia also put *Wolf* into production, starring multiple Oscar winner Nicholson and Michelle Pfeiffer – who had been nominated for three Academy Awards before joining the cast – and directed by Nichols, who was (and remains) best known as the director of the critically lauded dramas *Who's Afraid of Virginia Woolf?* (1966) and *The Graduate* (1967).

It is clear that Columbia intended that this would be a prestige picture in its production values, acting and direction. The film also leaves behind the grotesque transformations characteristic of 1980s werewolf films; here, Rick Baker's make-up is exceptionally minimalist – consisting of minor hair growth on the face and body and a stark change in eye colour during transformations – in an attempt to recall the classic wolf-men of the 1930s and 1940s (Figure 7.1). *Wolf*, then, was meticulously designed to be a critical and commercial success: a blockbuster with A-list appeal that consciously attempts to distance itself from the werewolf films of the 1980s. However, neither *Mary Shelley's Frankenstein* nor *Wolf* performed well and both were outshone by the success of Warner Bros' attempt at capitalising on the success of prestige horror: *Interview with the Vampire* (1994).[3] It is notable, however, that while *Wolf* seems to follow the formula established by *Bram Stoker's Dracula* in choice of cast and crew, the film itself is far removed from the gothic trappings of its immediate predecessors, all of which are period pieces.[4] In contrast, *Wolf* employs a contemporary setting, while the larger part of its narrative is concerned with office politics and the ruthless battle for masculine dominance between rivals in love and life. In fact, in its dramatisation of a white male recapturing his masculinity, *Wolf* has more of a thematic connection with *Teen Wolf* (1985) and *Teen Wolf Too* (1987) than it does with the prestige horror cycle. It is also part of a group of early-1990s films concerning the loss of traditional white patriarchy, notably *Falling Down* (1993) and *Groundhog*

Figure 7.1 The special make-up effects worn by Jack Nicholson in *Wolf* (1994) were designed by Rick Baker to recall the classic wolf-men of the 1930s and 1940s.

Day (1993).[5] While the posters for the film communicated that *Wolf* would be a love story by emphasising the relationship between Nicholson and Pfeiffer, the tagline communicated its real thematic preoccupation: 'The Animal Is Out.'

Wolf begins under a full moon as ageing professional Will Randall (Nicholson) is travelling home to New York City from Vermont. Blinded by a heavy snowstorm, Randall hits a wolf with his car and is bitten by the creature as he tries to move it to the roadside. Upon arriving in New York, Randall meets with his employer, Raymond Alden (Christopher Plummer). There, he discovers that he is soon to lose his job as editor-in-chief of a reputable publishing house to his ruthlessly ambitious protégé, Stewart Swinton (James Spader). Over the next month, Randall develops acute senses of sight, smell and hearing as well as peak physical and mental fitness. He also experiences periodic transformations into a feral wolf-man, though he does not remember them. Putting his highly attuned senses to use, Randall discovers that his wife, Charlotte (Kate Nelligan), has been having an affair with Swinton. His marriage over, Randall begins a new relationship with Alden's daughter, Laura (Pfeiffer), and embraces his newly merciless nature to win back his job and rebuild his life. But werewolfism comes at a cost: by the climax Randall is embroiled in an investigation into the murder of his estranged wife and facing the possibility of permanently transforming into a wolf at the next full moon.

What sets *Wolf* apart from the vast majority of the werewolf films that came both before and after it – with the notable exceptions of *Teen Wolf* and its sequel – is that at first it appears to depict werewolfery as a blessing rather than a curse. Randall is not condemned for his actions in werewolf form and for the greater part of the narrative we are led to sympathise with him: Randall is a man in crisis, and one who is facing the prospect of losing both his job and his marriage. His 'curse' brings about a new assertiveness in his personality that allows him to reclaim his career, leave his unfaithful wife and begin a new relationship. As Philip Kemp suggests, in *Wolf* 'the werewolf – animal id rampant – is clearly in touch with healthy natural instincts repressed beneath our over-civilised veneers'.[6] Despite Kemp's reference to the tradition that links the werewolf to psychoanalysis, his point stands: initially it is difficult to dismiss a sense that we are being asked to applaud Randall for railing against a society in which masculine traits carry negative connotations. This element of the film is inextricably linked to changing depictions of masculinity. As discussed in Chapter 6, the Reagan administration had endorsed staunchly traditional gender ideals. As a result, a socio-cultural movement developed in the late 1980s to combat media endorsements of aggressive masculinity, which became increasingly prominent in the early 1990s. As Susan Jeffords recounts:

> During the 1980s, a 'men's movement' was formed, modeled on the second wave of the women's movement in the United States and directed towards reassessing traditional roles and expectations for men's behavior in U.S. society. From this movement sprang discussion groups, therapeutic strategies, men's studies courses, conferences, music, artworks, newsletters, and magazines that took as their subject the question of men's changing roles in U.S. society.[7]

Jeffords asserts that because this movement began to highlight issues of gender construction, feminism and civil rights, Hollywood slowly ceased to portray men as highly masculine, aggressive, muscle-bound action heroes and instead began to communicate a sense that 'the hard-bodied male action heroes of the eighties have given way to a "kinder, gentler" U.S. manhood, one that is sensitive, generous, caring, and, perhaps most importantly, capable of change.'[8] Jeffords then points to a number of films released in the year 1991 that evidence this change by playing out transformation narratives in which male characters reassess their behaviour and values. It is of note that one of her examples, *Regarding Henry* (1991), was also directed by Mike Nichols.

Wolf is exceptionally interesting in this context because, of course, Randall does go through a transformation – but his is in the opposite direction. During the film's first act Randall is the embodiment of Hollywood's 'new man': a hard-working and caring husband, albeit one whose life is falling apart. In *Wolf*'s transformation narrative, the protagonist begins as a sensitive male and metamorphoses into the picture of animalistic hyper-masculinity. As Kemp points out in comparing *Wolf* with *Regarding Henry*, 'the two films are mirror images: Henry is a ruthless hot shot until an accident turns him gentle and caring, Will takes the opposite journey'.[9] Clearly, *Wolf* is connected to developments in gender politics and the changes in Hollywood's depiction of masculinity that resulted from them. But what, exactly, does *Wolf* have to say about Hollywood's new man? This is a complicated question to address as *Wolf* ultimately produces two opposing subtexts.

There were films released in the early 1990s which clearly railed against Hollywood's new interpretation of American masculinity. *Falling Down* is perhaps the quintessential cinematic depiction of a white male lashing out against a world in which traditional white patriarchy has been lost, and initially it is tempting to conclude that Will Randall is a brother-in-arms to *Falling Down*'s Bill Foster (Michael Douglas). Also known as D-FENS to the LAPD – a name taken from his vehicle registration plate – Foster has lost his family, his job and his sanity before he goes on a violent rampage

across Los Angeles. He eventually commits 'suicide by cop', preferring to
die than live in the modern world. For Denis Duclos, *Falling Down* is not
only a film about emasculation, but one of many cinematic revenge fantasies in which white males, or 'Mad Warriors', take revenge against those
who are perceived to be destroying traditional American society. He states:

> Never openly racist or sexist, *Falling Down* is an ambiguous response to the demands
> of political correctness. The film examines several aspects of the American social
> crisis and carries a message of anger against outsiders, deviants and the wealthy.
> Without actually saying so, it unmistakably suggests that, if nothing is done to stop
> the situation, it will degenerate . . . this film has the potential to become a fetish for
> any person in the United States and many other industrialized countries who thinks
> that the time has come to lead a white revolt against the mounting tide of these
> 'dregs of society'.[10]

Duclos's argument is somewhat overstated, but he is right to point out
Falling Down's reactionary themes. While Will does not resort to violence in the same visceral fashion as D-FENS, in some ways *Wolf* could
be considered to promote similar attitudes by playing out a narrative
in which Randall is able to have his metaphorical revenge against those
who have sought to hurt him physically, emotionally and financially by
embracing the feral instincts of the werewolf. He (literally) sniffs out his
unfaithful wife's affair and ends their marriage, taking particular joy in
turning her away when she attempts reconciliation; he does his utmost
to destroy the life and career of his backstabbing protégé and ultimately
succeeds; and even takes subtle revenge against his fickle and greedy
employer, Raymond Alden.

J. W. Whitehead argues that Alden's joy in life comes from his wealth
and materialism, stating 'He possesses people, too – his daughter Laura
(Michelle Pfeiffer) is among his key possessions, and he keeps her with
more ardor and less success than his stock acquisitions.'[11] Many of the
film's key scenes take place at Alden's gothic mansion, where Randall
never seems comfortable amongst the rich and ambitious – and Will's
contempt for his boss is the result of being treated like another negligible
asset, pushed aside to make way for the young and ruthless. But it is only
when he begins to embrace the instincts of the wolf that Randall has his
revenge. He is not able to diminish Alden's wealth or power, but he is able
to lure away his daughter, delighting in her father's dismayed disapproval.
As Whitehead asserts, by the end of the narrative Laura has broken free
of Alden only to have fallen under Randall's spell: 'Will has a kind of pos-
sessive power over Laura that comes, ironically, from truly loving rather
than possessing her.'[12]

A reading of Randall as Mad Warrior is particularly supported by a racially charged scene which sees Randall stalking in werewolf form through Central Park, where he encounters a trio of black and Hispanic characters (Jose Soto, Van Bailey and Dwayne McClary, each credited individually as 'Gang Member'). In a scene strikingly similar to an incident depicted in *Falling Down*, the gang attempt to intimidate Randall, asking him repeatedly for money. When one of the gang draws a gun, Randall savagely attacks in a moment symbolic of the white male retaking control.

The following day Will re-negotiates his contract with Alden on the condition that his wife's new lover is fired. Following the meeting, Randall encounters Swinton standing at a urinal and delights in delivering the news of his unemployment before urinating on his feet ('I'm just marking my territory'). As Randall washes his hands, he discovers two severed fingers in his jacket pocket. Clearly, he maimed and perhaps killed his would-be muggers. In just twenty-four hours, he has managed to prevent himself from becoming a victim of gang violence – here problematically associated with ethnic minorities – and assert his final dominance over a rival by embracing his lupine instincts for masculine aggression.

These points taken into account, it must be noted that the film does not necessarily endorse Randall's actions, nor does werewolfism ultimately bring him happiness. While the association formed between criminal activity and ethnic minorities in *Wolf* is troubling, it is made abundantly clear that Randall is horrified and guilt-stricken when he finds evidence of his savagery, and the film as a whole does not come to the conclusion that the loss of aggressive white patriarchy is necessarily something to lament. In fact, Will is made aware that his hyper-masculine existence is unsustainable and he will face dire consequences if he continues to embrace the instincts of the wolf. When he first begins to notice his changing physiology, Randall goes to see Dr Vijay Alezais (Om Puri), an expert on spiritualism and the occult, to obtain some understanding of what is happening to him. Randall asks what the doctor can tell him about his condition. Alezais replies:

> Only that the wolf rests by day and prowls by night, but is always present – that he grows inside the man he has entered until the first full moon. And then he consumes him, killing all but his nature and his heart . . . But of course, not all who are bitten change. There must be something wild within, an analogue of the wolf . . . Sometimes one doesn't even need to be bitten; only the passion of the wolf is enough.

During this discussion, Will says with some embarrassment that, 'Among my people I'm known as the guy least likely to have an analogue of the wolf.' Alezais simply replies, 'Your people are wrong.' The inference here, then, is that Randall has always possessed a potential for violence that he has thus far successfully contained. It is also clear that unless he chooses not to embrace these instincts, his fate will be to transform, wholly and irreversibly, into a wolf at the next full moon. Hyper-masculinity may help Will to regain control of his spiralling life in the short term, but he will ultimately have less than a month to enjoy his newfound dominance and virility.

It is also important to note that those personality traits we might be asked to applaud in Randall are the same as those we are pressed to despise in the film's principal antagonists. From Swinton he adopts cutthroat ambition, questionable ethics and a satisfaction in the demise of others; from Alden, a taste for power, control and influence. All three of these men also see women as objects to be owned and stolen. Swinton does not see a difference between his affair with Charlotte and his attempts to take his mentor's job. As Whitehead asserts, he is just attempting to rob Will of 'the most palpable symbols of his self-possession: his senior executive position and his handsome wife'.[13] In turn, Randall takes away Alden's most prized possession: his daughter. It would seem problematic to suggest that Randall's transformation renders him heroic for allowing him to develop personality traits displayed by the film's most despicable characters.

At the film's climax Will does, inevitably, go through a full anatomical change into a wolf, disappearing into the woodland surrounding Alden's secluded mansion. The chain of events that leads to this final metamorphosis begins when he bites Swinton on the night he discovers his protégé has been sleeping with his wife. This violent action sets in motion Stewart's own transformation, ultimately leading him to kill Charlotte in cold blood and frame Randall for the murder in the hope that Randall's arrest will restore his own career (clearly, both Randall and Swinton are prepared to do anything to establish their dominance as the alpha male). The two eventually meet at Alden's mansion and, in the throes of their final metamorphoses, clash in a battle of teeth and claws that only ends when Laura shoots Stewart dead. Set in full lupine form, Will disappears into the forest (Figure 7.2).

The ending of *Wolf* potentially produces two opposing interpretations of the film and two wildly different commentaries on Hollywood's new man. Perhaps Randall is aligned with D-FENS: a Mad Warrior who lashes out against a world he perceives as changing for the worse, preferring to return to the wilds of nature than have to relinquish his masculinity. Or perhaps Randall is damned: with his time up, he must live as the wolf forever as punishment for refusing to change his ways. As Whitehead highlights, even two of the film's creators disagree on this vital point.[14] In interviews conducted by Peter Biskind for *Premiere* magazine, Nichols and

Figure 7.2 Having chosen to embrace his werewolfism, Will Randall (Jack Nicholson) fully and irreversibly transforms from human to lupine form at the conclusion of *Wolf* (1994).

co-screenwriter Jim Harrison give very different accounts of the film's ending and its meaning.

As Biskind recounts, 'Harrison's script derived from Native American myths in which the souls of sick humans enter animals for therapeutic purposes.'[15] Harrison, then, maintains a romantic vision of the film's ending, seeing the wolf as a positive cleansing influence on Randall's life and his escape into the forest as, in Whitehead's words, 'a sloughing of civilization's bonds'.[16] On the other hand, Nichols does not see Randall as a traditional hero at all, but rather a man who is willing to sacrifice his humanity for short-term success in life and love. He comments: 'This is a story about somebody who loses his humanity, and you can't say that's something to be desired ... It's a sentimental lie.'[17] There is certainly enough evidence in the film to support either reading. However, one key scene ultimately bolsters Nichols's view: Randall's discussion of the rules of werewolfery with Alezais, which makes clear that if Randall wants to live like an animal, he will be forced to become one.

Wolf's thematic concerns are echoed in *Bad Moon* (1996), a feature adapted from Wayne Smith's novel *Thor* (1994). The film opens as Ted (Michael Paré) and his lover, Marjorie (Johanna Lebovitz), are attacked by a werewolf while having sex at their campsite in Nepal, where both are working as photo-journalists. Marjorie is killed and Ted, bitten and cursed, returns to the United States where he chooses to live in seclusion until his estranged sister, Janet (Mariel Hemingway), invites him to come and live with her and her son, Brett (Mason Gamble). It is here that *Bad Moon* begins to produce similar themes to *Wolf* by exploring a single male's reintroduction into the domestic sphere following years of careless adventure and isolation, where werewolfism acts as a metaphor for his difficulties in achieving reintegration into mainstream society.

This is primarily achieved through the contrast formed between Ted and the family's pet dog, a German shepherd named Thor who is unwaveringly loyal and fiercely protective of Janet and Brett. Thor represents family and domesticity, while Ted is, like *Wolf*'s Will Randall, a violent male whose monstrosity threatens to erase his humanity. Thor recognises immediately that Ted is a danger to his masters, and encounters the werewolf several times before Ted's affliction is made clear to his sister and nephew. Ultimately, Thor kills Ted in an affirmation of changing times: with Reagan's conception of masculinity eroded by progressive cultural movements, a figure representative of family life destroys the hyper-aggressive male.

Running with the Pack

Although its primary thematic concern is with changing attitudes to masculinity, perhaps the most problematic scene in *Wolf* – the racially charged confrontation between a white werewolf and a gang of minority criminals – is also the scene which has the strongest thematic connection with what I term the 'pack' films of the 1990s. Beginning with *Full Eclipse* (1993) and continuing into the 2000s, this is the first cycle of werewolf films to introduce the idea of werewolf packs that live, hunt and feed together.

This is not to say that *Full Eclipse* is the first pack film; *Werewolves on Wheels* (1971) and *The Howling* (1981) are isolated examples. However, the cycle that began in 1993 is set apart from its predecessors in that the werewolf packs in these films are exceptionally organised and work together to achieve common and often criminal goals. In an interesting twist on the werewolf's use as a metaphor for society's fear of youth culture in *I Was a Teenage Werewolf* (1957) and *Werewolves on Wheels*, this development in the werewolf film relates to a moment in history that witnessed the rapid expansion of street crime in America during the 1980s and 1990s, and to changes in criminal behaviour that saw gangs graduate from petty crime to more serious and organised activities. Writing in 1996, Jeffrey Fagan asserts:

> Until the 1970s, the term *gang* was synonymous with the large urban centers of New York, Chicago, Philadelphia and Los Angeles. That is no longer the case today. Gangs are now present in large and small cities in nearly every state. By 1992, police departments in over 85% of the nation's 250 largest cities reported the presence of

street gangs . . . Gangs today reflect the ethnic and racial diversity of U.S. society. New gangs have formed in small cities in Texas, in the midsize cities of California, and in urban areas throughout the South and the Midwest. Fundamental changes in gangs have accompanied their emergence . . . Traditionally, stealing and other petty economic crimes were the backbone of gang economic life. For some contemporary gangs, however, entrepreneurial goals, especially involving drug selling, have replaced the cultural goals of ethnic solidarity and neighborhood defense that have historically motivated gang participation and activities.[18]

With such a sharp rise in the proliferation of gangs and their graduation from theft to organised crime, it is not surprising that gang warfare would become a subject for the horror film. As Paul Robinson attests, it was an inevitable outcome of such issues being pounced upon and blown out of proportion by the mass media, which meant that gang violence 'became a favourite topic of news stories, television programming and Hollywood movies, both entertaining and frightening people all over the nation and around the world'.[19] And it was certainly not just werewolf films that incorporated organised crime into horror narratives during the 1990s: *Dark Angel* (or *I Come in Peace*, 1990) sees an extraterrestrial criminal drain the blood of heroin addicts for sale on his home planet, while *Predator 2* (1990) takes its alien hunter away from the jungle setting of *Predator* (1987) and transplants it into the concrete jungle: a near-future Los Angeles torn apart by gangland violence.

Yvonne Tasker has discussed *Predator 2* in this context at great length, examining its construction of race and gender through its dramatisation of turf wars and drug disputes.[20] Abbott suggests that gangs are also a central theme of many vampire films released since the late 1980s, specifically those set in Los Angeles: *The Lost Boys* (1987), *Blood Ties* (1991), *Blade* (1998) and *Revenant* (1999).[21] Though set in Pittsburgh, *Innocent Blood* (1992) also ties vampirism to gang violence; it sees an Italian Mafia boss and his loyal associates transformed into unwitting but vicious vampires. However, as yet no scholarly work has examined werewolf films in this context, but the 'pack' film is another product of this particular cultural moment.

HBO's made-for-television film *Full Eclipse* imagines Los Angeles as an urban war zone; the film's opening shot pans across a desolate neighbourhood, lingering on images of criminal gangs loitering on dank streets, selling firearms and vandalising public property. Following this opening scene, Detective Max Dire (Mario Van Peebles), and his partner, Jim Sheldon (Anthony Jon Denison), are called to intervene in an ongoing hostage situation. Both men are critically injured in a fire fight with the perpetrators, which leads them to be conscripted into an elite squad within the LAPD led by a high-ranking officer named Adam Garou (Bruce Payne). As is obvious from his name alone – though not revealed until the film's third act – Garou is a werewolf: he supplies his cranial fluid to his team as a drug, allowing them to transform partially into wolf-men and she-wolves. Garou's aim is to rid the city of crime and he is prepared to resort to violent vigilante tactics, including murder, to do so. Sheldon immediately finds his budding werewolfery difficult to reconcile with his humanity and commits suicide by silver bullet. On the other hand, Dire becomes heavily involved with Garou's squad – particularly officer Casey Spenser (Patsy Kensit) – and struggles to balance his personal morals with either his growing monstrosity or his team's brutal vigilantism.

Full Eclipse is a very interesting film in context, but one with a puzzlingly confused subtext. Its first half is an authoritarian power fantasy which depicts Los Angeles as a rotting city overrun with crime. The only havens for the law-abiding are depicted as those occupied solely by officers of the law; this is a city no longer safe for the average citizen. *Full Eclipse* avoids reactionary stereotyping – its gangs do not have any particular racial identity – but it is certainly guilty of endorsing authoritarian violence. Its conservatism in this regard is confirmed by Dire's first experience of the werewolf squad's full abilities: after introducing him to the team, Garou invites Dire to join them in intercepting an illegal firearms deal. In the first sequence that pits the partially transformed werewolf cops against organised crime, the squad's members are likened to a team of comic book superheroes in their appearance and abilities: the officers are uniformly dressed in black bodysuits and, after injecting Garou's drug, claws protrude either from their fingers or between their knuckles in an obvious allusion to Marvel Comics' Wolverine (Figure 7.3). The X-Men are name-checked in earlier dialogue to ensure the allusion is not missed.

Despite their willingness to tackle organised crime by any means necessary – including by slaughtering suspected criminals without following proper judicial procedure – the werewolf cops are painted as heroes to be applauded. The squad's ferocious and fatal attack on the arms dealers is a rapidly edited action sequence clearly designed to inspire awe rather than revulsion at the police brutality on display. The same is true of many of the film's other action scenes: Dire and Spenser clear out an apartment block filled with armed criminals, leaving many dead; a group of hoodlums attempt to kill the squad with a car bomb, only for the werewolves to emerge coolly from the flames and execute their attackers; later, the would-be assassins' mutilated bodies are delivered to their boss. These are horrifying examples of police officers acting outside of the law, but by framing their violent vigilantism in high-energy setpieces, the film transforms corrupt cops into action heroes.

Figure 7.3 The werewolf cops central to *Full Eclipse* (1993) are designed to recall comic book superheroes such as the X-Men.

In its second and third acts, however, *Full Eclipse* contradicts itself by asserting that the behaviour of the werewolf cops – and especially Garou – is reprehensible. This first becomes clear when Garou finds out that Spenser and Dire are in a relationship. He reminds Spenser that he is 'top dog' and brutally rapes her: only the first sign that he is capable of horrifying violence against innocents. Dire then comes to discover that Garou has a long history – too long, in fact, for him to be human – of forming elite police units, only to kill off his team and move to a new city. Having realised that not only is Garou a true werewolf but the source of the group's powers, Dire sets out to stop his leader.

Dire's motives here are murky. The realisation that Garou is a full-blooded werewolf leads him to deplore his leader's authoritarianism but, despite some initial reservations, he not only supports but actively participates in vigilante activity earlier in the narrative. Regardless, Dire's sudden determination to put a halt to Garou's war on crime is an interesting narrative twist and one that begins to question the film's initial conservatism. After all, the revelation that Garou is a monster – and that he has historically used his position as a police officer as an outlet for his curse – suggests that he is less interested in seeking justice than in being able to embrace his bestial side without fear of legal retribution. Despite *Full Eclipse*'s evasion of racial politics, this interpretation taps into a popular feeling in the early 1990s – especially among black communities in Los Angeles – that police officers were using gang activity as an excuse to justify sadistic behaviour as part of larger institutional racism. As Robinson states, 'Many black Angelenos viewed police actions to stop the gang turf wars as anything but heroic. For many in Black Los Angeles, gangs were seen as an excuse for police to brutalize blacks who weren't actually affiliated with gangs.'[22]

And Dire soon learns that his actions throughout the rest of the film – including his brutal vigilantism – have all been influenced by Garou in a very direct way. Garou's drug is, after all, his own cranial fluid; it has been changing the team's behaviour and altering their thoughts. This is confirmed by a meeting between Dire and Detective Tom Davies (Joseph Culp), an officer who served under Garou in Miami. Dire finds Davies cowering in an LAPD holding cell, a physically deformed and mentally unstable shadow of his former self. His body and mind have been destroyed by Garou's serum: a drug that is so addictive that he tries to steal a dose from Dire despite the damage it has already done to him. This reference to substance abuse aligns *Full Eclipse* with other gang-focused genre films of the period; as Tasker notes, 'In *Predator 2*, drugs are part of the scenery.'[23] Of course, in *Full Eclipse* it is the police, rather than the criminals, who are addicts. Garou's drug thus becomes a further metaphor for corrupt law enforcement, in which junior officers learn brutality and sadism from their superiors.

Full Eclipse comes to contradict itself for the second time in its ending. Garou chooses the night of an eclipse to finish off the city's criminal element, while Dire attempts to assassinate his former superior with a silver bullet. Then Garou reveals the meaning of the film's title: a werewolf cannot be harmed during a total lunar eclipse. He transforms, for the first time, into a true werewolf: a huge bipedal beast with a ferocious lupine head. Dire survives long enough for the eclipse to end, and injects Garou with his secret weapon: a silver nitrate solution. Dying, Garou urges Dire to lie in his blood, absorb his power and continue his mission. For reasons that are narratively unclear, Dire complies and goes on to become a werewolf vigilante.

This climax further confuses the film's ideology: at the outset, *Full Eclipse* is an authoritarian fantasy in which werewolf police officers slaughter criminals for the good of society; then it sheds the conservatism of its first act to reflect on vigilantism, corruption and social justice; then its ending threatens to reinstate the opening's reactionary themes. However, it is possible to suggest that Dire's corruption has simply become so entrenched that he is unable to shed Garou's influence or resist the temptation of inheriting his occult powers. However the movie is interpreted as a whole, though, it is clear that this is the product of a specific cultural moment: a frustrating film that earnestly attempts to reconcile the perceived threat of gang violence with issues surrounding substance abuse and state-sanctioned brutality.

Much more straightforward is the next film in the pack cycle: *An American Werewolf in Paris* (1997), a loose sequel to *An American Werewolf in London* (1981). From the earlier film, *An American Werewolf in Paris* retains the notion that werewolves are haunted by the ghosts of their victims but removes its emphasis on body-horror, instead rendering its werewolves with CGI and concentrating on the threat posed by gang-related activity. The story concerns Andy McDermott (Tom Everett Scott), an American tourist visiting Paris with friends Brad (Vince Vieluf) and Chris (Phil Buckman). There they meet Sérafine (Julie Delpy), who is heavily implied to be the daughter of *An American Werewolf in London*'s Alex Price.[24] A troubled French she-wolf, Sérafine has come to be connected with a werewolf gang that regularly feeds on unwitting tourists. McDermott first encounters Sérafine atop the Eiffel Tower, where she is contemplating suicide; after talking her down, McDermott becomes romantically obsessed with her and gets entangled with both her and the gang.

Unlike *Full Eclipse*, *An American Werewolf in Paris* is sure of its stance on street crime. The werewolf gang in this film, led by the charismatic Claude (Pierre Cosso), is made up of calculating and sadistic murderers. The film preys specifically on a fear of becoming a victim of gang violence, in this case at the hands of what Kim Newman calls 'a gang of racist, skinhead lycanthropes'.[25] Just as America's gangs graduated from petty theft to murder and criminal enterprise, the skinhead gang in this film is bloodthirsty and devilishly organised. Upon realising that McDermott is becoming romantically involved with Sérafine, Claude invites him and his friends to a party at 'Club de la Lune' ('Club of the Moon'), a supposed nightclub where he claims Sérafine will meet them. Instead, the club turns out to be a smokescreen to aid in the gang's horrific crimes: a confined space into which the werewolves herd huge numbers of tourists to prey upon during the full moon. Unlike the bikers in *Werewolves on Wheels*, this gang consists of organised pack animals that openly embrace their werewolfery and have established elaborate front operations through which to attract their prey. McDermott emerges from the club alive (although he does become a werewolf as a result of being bitten by Claude during his escape) but others are not so lucky. Many in attendance – including McDermott's friend and travelling companion Chris, who later appears as a ghost – have their hearts eaten from their chests.

As well as being more straightforward in its fearful depiction of gangs, *An American Werewolf in Paris* is also more explicit in linking gangs with drug abuse. As Fagan asserts, 'Few phenomena have been stereotyped as easily as gangs, violence and drug use, especially when they are taken in conjunction.'[26] *An American Werewolf in Paris* perpetuates this stereotype: the werewolf gang steals a serum initially developed for Sérafine to halt the effects of werewolfism, but which actually has the opposite effect: it allows the user to transform without the full moon. This concoction is injected intravenously, which immediately creates a symbolic connection between the serum and heroin. However, as the drug's use leads to an immediate, horrifying transformation, the film decisively connects narcotics to monstrous acts of violence, which is perhaps more accurately interpreted as a metaphor for the use of substances, such as phencyclidine (or PCP), which have been widely hypothesised to have a radical effect on the behaviour of the user.[27] PCP's reputation for causing violent aggression is such that it has even been perpetuated by criminals; Fagan asserts that gang members have been known to prepare 'for imminent fights with other gangs by drinking and smoking PCP-laced cigarettes'.[28] Through its allusions to recreational substance abuse, *An American Werewolf in Paris* makes an explicit link between gangs, drugs and violence and perpetuates the perception that gang-related violence is often the result of intoxication.[29]

In another contrast to *Full Eclipse*, this gang is also given a clear racial identity: with every member a white male sporting a shaven head and military jackboots, the werewolves are aligned with white supremacist criminal organisations such as the Aryan Brotherhood. While the group never explicitly expresses hatred towards anyone but American tourists, Claude does have delusions of grandeur that lead him to believe his followers have a higher purpose beyond their petty criminality, which he articulates in a speech that has decidedly fascist overtones:

> We have a mission, Andy, to purify the world. That's why we pick our victims from the scum of society. The governments of the world spend billions on medicine, welfare, charity, to what effect? It only keeps alive the weak, the stupid, the lazy, who breed and multiply, weakening the human race. All my men I have chosen for their loyalty, their dedication to the coming age.

In fact, the most interesting element of *An American Werewolf in Paris* is that it is a Hollywood studio picture which suggests gang violence – and specifically white supremacist gang violence – is a European problem, despite the widespread presence of neo-Nazi organisations in the American prison system.[30] The film's attempt to distance white supremacist gangs from the United States is most obvious in Claude's appetite for eating Americans. Upon finding that their werewolf serum will allow them to transform at will, the first thing the werewolves do is throw a party on the Fourth of July, to which this time only American tourists are invited. Having herded hundreds of people into an abandoned church, the skinheads inject their serum, transform and begin to feed in a sequence that eventually leads to McDermott killing Claude, putting an end to both the gang's reign of terror and his own curse.

It seems ironic, however, that the film posits neo-Nazi gang activity as a European issue. The 1990s saw a dramatic rise in the membership and proliferation of such gangs in America, as explored in two of the film's contemporaries: *American History X* (1998) and *Pariah* (1998). As Ronald M. Holmes, Richard Tewksbury and George E. Higgins assert, 'Whilst in 1991, only 27 percent of prison wardens reported the presence of separate white gangs in their prisons, the prevalence increased to 56 percent in 1993, 70 percent in 1999.'[31] *An American Werewolf in Paris*, then, is a film that geographically evades but thematically confronts growing problems in America: drug abuse, racism, criminal violence and the rapid growth of gang membership.

High School Howlers

While the pack cycle would continue into the 2000s, the dawn of the new millennium saw the release of *Ginger Snaps* (2000), a film that also expresses a fear of youth culture but shifts the focus of this anxiety away from working-class criminals and towards troubled teenagers. Set in the Canadian suburban town of Bailey Downs, *Ginger Snaps* follows Ginger (Katharine Isabelle) and Brigitte Fitzgerald (Emily Perkins), sisters and social outsiders who are a mystery to their parents and ostracised by their peers due to what Estella Ticknell calls 'a mutual interest in the subcultural pleasures of a gothic obsession with death and self-mutilation.'[32] The two have established a suicide pact before Ginger, the elder sister, is bitten by a werewolf ('The Beast of Bailey Downs') and slowly – gruesomely – begins to transform into a monstrous wolf. While Ginger indulges newfound urges for sex and violence, Brigitte attempts to cure her sister with the help of Sam MacDonald (Kris Lemche), a drug dealer. By the time they discover that Ginger could be treated with a chemical synthesised from monkshood, she has already spread her infection to a classmate and killed several people.

The subject of a great deal of academic work, *Ginger Snaps* is notable for making an explicit connection between the werewolf's monthly transformation and the menstrual cycle. As a result, it has been the recipient of feminist readings.[33] This is certainly not difficult to understand; she-wolves had been relatively rare in the werewolf films that preceded *Ginger Snaps*, and it is the first to place a female werewolf in a high-school setting. The film's creators certainly viewed it in this light, though from different perspectives. Screenwriter Paula Devonshire suggests that *Ginger Snaps* is feminist in its depiction of 'women helping themselves', continuing, 'they don't need men to come and rescue them, these girls contain an inner strength that the male characters could never possess'.[34] Conversely, director John Fawcett feared that the film projected a negative message: 'I actually thought that women would be very offended by this film. I was worried that what we were saying thematically was that to go through adolescence and become a woman was like becoming a monster.'[35]

Though both Devonshire and Fawcett perceive *Ginger Snaps* as a film primarily concerned, for better or worse, with female adolescence, it would be received – along with its sequel, *Ginger Snaps 2: Unleashed* (2004) – in a specific cultural context. Both films were released amidst a moral panic that followed several incidents of high-school violence, the most infamous and fatal of which, the Columbine High School massacre, occurred during the first film's pre-production.

In the year 2000, then, the threat of a violent teenager harbouring obsessions for death and suicide was immediately relevant in North America and, as Linda Ruth Williams attests, *Ginger Snaps* is 'haunted by stories of high school massacres'.[36] On 20 April 1999, the Columbine shooting had occurred, a tragedy in which Eric Harris and Dylan Klebold – two heavily armed seniors – killed twelve students, one teacher and themselves, injuring a further twenty-four in the most infamous high-school rampage in American history.[37] In its aftermath, Harris and Klebold were demonised by the press and falsely connected to the same goth sub-culture that Ginger and Brigitte subscribe to.[38] Only eight days later, Canadian fourteen-year-old Todd Cameron Smith took a gun to the W. R. Myers High School in Taber, Alberta, and shot two fellow students, one fatally. When news of the Alberta shootings broke, any illusion that high-school violence was an exclusively American problem was shattered. The perceived threat of teenage violence became immediately relevant for the Canadian public, the domestic audience for *Ginger Snaps*. The film would begin shooting in the Toronto suburbs later that year. In fact, as Ernest Mathijs notes, six casting directors based in Canada announced that they would be boycotting the film due to its subject matter.[39]

Benjamin Frymer argues that in the aftermath of Columbine – at that time the most recent in a barrage of violent incidents in American high schools – youth culture came to be demonised in the mass media. He suggests that coverage of the massacre generally worked to construct youth as pathological aliens who, like Goths, formed strange new alien subcultures . . . the media's real power and consequence lies in the overarching narrative spectacle provided for its American audience – one that turned Columbine into a story of new, vicious, alien creatures to be feared by the public.[40]

Although *Ginger Snaps* was in pre-production when the massacre occurred, it was released in a post-Columbine culture, only seventeen months after school shootings on both sides of the Canada–United States border. And while Mathijs argues that 'most of the controversy had been brushed away' before production even began,[41] the film's themes remain closely linked to troubled teenagers and high school violence. In the eyes of their parents, teachers and peers, Ginger and Brigitte are 'alien creatures' in the same mould as the twisted media portraits of Harris and Klebold: distant adolescents preoccupied with dark thoughts of killing themselves and others. Before Ginger is bitten, the sisters have already discussed how they would like classmates to die; made plans to kill a fellow student's dog; and, in an extended opening sequence, photographed mock-ups of their own suicides.

In short, Ginger and Brigitte are depicted as troubled long before the curse; werewolfism simply unleashes a thirst for sex and violence in Ginger and allows her to turn her morbid thoughts into a reality, her behaviour escalating in tandem with her slow metamorphosis (Figure 7.4). By indulging what she believes to be sexual desires, Ginger spreads her infection to

Figure 7.4 In *Ginger Snaps* (2000), the eponymous Ginger Fitzgerald (Katharine Isabelle) becomes increasingly monstrous as her behaviour spirals out of control.

fellow student Jason McCardy (Jesse Moss). Here, werewolfism is treated as a volatile sexually transmitted infection. Clearly, then, *Ginger Snaps* also might be seen to express a fear of budding female sexuality, and the sexual themes of the film have been discussed at length by both Bianca Nielsen and Barbara Creed.[42] However, dialogue reveals that teenage sexuality is not as important here as the perceived threat of teenage violence. During her transformation, Ginger admits: 'I get this ache. I thought it was for sex, but it's to tear everything to fucking pieces.' It is notable that two of Ginger's three victims are killed within the walls of her high school.[43] Even the film's title is a reference to Ginger's homicidal impulses: it suggests that her werewolfery causes her to psychologically 'snap'. Similarly, in coverage of high-school shootings, the media often (falsely) hypothesise that teenagers 'snap' immediately before taking guns into classrooms.[44]

In fact, the paranoia at the heart of *Ginger Snaps* can be convincingly linked with the fear school shootings inspire in society. As Katherine S. Newman et al. assert:

> Rampage school shootings terrify us because they contradict our most firmly held beliefs about childhood, home and community. They expose the vulnerable underbelly of ordinary life and tell us that malevolence can be brewing in places where we least expect it, and that our fail-safe methods (parental involvement in children's lives, close-knit neighbourhoods) do not identify nascent pathologies as well as we thought.[45]

While the sisters' father (John Bourgeois) is bemused by their behaviour, their mother Pamela (Mimi Rogers) is determined to be involved in their lives. However, she is completely oblivious to what is actually going on in them. Despite several near misses, she does not notice Ginger's escalating violent behaviour until she discovers a corpse hidden in her garden shed, at which point – rather than talking to her children or contacting the authorities – she suggests concealing the crime by burning down the family home. *Ginger Snaps* is in many ways an intentionally comedic film and much of its humour arises from suggestions that Ginger and Brigitte's parents are liberal to a fault. Even in finding concrete evidence that her daughters have been involved in the death of a classmate, Pamela just wants to protect her children. In fact, there is no sign of any real authority in *Ginger Snaps* at all. The police are strangely absent throughout. Ginger even makes a point of murdering her guidance counsellor; just as in *I Was a Teenage Werewolf* (1957) and *The Boy Who Cried Werewolf* (1973), therapy is clearly useless here. Despite living in a middle-class, close-knit suburban community with at least one parent who earnestly – if naïvely – attempts to take an active interest in her life, Ginger's transformation still turns her into a malicious murderer while figures of authority are nowhere to be seen.

Ginger Snaps offers only three ways in which such antisocial behaviour can be resolved. Firstly, adolescents can resist morbid obsessions; as the film's primary protagonist, Brigitte loses her interest in death and mutilation when she is confronted with their consequences. At the film's climax, trapped in the family home with a fully transformed Ginger, Brigitte breaks their suicide pact, declaring: 'I'm not dying in this room with you.' Secondly, they can continue to act on their impulses until they are destroyed; Brigitte attempts to reason with Ginger but eventually is forced to kill her. However, *Ginger Snaps* primarily endorses a third option for resolution that is further explored in *Ginger Snaps 2*.

The only treatment for werewolfism in the *Ginger Snaps* universe is a drug, proven to be temporarily effective when it is used on Jason. In *Ginger Snaps*, this potentially life-saving chemical never reaches Ginger. In the sequel, Brigitte is reliant on the drug to halt her transformation, having purposely infected herself with the werewolf's curse in the previous film to feel closer to her sister. It is revealed that monkshood is not a cure but a treatment: it needs to be taken consistently and indefinitely. Brigitte's metamorphosis advances whenever she withdraws from the drug; she also experiences vivid hallucinations in which her dead sister urges her to give in to her bestial desires. Where *An American Werewolf in Paris* suggests that drugs contribute to violence, *Ginger Snaps* and its sequel use a chemical treatment as a metaphor for pharmacology: the only possible remedy for antisocial behaviour in their universe. Furthermore, because monkshood is a treatment rather than a cure, the two films articulate a sense that such behaviour can only be controlled through its perpetual use until the unwanted behaviour is brought under control.

This thematic concern coincides with a dramatic change in the treatment of adolescent mental illness. In the 1990s, a meteoric rise was recorded in the number of psychiatric drugs prescribed to minors.[46] Such a dramatic increase in prescriptions for medication suggests that Western society now relies more on pharmacology than talk therapy to suppress undesirable behaviour in children. It is certainly the only thing that can help Brigitte; she is institutionalised in *Ginger Snaps 2* and holds nothing but contempt for her therapists. Once more, psychiatry is ineffectual. A drug alone can halt Brigitte's transformation, and she pointedly refuses to engage with peers in group therapy or counselling sessions.

It is of note, however, that the scenes in which Brigitte uses monkshood are blunt in their allusions to substance abuse through extreme close-ups of intravenous injections and Brigitte's use of items – tourniquets, spoons, cigarette lighters – which are heavily associated with the recreational use of heroin. The negative connotations of these scenes are enhanced by their close proximity to scenes of self-harm; Brigitte is also prone to slicing herself open in order to measure the advancement of her metamorphosis based on how long it takes her skin to heal. However, despite these allusions to self-harm and addiction, the fact remains that monkshood suppresses Brigitte's symptoms. Without it, her metamorphosis advances to the point that even the drug is incapable of saving her. In fact, by the film's end she has permanently transformed. So even if the film links monkshood with substance abuse, the fact remains that only a drug can prevent Brigitte from transforming into a monster.

Ginger Snaps 2 also makes the first film's thematic concern with teenage violence surprisingly explicit. Although *Ginger Snaps* was still in production while attitudes to youth culture were changing in North America, by the time of its release its themes were rendered inseparable from media rhetoric surrounding a then unprecedented tragedy. *Ginger Snaps 2*, however, was written and produced after many of the details surrounding the Columbine massacre had come to light and released at a time when school violence continued to haunt the headlines – only two weeks before its theatrical run began in Canada, two Louisiana teens were arrested for allegedly planning to recreate the Columbine massacre on its fifth anniversary.[47] It is perhaps no surprise, then, that the sequel intensifies the first film's thematic preoccupation with troubled adolescents. It primarily does so through the character of Ghost (Tatiana Maslany), while simultaneously projecting a more progressive message by using her to satirise the media response to Columbine.

Brigitte first meets Ghost in the psychiatric clinic she is taken to when the authorities become aware that she is using monkshood, which they assume to be an addictive recreational drug. Ghost is not a patient, but rather a seemingly contented young girl – possibly even a pre-teen, although her age is never explicitly disclosed – who is living at the clinic while the authorities try to find her a foster home. Her only living relative, her grandmother Barbara (Susan Adam), is unable to care for her, having suffered severe burns in a house fire. Ghost is immediately depicted as Brigitte's polar opposite: while Brigitte continues to be associated with goth sub-culture, Ghost is an outgoing young girl with blue eyes, a blonde ponytail and an eccentric wardrobe of brightly coloured clothes. However, as the narrative progresses, it becomes clear that while Brigitte is terrified of hurting others and desperate to slow the onset of her transformation, Ghost is extremely dangerous beneath her façade.

The younger girl is shown to be something of a pyromaniac, which foreshadows the later revelation that her grandmother's burns were not an accident: Ghost intentionally set her alight. She also helps Brigitte to escape from the clinic, but her motives are far from noble; she fantasises about keeping a werewolf as a pet and using it to kill her enemies. She achieves this at the film's climax, when she locks the fully transformed Brigitte in the basement of her grandmother's house. Here, then, the media's assumptions about teenage killers are subverted. Brigitte – who possesses the physical appearance, apparent mental health troubles and sub-cultural obsessions of the media's teenage spree killers – is desperate to prevent anyone from coming to harm at her hands; Ghost, on the other hand – an outwardly innocent, all-American, extroverted young girl – is harbouring dark thoughts of murder and revenge.

However, while *Ginger Snaps 2* subverts common media perceptions, the threat of violent children remains central to its creation of fear and the film continues to perpetuate ideas that have their origin in media responses to Columbine. Ghost is seen throughout the film to read lurid horror comics, though she hides them for fear of having them confiscated by her carers. These comics are directly linked to her crimes. For example, she reads a story about a warrior woman who is accompanied by a pair of huge demonic dogs. It is the influence of this comic that leads Ghost to begin entertaining fantasies that she will enslave the fully transformed Brigitte as a loyal pet to be used as a weapon. As Augusto de Vananzi notes, popular culture has often been blamed for crimes committed by teenagers, especially in connection with school shootings:

> The violent messages and images contained in TV series, movies, and video games have been blamed by parents, politicians, and segments of the academic community for producing a detrimental effect on teens' psychological wellbeing, even offered as direct causal variables in the explanation of rampage school shootings. The fact is that violent movies and video games, together with the sophisticated audio–visual technologies that go into their making, have been converted into objects of fear.[48]

Various forms of pop culture were blamed for the violent actions of Harris and Klebold. In particular, the media drew attention to the killers' apparent love for *Natural Born Killers* (1994).[49] It is possible that Ghost's fixation on horror comics is intended to be satirical; films, music and video games were the most commonly demonised forms of pop culture in the aftermath of Columbine, while paranoia surrounding the comic book medium is something more contemporaneous to the release of *I Was a Teenage Werewolf* than *Ginger Snaps 2*. However, the film's ending does not support this reading. In a final scene clearly intended to shock, the camera tracks around the empty house that once belonged to Ghost's grandmother. Brigitte has undergone her final metamorphosis in the basement, the door rattling as the werewolf tries to escape. On the wall is a sign that reads 'Welcome Home Barbara', suggesting that Ghost's recently healed grandmother is soon to fall victim to her pet werewolf.

Upstairs, Ghost is working on a drawing in her bedroom: a picture of herself holding an automatic weapon with a werewolf standing at her feet, a crude tribute to the illustration in her favourite comic book. In voiceover, Ghost speaks of herself in the third person as she discusses her plans for the werewolf: 'Growing steadily stronger beneath the floorboards, her faithful companion with a deadly hunger for human flesh waited to unleash the darkness and fury of hell on her mistress' enemies, of which there were many. And so began Ghost's reign of moral terror.' *Ginger Snaps 2*, then, is a somewhat confused film in its position on teenage violence. While it eschews the media response to Columbine by depicting a seemingly innocent young girl as a calculating psychopath, it perpetuates much of the rhetoric that dominates popular commentary on high-school shooters.

The third entry in the *Ginger Snaps* series, *Ginger Snaps Back: The Beginning* (2004), removes itself entirely from the first two films' contemporary setting. In 1815, Ginger and Brigitte (portrayed by the same actors playing ostensibly the same characters) stumble across a fort on the Canadian frontier that has been besieged by werewolves for some time. The shift to a period setting is jarring, but could be considered to serve a thematic purpose; Sunnie Rothenburger argues that all three *Ginger Snaps* films are concerned with Canada's colonialist history, and clearly a shift to a period setting would aid in communicating such themes.[50] However, this also has the effect of distancing *Ginger Snaps Back* as far as possible from the high-school violence evident in *Ginger Snaps* and *Ginger Snaps 2*. But there would be numerous teenage werewolves to come, with teenage protagonists taking a central role in a large number of twenty-first-century werewolf narratives. However, none of these films are as clearly concerned with high-school violence as the *Ginger Snaps* series. Rather, they revive a thematic preoccupation common in werewolf films of the 1980s and 1990s: gender politics. A number of other thematic cycles would also develop throughout the 2000s and 2010s as the werewolf became a prolific figure in popular cinema like never before.

CHAPTER 8

Shapeshifters

Lunar Cycles

Since the turn of the millennium, the werewolf film has proliferated like never before. For much of the twentieth century, the werewolf experienced peaks and troughs in popularity, and was often contained to brief cycles made in specific geographic areas. Werewolf films are now produced in ever-increasing numbers and by several indigenous film industries. The year 2014, for example, witnessed the release of eight werewolf films produced in five different countries: America's *Late Phases*, *Werewolf Rising* and *Bubba the Redneck Werewolf*; Canada's *Wolves* and *WolfCop*; Britain's *Blood Moon*; Denmark's *When Animals Dream*; and New Zealand's *What We Do in the Shadows*, which features an exceptionally polite werewolf pack as supporting characters. So many werewolf films have been produced over the last twenty years – from major Hollywood releases such as *The Wolfman* (2010) to low-budget fare like *The Snarling* (2018) – that it would be impossible to discuss all of them here. However, this chapter will offer a survey of some of the most culturally important examples produced in the last two decades and will explore how their lupine monsters have arisen from and engaged with contemporary – and often transnational – concerns.

As the 2000s began, though, the most prolific themes of the previous decade continued to dominate a number of millennial cycles. For example, following *An American Werewolf in Paris* (1997), a new series of pack films perpetuated the notion of werewolf packs as violent and organised criminal gangs. The films in this cycle see clans of werewolves either warring against each other or against other supernaturally powered groups and often engaging in violent clashes over turf, resources or conflicting ideologies. They include: *Skinwalkers* (2006), *Bloodz vs. Wolvez* (2006) and *Underworld* (2003), which has been followed by four sequels, *Underworld: Evolution* (2006), *Underworld: Rise of the Lycans* (2009), *Underworld: Awakening* (2012) and *Underworld: Blood Wars* (2016).

In addition to the case studies discussed in the previous chapter, another key werewolf film of the 1990s is *Project: Metalbeast* (1995), the first film since *The Mad Monster* (1942) to focus on a werewolf used as weapon of war.[1] *Project: Metalbeast* was produced in the wake of the Gulf War and concerns a CIA agent named Donald Butler (John Marzilli) who is tasked with investigating a werewolf's island castle on behalf of the United States government. He returns with a sample of the beast's blood in hand; tests yield few results and eventually, impatient, Butler chooses to inject the last of the werewolf blood into his veins. Uncontrollable, werewolf Butler is shot with silver bullets and cryogenically frozen by the military. Twenty years later, his supposedly dead body is used as a test subject for a new type of metal skin graft at the behest of the corrupt Colonel Miller (Barry Bostwick); during the procedure, scientist Anne De Carlo (Kim Delaney) and her team remove the silver bullets from Butler's body, reviving him. Faced with a werewolf sporting impenetrable metal skin (portrayed by Kane Hodder), the scientists destroy Butler before he can escape (though the film's ending suggests he is not quite dead).

The Mad Monster was released at a time when the world was growing anxious due to the rapid advancement of weapons technology; the Gulf War reinvigorated these fears, especially in relation to chemical and biological agents. Paranoia surrounding chemical warfare was fostered by the Western media, but was not entirely unfounded in truth. The Iraqi military did, in fact, possess biological weapons: 'During the Persian Gulf War, coalition forces recognized that Iraq possessed nerve agents, including sarin, and had prepared them for use in rockets, bombs and missile warheads.'[2] As Ella Shohat notes, the American media were particularly interested in exploiting Saddam Hussein's use of biological agents as a propaganda tool. She points out that the nation's own history of using such weapons – particularly in Vietnam – was purposely obscured.[3] *Project: Metalbeast* is a countercultural film, then, that draws attention to the fact that America has been equally guilty of pursuing the development and use of volatile weapons technology; it is no coincidence that the opening scenes take place in 1974, shortly after America's withdrawal from Vietnam the previous year.

This is another theme of the 1990s werewolf film that resurged in the twenty-first century, following the 9/11 terrorist attacks and the beginning of the War on Terror. The British *Dog Soldiers* (2002) is an early example of a film released in a post-9/11 context: it pits a squad of British servicemen against a pack of vicious werewolves during a training exercise in remote Scotland. Only later do they learn that it is not a training exercise at all. Rather, they have been tricked into serving as bait for the werewolves so that a special operations team can capture, study and attempt to weaponise one of the creatures. *Dog Soldiers* was filmed in 2001 and released in 2002; as such, it was clearly not intended to be viewed as a political allegory. However, it began its theatrical run in cinemas just six months after the onset of the War on Terror, and contained some exceptionally prescient themes: its story of soldiers fighting off cunningly intelligent foes as a result of betrayal by their superiors would become all too relevant as public opinion against British involvement in the War on Terror began to sour. It clearly struck a chord with military personnel; writer-director Neil Marshall claims that 'it was for a long period of time the most watched movie by British forces out in Afghanistan and Iraq'.[4]

Dog Soldiers would be followed by *War Wolves* (2009), *Battledogs* (2013) and *Silverhide* (2015). *War Wolves* creates an explicit link to the War on Terror: its narrative sees a group of American soldiers attacked by a werewolf during a tour of the Middle East. On arriving home, they begin to transform into monsters, rendering the film an interesting allegory for the psychological ravages of war and particularly PTSD. Both *Battledogs* and *Silverhide* possess similar plots to *Project: Metalbeast*. In *Battledogs*, an army general attempts to create an army of super-soldiers after collecting DNA samples from werewolves, while *Silverhide* sees conspiracy theorists discover that the British military is hiding a werewolf-like monster (codenamed 'Silverhide') with the ability to become invisible under moonlight. By borrowing the concept of weaponised werewolves from *The Mad Monster* and *Project: Metalbeast*, both *Battledogs* and *Silverhide* express a distrust of the military-industrial complex in a post-9/11 world.

Gender identity is another theme common in the 1990s werewolf film (though it has been a thematic concern that has recurred several times since the 1940s) that has grown increasingly evident in contemporary examples. These films are, like *Teen Wolf* (1985), *Teen Wolf Too* (1987), *Wolf* (1994) and *Bad Moon* (1996), largely concerned with problematising traditional masculinity. This is not at all surprising; gender equality is far from a reality in the twenty-first century. Writing in 2000, bell hooks suggests that the distinction between what is considered traditionally 'masculine' (i.e. dominant) and feminine (i.e. subordinate) remains deeply problematic in the new millennium. Following decades of campaigning, hooks argues that patriarchy continues to be the norm and that:

> Males as a group have and do benefit the most from patriarchy, from the assumption that they are superior to females and should rule over us. But those benefits have come with a price. In return for all the goodies that men receive from patriarchy, they are required to dominate women, to exploit and oppress us, using violence if they must to keep patriarchy intact. Most men find it difficult to be patriarchs.[5]

As social and cultural conceptions of gender identity have continued to develop in the new millennium, the themes of gender crisis common to the werewolf film since the 1940s have reappeared in two closely related cycles of werewolf films. The first, comprising *Big Bad Wolf* (2006), *Blood and Chocolate* (2007), *Wolves* and the latest instalment in the *Howling* series, *The Howling: Reborn* (2011), updates the 'pack' film to unpick the problematic nature of patriarchal societies through dysfunctional werewolf families. The second includes three films featuring she-wolves – *When Animals Dream*, *Female Werewolf* (2015) and *Wildling* (2018) – and arises from the birth of fourth-wave feminism.

Big Bad Wolf is a clear continuation of the masculine crisis palpable in *Wolf* and *Bad Moon*. A truly unusual werewolf film, *Big Bad Wolf* features a werewolf who retains human consciousness and is even able to speak in his transformed state. At the film's opening, Derek Cowley (Trevor Duke) steals the keys to his stepfather's remote cabin so that he and five friends – including his best friend Samantha Marche (Kimberly J. Brown) – can hold a party. During their stay in the rural shack, they are ambushed by a sadistic werewolf who gleefully massacres the teenagers, even graphically raping one of Derek's female friends. Derek and Samantha are the only survivors of the attack and, arriving home, soon come to suspect that the werewolf is Derek's stepfather, Mitchell Toblat (Richard Tyson).

Like *Wolf* and *Bad Moon* before it, *Big Bad Wolf* muses on outmoded notions of masculinity: in human form, Toblat is a misogynist and domestic tyrant who rules over his stepson and wife, Gwen (Sarah Aldrich), with fear. His only interests are in drinking, pursuing extramarital sex and weightlifting to maintain a traditionally masculine appearance. In werewolf form, he is a vicious rapist and murderer. Moreover, he is entirely aware of his actions once transformed and does not suffer any sense of guilt; rather, his transformations just serve as an outlet for him to indulge his more violent urges. Similar to *Bad Moon*, then, *Big Bad Wolf* is the story of an impressionable male learning to reject toxic masculinity as represented by a dysfunctional father figure; in fact, Derek learns from his uncle Charlie (Christopher Shyer) that Toblat was responsible for the death of his real father, Scott (Andrew Bowen).

Before long, Toblat comes to suspect that his wife is attracted to Charlie and kills him in cold blood. Shortly afterwards, Derek is finally able to prove that Toblat is a werewolf, and confronts his stepfather back at the cabin. There, he and Samantha face Toblat in werewolf form, attacking him with silver and fire. In an echo of *The Boy Who Cried Werewolf* (1973), Toblat bites Derek on the arm before he is eventually destroyed, uttering 'my curse is now yours'. As he leaves the scene, Derek is visibly worried as to what his future may hold. Unlike *The Boy Who Cried Werewolf*, though, *Big Bad Wolf* ends on a comforting note. Toblat is framed throughout the film as a sadist who also happens to be a werewolf; the man, not the monster, is responsible for his crimes. Having destroyed his hyper-masculine stepfather, Derek is free to take his father and uncle as role models, regardless of the werewolf's curse.

Following the release of *Big Bad Wolf*, a new cycle of closely related werewolf films emerged. The films that make up this cycle – *Blood and Chocolate*, *The Howling: Reborn* and *Wolves* – share a great deal in common: they all concentrate on young, adolescent protagonists, both male and female, who are either brought up as members of a werewolf pack or discover that a hereditary history of werewolfery has been hidden from them as children; they all see these teenage werewolves attempt to come to terms with the traditions of their unusual families before they attempt to break free of the pack; and they all detail the attempts of these monstrous families to assimilate or otherwise eliminate their rebellious children. In this regard, they might be considered to form a new type of 'pack' film, in which the pack is no longer representative of organised criminal violence but outmoded patriarchal attitudes.

The Howling: Reborn and *Wolves* are strikingly similar narratives in which young men of high-school age come to discover that their biological parents are werewolves. In *The Howling: Reborn*, eighteen-year-old Will Kidman (Landom Liboiroh) believes his mother, Kathryn (Ivana Miličević), is dead, having been killed – the victim of a sadistic attack by a male member of a werewolf cult – while she was pregnant with him. Raised by his father, Will is a normal teenager until he discovers two guarded secrets: that he himself is a werewolf, having been infected during the attack on his mother, and that his mother is alive and living with the pack. The narrative details his mother's attempts to bring him into the fold; she suggests that Will's father has 'domesticated' him and 'made him soft' through a liberal upbringing. But Will refuses to conform to the pack's preferred mode of aggressive masculinity. He eschews their animalistic nature, choosing to kill his mother and her kind before exposing their existence to the world in an echo of *The Howling* (1981).

Similarly, in *Wolves*, adolescent Cayden Richards (Lucas Till) discovers that he is a werewolf following a series of disturbing events: first, he exhibits enormous strength during a high-school football game, severely injuring a rival player; second, he partially transforms and attempts to rape his girlfriend when his aggressive sexual behaviour causes her to rescind consent; third, later that night he appears to kill his adoptive parents in werewolf form. Wanted for murder, he becomes a drifter and eventually finds his way to Lupine Ridge, a rural town home to numerous werewolves. There, he discovers that he is a child of rape and that his biological father, Connor Slaughter (Jason Momoa), is the patriarch of a violently misogynistic werewolf pack. Furthermore, Slaughter intends to mate with an unwilling young she-wolf, Angelena 'Angel' Timmins (Merritt Patterson), in the hope of producing an heir. Appalled by his biological father's values, Cayden enlists the help of Angel to destroy the pack: he thus redeems himself by condemning the wholly negative masculine behaviours he exhibits in the film's first act. Like *Bad Moon*, *Big Bad Wolf* and the *Teen Wolf* films before them, both *The Howling: Reborn* and *Wolves* concentrate on young male protagonists doing battle with patriarchal forces that would like to see them conform to an archaic conception of masculinity.

Blood and Chocolate is perhaps the most interesting entry in the contemporary pack cycle because, while its narrative and themes are familiar to *The Howling: Reborn* and *Wolves*, it is the only example to concentrate on a female protagonist. *Blood and Chocolate* follows Vivian Gandillion (Agnes Bruckner), a young member of a werewolf pack living in Bucharest, Romania. The fiercely traditional group – hundreds of years old, its members refer to themselves as *loups-garous* – is ruled over by patriarch Gabriel (Olivier Martinez), who routinely executes traitors and interlopers by allowing his followers to hunt and kill them. Gabriel has chosen Vivian as his next mate but, much to the chagrin of the pack's males, she instead begins a relationship with a sensitive American artist, Aiden (Hugh Dancy), who has come to Bucharest to research the region's werewolf lore. Thus, Vivian is forced to choose between her family and her freedom: she must either surrender her body to the pack's dominant male or risk exile and death. Ultimately, Vivian chooses to pursue her own happiness rather than a life of subordination; she kills Gabriel at the film's climax in an act of rebellion against his regressive patriarchal values. In a scene that functions as a prologue, it is suggested that Vivian will lead the pack into a prophesised 'age of hope' in which they will abandon tradition and embrace a new and equal society.

She Bites

While *Blood and Chocolate* is the only film in the new pack cycle to feature a she-wolf, it is certainly not the only modern werewolf film to concentrate on a female protagonist, or to explore the effects of patriarchal oppression on women. In fact, since the dawn of the 2010s, this has become a consistent and transnational theme in a second cycle of werewolf films concentrated on individual women afflicted with werewolfism. These films – *When Animals Dream, Female Werewolf* and *Wildling* – explore the oppression suffered by women in contemporary society and are products of cultural shifts ushered in by fourth-wave feminism, which has reinvigorated the struggle for gender equality in the twenty-first century.

The fourth wave of feminism has been defined by two primary developments: the first is an emergent emphasis on intersectionality and inclusivity.[6] The second is an increasing use of the internet as a tool for activism: a site for shedding light on the abuse and harassment suffered by women in their day-to-day lives. These developments began in the early 2010s, made possible through the explosion of social media platforms that have allowed women from many different backgrounds to share their experiences with each other and appeal for social, cultural and political change. Writing in 2013, Ealasaid Munro suggests that, for many, 'the internet itself has enabled a shift from "third-wave" to "fourth-wave" feminism. What is certain is that the internet has created a "call-out" culture, in which sexism or misogyny can be . . . challenged'.[7]

Social media has allowed women to speak out about instances of harassment, sexual assault and rape suffered at the hands of male abusers and call attention to the prevalence of patriarchal violence and oppression in contemporary society. Perhaps the most famous example of this is the 'Me Too' movement, which reached its apex following the numerous allegations of sexual misconduct levelled at film producer Harvey Weinstein in October 2017. Me Too, popularised as a Twitter hashtag by actor Alyssa Milano, encouraged women to publicly share their own experiences. In the years following the birth of Me Too and the subsequent establishment of 'Time's Up' (an organisation founded by Hollywood personalities and dedicated to putting an end to sexual harassment), a number of prevalent and powerful men have been the subject of similar allegations, including both United States President Donald Trump and British Prime Minister Boris Johnson.

Though both the Me Too and Time's Up movements have been centred in the United States, social media has allowed them to have an international impact, and this has been true of fourth-wave feminism, a truly global movement, in the 2010s. As such, the feminist she-wolf films released in the last decade have arisen from different national contexts. *When Animals Dream* was produced in Denmark, *Female Werewolf* in Canada and *Wildling* in the United States, but all three films are united by a resolutely dark tone and a thematic preoccupation with the systemic oppression of women. Like the earlier *Werewolf Woman* (1976), they recast werewolfism as a symbol of empowerment rather than monstrosity: a marker of difference, individuality and power that allows their werewolf women to slip the bonds of patriarchal societies and escape the control of men who have subjugated and abused them.

Denmark's *When Animals Dream* follows Marie (Sonia Suhl), a sixteen-year-old girl living in a remote coastal village with her father, Thor (Lars Mikkelsen) and her unresponsive mother (Sonja Richter). As the narrative progresses, Marie discovers that she is a werewolf – a condition inherited from her mother, whose apparent catatonia is actually the result of medication designed to suppress her feral instincts. The teenager embraces her budding werewolfery, resisting any and all attempts to treat her condition. However, the male-dominated society that surrounds Marie insists that she be kept under control by any means necessary – leading to a climax in which several members of the community trap her aboard a fishing vessel and attempt to kill her.

When Animals Dream is set on the west coast of Northern Jutland, an area sustained by the farming and fishing industries and commonly associated with Christian conservatism; it has long been the stronghold of the Church Association for the Inner Mission in Denmark, a Lutheran revival movement. As David Arter notes, even in the twenty-first century it remains a socially conservative region in which the Inner Mission thrives and Denmark's left-leaning parties have enjoyed little support.[8] It is, then, an area associated with deeply regressive ideologies, and the film introduces it as a bleak and isolated place. The opening credits appear over portraits of coastal Jutland cast in murky sepia tones; drained of all colour and vibrancy, images that should otherwise be beautiful – beaches, hills, crashing waves – instead become indicators of loneliness and detachment. This feeling is reinforced by the fact that several of these shots are devoid of human life: they depict nothing but the landscape, and when the film's title finally appears at the end of this montage, it is pictured over a barren hillside beneath a blackened sky. Intercut with these desolate images are shots of the house Marie shares with her parents, illustrating that she feels just as alone in her own home as she does in Jutland as a whole; lingering wide shots of empty rooms and corridors, rendered in shades of grey, create a sense of alienation. And when an establishing shot of her village appears, it is framed from a canted angle – hinting at the repressive atmosphere that clouds this ostensibly idyllic community.

As the film begins in earnest, it soon becomes clear why Marie might feel oppressed by her environment. The first shot of the film, following its opening montage, is of her flesh under a microscope. We soon learn that she is being examined by a physician, Dr Larsen (Stig Hoffmeyer), but this image is a striking metaphor: over the film's first act, Marie is

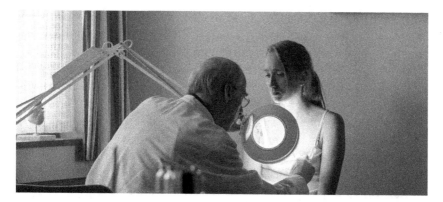

Figure 8.1 *When Animals Dream* (2014) opens as Marie (Sonia Suhl) is enduring an invasive examination by Dr Larsen (Stig Hoffmeyer), establishing her distaste for being objectified.

routinely sexualised by men, and this opening scene – in which her flesh is pictured in extreme close-up before being invasively examined by the doctor – establishes her distaste for being objectified (Figure 8.1). This theme continues as Marie experiences her first day working in a fish packing plant; while she is attempting to learn the skills of the trade from her new colleague Felix (Mads Rilsom), she is forced to endure being suggestively stared at by another co-worker, Esben (Gustav Giese). When Marie sparks a relationship with the meek Daniel (Jakob Oftebro), Esben subjects her to a number of violent and humiliating hazing pranks, culminating in a scene where he and two other male colleagues corner her in a locker room, strip her to her underwear and threaten her with rape. Marie does not speak out because – as is illustrated in an earlier scene that sees the teenager pushed into a vat of fish heads in front of the plant's entire workforce – this behaviour is excused and normalised by the wider community.

This abuse of patriarchal power is evident even in Marie's relationships with men she should be able to trust. Aside from Daniel, who rejects the toxic masculinity represented by every other male character in the film, all of the men in Marie's life eventually betray her. Felix, who becomes a close friend of Marie's during the course of the narrative, does not come to her aid when the community turns against her. Earlier, she discovers through her mother's medical notes that Dr Larsen is aware of her hereditary werewolfism and has simply been examining her so that he can decide on the correct time to begin her own 'treatment'. That discovery leads her to the realisation that Thor, her own father, has been allowing Larsen to medicate her mother: he has been quite literally subjugating his wife, and plans to do the same to Marie. And Thor plays an active part in this: in addition to helping the doctor to administer his wife's medication, Marie catches him shaving her back. As noted in Chapter 6, female body hair has long been 'viewed as a manifestation of animalistic lust'.[9] In having Thor shave his wife against her will, *When Animals Dream* suggests that he is not only trying to conceal her apparent 'monstrosity' but suppress her sexuality.

In fact, Marie's mother suffers many of the same patriarchal abuses as her daughter, and the film makes clear that she has been suffering them for years. She does not have a single line of dialogue, illustrating that she was long ago robbed of her voice both figuratively and literally, and after she kills Dr Larsen – attacking him as he attempts to medicate her daughter – she is stripped to her underwear and, in a mirror of the film's opening scene, humiliatingly examined for signs of werewolfery by members of the community. She eventually commits suicide, preferring to die rather than continue to live under the control of her husband; when Marie finds her body, drowned in the family bath, the camera lingers on her wedding ring – a potent symbol of her long-standing subordination.

It is after her mother's death that Marie truly begins to embrace her werewolfery, but there are earlier suggestions that she finds comfort in it. She experiences fantasies of bodily metamorphosis, and initiates her first sexual encounter with Daniel by whispering, 'I'm transforming into a monster and I really need to get laid before.' She then experiences a partial transformation as she has sex with him, revealing that here werewolfism represents little more than a woman's natural desires – rendered monstrous only because a conservative society considers them to be so. This idea is reinforced by two shots that bookend the film's sex scene: before Daniel and Marie arrive at the beach where they will have sex for the first time, they pass a church adorned with an illuminated crucifix that represents the community's religious repression; and immediately after this scene, the film cuts to Thor sitting awake in bed next to his clothed and sleeping wife, all intimacy between them long absent.

Later, Marie begins to openly indulge her instincts. At her mother's wake, she notices her fingernails are falling out, blood seeping from underneath; she purposely displays them to the mourners, delighting in their disgust. She then bites into a drinking glass during a meal with her father, chewing the shards and allowing her mouth to bleed profusely – illustrating to him that she has no intention of being controlled like her mother. In the film's final act, she finally experiences her first full transformation and takes violent revenge on the men that have oppressed her, killing Ebsen and several others. At the film's end, she is reunited with Daniel, the only man who has consistently encouraged her to be herself.

In an interview with the Danish Film Institute, *When Animals Dream* director Jonas Alexander Arnby expresses that it was his intention 'to show Marie's quiet rebellion, how she stands outside the community, while she is forced to go on a journey where she learns who she is'.[10] Here, then, werewolfism importantly does not represent monstrosity but rebellion, quiet or otherwise: the wolf inside Marie represents everything she has been taught to repress, and in embracing the animal she shows that she will no longer allow herself to be brutalised or controlled.

Canada's *Female Werewolf* similarly reflects on the consequences of sexual repression. It concentrates on an alienated woman, credited as She (Carrie Gemmell), who spends her days working a monotonous office job and her nights alone in a motel suite. Her terminally dull existence is broken up by erotic fantasies centred on her female co-worker, credited as Office Girl (Cheryl Singleton). As these daydreams dominate her thoughts, She begins to believe that she is turning into a werewolf (and is particularly fixated on her canine teeth, which appear to be growing into fangs). Eventually, She invites Office Girl back to her motel and kills her during a violent and sexualised encounter. Having murdered the object of her desires, She then lures another woman, Street Girl (Elena Pilipaitis) to her suite and claims her second victim as a monstrous lupine creature emerges from her mouth. At the film's end, She stands in open woodland, at peace with her animal instincts.

Many of the techniques *Female Werewolf* uses to express its themes are remarkably similar to those employed by *When Animals Dream*. Echoing the earlier film's credit sequence, *Female Werewolf* reveals the oppressive nature of this society through lingering images of dull and empty streets. Here, though, these shots reoccur throughout the film: a constant reminder that its protagonist feels both trapped in and detached from the world around her. In fact, the later film takes this idea to its extreme; it features several long and often recurring takes designed to reflect the terminal boredom of its budding she-wolf, including a dripping kitchen tap. And while *When Animals Dream* renders Marie's mother mute to represent her lack of agency, *Female Werewolf* extends this idea to its entire cast: the film contains only one line of dialogue. Its three characters, all of them women, are rendered voiceless by patriarchy – one scene, for example, sees She and Office Girl simply staring into each other's eyes, unable to speak. It is notable that there are no male characters in *Female Werewolf* – and yet a sense of overbearing patriarchal control is ever present in the silence of its women.

She's repression means that she is only able to express her sexuality within the confines of her mind, her fantasies cleverly intercut with her dull reality; the film begins with an extended shot of her licking her lips while staring directly into the camera, while the rest of the narrative is littered with dream sequences, bathed in red lighting, in which she is able to act out her deepest desires. The contrast created between these fantasies and the oppressive nature of the she-wolf's real existence – that dripping tap, those empty streets, endless days spent in a dreary office building – make clear that She should not be blamed for her horrifying actions later in the film; instead, it suggests that the society that surrounds her is stifling and suffocating her, forcing her to hide her true self until it erupts from within her in a flurry of violence.

The film's final transformation scene, in which that eruption finally occurs during a surreal sequence saturated in violet, blue and red, is therefore enormously important to communicating the film's themes. Like *Cat People* (1982) and *The Company of Wolves* (1984) before it, *Female Werewolf* does not have its protagonist go through a full bodily transformation, but rather depicts a demonic lupine creature literally bursting from her mouth: it emerges, fully formed, during a sexual encounter with her second victim. By choosing to depict its werewolf as a separate being lurking inside the body of its troubled protagonist, *Female Werewolf* uses its transformation sequence as a final metaphor for repressed sexuality. The desires that She has suppressed finally surface, twisted into something violent and monstrous by the society that has forced her to conceal them. This metaphor becomes even more explicit when we finally hear the only words spoken throughout the entire film; as She leans over her victim's body, a harsh and distorted voice can be heard on the soundtrack. It hisses: 'Let it out.'

Wildling significantly intensifies the themes of patriarchal control and abuse evident in both *When Animals Dream* and *Female Werewolf*. It focuses on Anna (Bel Powley), a teenage girl who is forced to enter mainstream society after a childhood of seclusion under the care of Gabriel Hansen (Brad Dourif), the man she thought was her biological father (and refers to as 'Daddy'). Having been brought up to believe she was being protected from a ferocious werewolf named a 'Wildling', Anna is eventually freed from captivity when she falls ill and her surrogate father attempts to commit suicide. After awakening in a hospital bed, she is taken in by the local Sheriff, Ellen Cooper (Liv Tyler), falls in love with Ellen's younger brother, Ray (Collin Kelley-Sordelet), and begins attending high school. But the teenager soon discovers that she herself is a werewolf (or Wildling); her 'father' is in fact a hunter who killed her biological mother. As she begins to go through a slow transformation, Anna finds herself hunted after she attacks and kills a would-be rapist. She flees north into open woodland and, eventually, finds peaceful seclusion in the snowbound wilderness.

Wildling establishes its concern with patriarchal oppression in its first few scenes, which detail Anna's childhood. Like Marie in *When Animals Dream*, Anna lives with a father figure who seeks to dominate her. Gabriel keeps Anna locked inside a shoddily decorated attic room filled with little more than a bed and a writing desk; the door is electrified, preventing escape. This desaturated room is all that Anna knows for the first sixteen years of her life: a prison in which her thoughts and actions are shaped by an overbearing patriarch. Anna's 'father' exerts his power over her in three ways. First, he makes her fearful of the outside world through his stories of the Wildling, leading Anna to have traumatic nightmares about the creature. Second, he uses hypnosis to reinforce these lies. Third, he uses leuprolide to quash her werewolfery. Importantly, this drug is an estrogen suppressant that Gabriel begins administering to his 'daughter' following her first period, communicating that here – just as in *When Animals Dream* and *Female Werewolf* – the she-wolf's apparent 'monstrosity' equates to sexuality. Like Thor in *When Animals Dream*, then, Gabriel wants to keep his 'daughter' under his authoritarian control, restrict her freedoms and prevent her from discovering her true nature.

Anna begins to encounter the workings of real-world patriarchy as soon as she wakes up in hospital – and resists male domination at every turn. First, she refuses to be sent to a psychiatric unit, quite literally standing up to a male doctor on her hospital bed. Then she witnesses Laurence Fowler (Mike Faist), a student at her high school, lifting a classmate's skirt in the street; shortly afterwards, she physically attacks Laurence and his friend Hugo (Keenan Jolliff) when she catches them harassing Ray. These instances of Anna refusing to be subordinated by men reach their apex when Laurence attempts to rape her after she has fled from a high-school party. Playing on the common conception of the werewolf as a symbol of masculine aggression, the film initially depicts Anna's attacker as the Wildling of her nightmares: a ferocious, lupine beast. It is only once she has torn out Laurence's throat that we realise he is the assailant: a stark metaphorical reminder that teenage boys can also be monsters. By the time Gabriel recovers from his injuries enough to find his 'daughter' and offer a lethal dose of the medication he gave to her in childhood, she refuses it – proving that she has finally broken free of his will.

As these events occur, Anna's sexuality begins to develop in tandem with her slow transformation into a Wildling. Once her body is no longer under the influence of leuprolide, her menstrual cycle resumes, her leg hair begins to grow, she takes an interest in feminine clothing and she experiences her first sexual attraction – she stares in fascination at Ray's naked body when she walks in on him in the shower. Meanwhile, her teeth fall out and are replaced by fangs, unnaturally coarse hair begins to grow on her back, and her nails develop into claws. It is important to the film's themes that Anna's awareness of patriarchy, her sexual maturity and her werewolfism all occur in tandem; as Sheriff Cooper tells her, Anna is becoming a woman – and she soon learns that becoming a woman means she will be abused, objectified and perceived as monstrous for any deviation from patriarchal norms.

In all three of the films in this cycle, in fact, werewolfism represents both overt female sexuality and a refusal to conform. In *When Animals Dream*, Marie desperately wants to break free of her repressed community; in *Female Werewolf*, She wants nothing more than to act on the desires that society has taught her to conceal; and in *Wildling*, Anna ultimately comes to reject stereotypical conceptions of femininity and embrace her difference. Initially, she is fascinated by what is traditionally feminine: as Sheriff Cooper teaches her to shave her legs (itself an act of conformity to gender norms), Anna stares longingly at Ellen's painted toenails, and soon after delights in wearing a yellow dress that her new guardian has bought for her. But it is while she is wearing that dress at a high-school party that her teeth fall out as her mouth gushes with blood, revealing that Anna is suppressing her true identity in order to conform to society's expectations of women.

In fact, it is only as it grows increasingly 'monstrous' that Anna comes to be comfortable with her body. Just as in *When Animals Dream*, a moment of realisation – that the young she-wolf is able to accept herself – occurs during a sex scene. Having fled into the woods to escape police investigating the death of her attempted rapist, Anna is alone until Ray sets out to find her. There, in the seclusion of the woodland, Anna kisses Ray and allows him to run his hand over the coarse hair growing from the bottom of her spine. Ray – like Daniel in *When Animals Dream* – is depicted positively because he accepts her individuality and difference. But, more importantly, this scene illustrates that Anna is finally at peace with herself: as Anna and Ray have sex, a wolf's howl can be heard on the soundtrack and the final stage of her transformation begins. It is notable that Anna's metamorphosis is irreversible: she will soon no longer be able to present herself as traditionally feminine – but, of course, she also no longer wants to.

From this moment onwards, Anna accepts her werewolfery (and, in metaphorical terms, her womanhood), and exacts her revenge on the men who have oppressed her. As a posse of hunters led by Gabriel enter the woods to track her down, Anna allows her animalistic instincts to take over. She ferociously attacks the men, and eventually kills her 'Daddy' in a cathartic scene that symbolises her final emancipation. Having fallen pregnant with a child from her encounter with Ray, she flees north. The final shot shows Anna standing on a mountainside, her baby in her arms, as she hears a howl in the distance – a suggestion that there are other Wildlings that have chosen, like her, to live outside of human (and thus patriarchal) society. Ultimately, then, as suggested by Bel Powley, *Wildling* is 'symbolic of what every girl goes through [and] the obstacles that society puts up against young girls when they grow into women'.[11]

When Animals Dream, *Female Werewolf* and *Wilding* are all staunchly progressive films that depict their werewolves as women who refuse to be silenced, controlled and abused; in this, they owe a great deal to *Werewolf Woman*. And, it must be noted, all three films are also indebted to the *Ginger Snaps* series, but they are far less problematic. For example, *Ginger Snaps* (2000) and *Ginger Snaps 2: Unleashed* (2004) suggest that monstrous women should be controlled with drugs; Brigitte attempts to medicate her sister before administering the same treatment to herself. The she-wolves of *When Animals Dream* and *Wildling*, on the other hand, reject any pharmaceutical solutions to their werewolfery (which are, importantly, forced upon them by men). This is because, unlike Ginger and Brigitte, the women central to these more recent she-wolf narratives do not see themselves – or their werewolfism – as monstrous. On the contrary, their transformations are representative of their refusal to be oppressed and their determination to express their feelings and desires without judgement or consequence. In the age of fourth-wave feminism, their werewolfism is something to be embraced: it represents not monstrosity, but emancipation.

Underdogs

Parallel to the she-wolf films of the 2010s, a second transnational cycle of werewolf films has been unified by an overarching thematic concern with the resurgence of fiscal and social conservatism in the twenty-first century. The films in this cycle were produced in three different countries – *Werewolf Fever* (2009) and *WolfCop* in Canada, *Bubba the Redneck Werewolf* and *Late Phases* in the United States and *Howl* (2015) in Britain – but all of them use the werewolf narrative to critique conservative ideology and particularly unchecked capitalism; they generally concentrate on the struggles of characters – and often werewolves – that are figured as distinctly working class. They can be further sub-divided by their approach to this theme; *Werewolf Fever*, *Bubba*

the Redneck Werewolf and *WolfCop* are all satirical horror-comedies, while
Howl and *Late Phases* strike a far more serious tone.

In many ways, these films are indebted to the community horror cycle
of the 1980s; they have a concern with conservative politics, social conservatism and economic disparity. The resurgence of such themes in contemporary genre cinema is not difficult to explain: these films emerge from
the years following the financial crisis of 2007–8 and the subsequent Great
Recession, a period defined by economic instability. The financial crisis
had two primary causes: the birth of free-market capitalism and irresponsible lending on the part of leading financial institutions in the United
States, largely in the form of mortgage loans that heavily outweighed
their assets. Leigh Gallagher suggests that this created an unsustainable
housing bubble.[12] As Peter Hough notes, 'When it became obvious that
banks had been lending sums far in excess of what they owned, businesses
lost confidence in them and the whole financial system was plunged into
chaos.'[13] The housing bubble burst, resulting in the worst global economic
downturn recorded since the 1930s.[14] The onset of the Great Recession
had several dire consequences. In the United States – during the Barack
Obama administration – unemployment doubled between December
2007 and February 2010;[15] foreclosures reached their highest ever levels
between 2009 and 2010;[16] and economic suicide rates accelerated, while
they reversed in the UK and Canada, where they had been in decline
before 2007.[17]

In Canada, the recession did not hit as hard as it did in either the United
States or the United Kingdom. However, the nation did experience an
increase in unemployment, a manufacturing crisis and an overall economic
decline.[18] In Saskatchewan, where *WolfCop* was produced, the mining, oil
and gas industries were most affected, creating a steady rise in unemployment.[19] The response of Stephen Harper's Conservative government was
to enforce austerity measures; Harper simultaneously introduced cuts to
taxes and public spending, openly expressing 'a commitment to leave as
much as possible to the private sector'.[20] Toby Sanger suggests that this
was not just a response to the recession, but a veiled attempt to further the
Conservative Party's pro-business agenda; he suggests that the government also used the country's economic troubles as a reason to introduce
measures to suppress wage rises and 'to further entrench a shift in the
national income away from labour to capital at the expense of stronger
economic growth'.[21] Harper's austerity measures, then, bolstered business
at the expense of Canada's working citizens.

The response in the United Kingdom was similar; in 2010, the Conservative Party won a parliamentary majority, following a campaign

heavily centred on a promise to reduce national debt and stabilise the UK economy in the aftermath of the financial crisis. Prime Minister David Cameron introduced a raft of austerity measures, making significant cuts to government support for local councils, public services and the welfare state. However, as Craig Berry states in his study of austerity in twenty-first century Britain, 'the most important implication of austerity is its success in generating the *illusion* of change in fiscal management, and shielding from scrutiny the considerable effort of policymakers to actually *prevent* change in the way that the UK economy operates'.[22] In short, Cameron used austerity in exactly the same way as Harper: to aid business and suppress labour.

In Canada, genre films attacked austerity politics through a style of cinema that Sarah Wharton refers to as 'neo-grindhouse'.[23] Neo-grindhouse, Wharton argues, 'shares characteristics of the style of films exhibited in grindhouse theatres through the 1970s and early 1980s'.[24] These are genre films that employ high-concept narratives, exaggerated performances and are, as Wharton suggests, particularly preoccupied with graphic sex and gratuitous violence.[25] In addition to these narrative and aesthetic elements, however, Canada's neo-grindhouse films often concentrate on downtrodden protagonists oppressed by capitalism; see, for example, *Hobo with a Shotgun* (2011), in which a homeless man (Rutger Hauer) goes to war with a rich and powerful gangster (Brian Downey), or *Turbo Kid* (2015), which sees a teenager (Munro Chambers) dethrone a tyrannical despot (Michael Ironside) who controls the water supply in a dystopian wasteland.

Several of the werewolf films produced in Canada during this period also employ the grindhouse style. *Werewolf Fever*, for example, concentrates on a group of Ontarian fast-food workers – Mandy (Heather Duthie), Sandy (Megan Fortier), Stubs (Kevin Norris), Frank (Richard Glasgow) and Ronny (Mark Singleton) – beset by a werewolf on the night of a full moon. The film is a horror-comedy with all the hallmarks of a neo-grindhouse film: its performances are exaggerated for comic effect; it contains scenes of gratuitous violence that border on the ludicrous; and it is filled with self-conscious dialogue ('toss the burgers or die, take your pick!'). It is also a satirical film that uses a story of workers besieged by a monster to critique a society in which business thrives while labour suffers.

The film's first act is dedicated to establishing that these workers are downtrodden and exploited as they are bullied and chastised by Odi Buckmeyer (Ian Lloyd), the owner of the 'Kingburger' drive-in restaurant. In the film's first ten minutes, Odi rebukes every single member of his staff for tiny transgressions: talking, taking a break, and even flipping burgers in a way not to his satisfaction. Odi's costume design is particularly telling. Dressed in a Stetson, bolo tie and giant belt buckle, he is dressed more like a Texan oil baron than the owner of a fast-food joint in Ontario: the picture of North American capitalism. Before he leaves his business for the night, he has ordered Ronny to mop up spilt cream, clean the inside of an industrial waste bin and even wipe his spit from the ground, and then orders all of his employees to remain at the restaurant after closing time to help Ronny's twin brother Donny (also played by Mark Singleton) unload a delivery later that night.

It is only because of Odi's immoral business practices, then, that his employees are still present in the restaurant when the werewolf attacks, having been forced to remain at the Kingburger against their will – a rather literal interpretation of a 'dead-end job'. Importantly, it is also because of the restaurant's owner that the werewolf attacks at all; at the beginning of the film, the owner sends Donny to fetch supplies and demands that he return within a few hours. Donny is so brainwashed by his belligerent employer that, even after he has been bitten by a werewolf out in the wilderness and turned into a ferocious creature, he dutifully returns to his workplace – illustrating that his unconscious mind is still driven by a need to work and thus survive.

There, he systematically tears through Sandy, Ronny and Frank, who all die in and around the building they despise. Perhaps the film's most cathartic moment arrives when Odi returns to reprimand his staff. As he screams at his employees, Donny tears Odi to pieces in an act of revenge against his greedy employer. Eventually the werewolf is destroyed, but the film's anti-corporate satire doesn't end with its demise. Stubs and Mandy – the only survivors – give in to their own greed and decide to sell 'wereburgers' using the monster's meat. Having now become unscrupulous capitalists themselves, they will soon be punished: the ending reveals that everyone who has consumed the werewolf's flesh will transform at the next full moon.

WolfCop also employs the neo-grindhouse style; the film's high concept revolves around an inept and alcoholic police officer (Leo Fafard) – named Lou Garou in a nod to the French *loup-garou* – working in the fictional Canadian city of Woodhaven. Lou is cursed with werewolfism when he is subjected to an occult ritual in secluded woodland and, after coming to terms with his affliction, becomes a werewolf vigilante: the eponymous 'WolfCop'. Like *Werewolf Fever*, *WolfCop* also features over-the-top performances, graphic gore and sexual imagery. Garou's first transformation, for example, sees a werewolf penis burst through his skin as he urinates, and the film features a comically prolonged sex scene involving the fully transformed WolfCop.

But *WolfCop*, too, tackles serious themes. As Lou drives his squad car through his town in the film's opening sequence, we see shuttered buildings, walls scrawled with graffiti and dishevelled citizens fighting on street corners. These are all pointed shots that establish Woodhaven as a deprived community; when Lou arrives at the police station, even its door is boarded up. Amongst these images of a broken town are shots of vibrant placards displayed in support of Mayor Bradley (Corinne Conley) and Terry Wallace (Ryland Alexander), candidates in Woodhaven's upcoming mayoral election, satirically suggesting that this community's local politicians – and, by extension, the Canadian government as a whole – are out of touch with the daily struggles of its working people. But at least one of the candidates wants to see a change; in a thinly veiled attack on Harper's pro-business rhetoric, a later scene sees Wallace tell the people of Woodhaven that their current mayor 'is more concerned with selling this town than with running it'.

A police officer – werewolf or otherwise – might seem like an odd choice of champion to fight for working people. Lou's profession would suggest that he is a member of the establishment himself – and it is worth pointing out that he fights crime in his uniform even in his transformed state (Figure 8.2). However, the most important elements of his character are his low status and, following his transformation into a werewolf, his vigilantism. As a low-ranking officer with little social capital, Lou's

Figure 8.2 In *WolfCop* (2014), vigilante werewolf Lou Garou (Leo Fafard) fights crime in his uniform even when transformed, but ultimately does not represent the establishment.

werewolfery lends him the courage he needs to defy his superiors, call out corruption and take matters into his own hands – or, in other words, stand up to the establishment he ostensibly represents. Of course, this is complicated by WolfCop's attacks on Woodhaven's criminal underclass. As writer-director Lowell Dean suggests, Lou is an 'anti-hero',[26] and he is initially willing to use any means necessary to clean up his town. But, importantly, he increasingly becomes aware that the crooks he is waging war on are puppets of far more insidious enemies.

For in *WolfCop* – just as in several of the community horror films of the 1980s – the real monsters in Woodhaven are its community leaders. By the film's end, Lou discovers that the town's criminal element is controlled by a group of humanoid shapeshifters who are posing as figures of authority; both Woodhaven's mayor and chief of police (Aidan Devine) are revealed to be among their number. These reptilian monsters are not only responsible for Lou's curse, but have used occult means to maintain their wealth and influence over several decades – and, in a potent metaphor for the exploitation of the working class by the financial elite, intend to sacrifice the werewolf during a blood moon to further increase their power. Thus Lou learns that he has been misdirecting his aggression and destroys the supernatural capitalists that have fostered an unequal society, blighted by destitution and criminality, to serve their own interests. The film's sequel, *Another WolfCop* (2017), continues to indict Harper's politics even after the end of his time in office; it pits WolfCop against a corrupt business-man and right-wing politician, Sydney Swallows (Yannick Brisson), who builds a new brewery in Woodhaven as a front for an alien invasion.

Bubba the Redneck Werewolf was made in America, but it shares its neo-grindhouse aesthetic and recessionary themes with *Werewolf Fever* and *WolfCop*. It follows Bubba (Chris Stephens), a working-class dog catcher living in the fictional Floridian town of Broken Taint. Tired of being a laughing stock, he signs away his soul to the Devil (Mitch Hyman) in exchange for power, strength, respect and a full head of hair – all things that he believes will help him to win back his high-school sweetheart, Bobbie Jo (Malone Thomas). But a deal with Satan is never that simple; he wakes up the next morning to find he has been permanently transformed into a werewolf (played by Fred Lass). The Devil then offers deals to people all over town, and Bubba is tasked with winning back their souls.

As its title would suggest, *Bubba the Redneck Werewolf* is in many ways purposely ridiculous: like both *Werewolf Fever* and *WolfCop*, it is played largely for comedy, but its thematic preoccupations are as unsubtle as its satirical humour. Bubba's working-class status is quickly established; the first shot we see of him is in his workplace, where he is feeding dogs in cages. Shortly afterwards, we see him accidentally rest his head in dog faeces, before – in an echo of *Werewolf Fever* – he is chastised by his boss (Karen Poulsen) for his apparent laziness and stupidity. In between these two scenes is a credit sequence, set to a bluegrass song that works to further entrench the character's social and economic status:

> Imagine now, if you will, a man of meagre means
> Who stumbled across lycanthropy
> But he don't know what that means!

Bubba, then, is a low-paid working man with very few prospects. The Devil, on the other hand, is here firmly associated with the financial elite: when he first appears to Bubba, he is wearing a sharp suit and tie (in stark contrast to Bubba's vest, baseball cap and ripped flannel shirt). Satan is explicitly referred to as a 'lawyer' in the film, but he actually shares more in common with a corrupt businessman; when Bubba seems reluctant to sell his soul, the Devil tempts him with superficial consumer goods designed to appeal to his desire for social status: a toaster, a smokeless ashtray and a potato peeler. By exploiting the working man's naïve materialism and employing deeply unethical sales patter, the Devil manages to manipulate his mark and close the deal.

The Devil's other victims, too, are explicitly framed as working class: his second is a butcher, his third a struggling single mother ('I just wanted my hubby back and the damn kids gone!'). And the film further aligns Satan with big business through a satirical television commercial, in which he declares: 'Hell is full, and so we're franchising!' In an echo of *WolfCop*, then, *Bubba the Redneck Werewolf* ultimately figures werewolfism as a blessing rather than a curse; it provides a working-class hero with the strength and courage he needs to be able to stand up to an antagonist representative of the wealthy elite – here quite literally depicted as the ultimate evil – that created the financial crisis by exploiting, manipulating and profiting from those at the bottom of the economic ladder.

Howl strikes a far more serious tone than the neo-grindhouse werewolf films of the 2010s, but it is thematically bound to them through a concern with capitalism and class – here in the context of austerity Britain. The film follows Joe (Ed Speleers), a young train guard working for the fictional 'Alpha Trax' rail service. At the beginning of the film, Joe is forced to work a double shift when a colleague calls in sick. He boards a train departing London at midnight, but it never reaches its destination. Under the light of a full moon, it comes to a halt in dense woodland, and Joe – along with his colleague Ellen (Holly Weston) and a diverse group of passengers – becomes trapped in the train as it is attacked by a pack of werewolves.

Howl establishes a concern with class long before its werewolves enter the narrative. Its opening follows Joe as he walks across a train platform; with his slumped shoulders and heavy eyelids, he is visibly overworked. He is also obviously desperate to improve his circumstances; he arrives at his locker to find a letter confirming that he has been denied a promotion, screwing it up in frustration. Like the protagonists of *Werewolf Fever*, *WolfCop* and *Bubba the Redneck Werewolf*, this is another modern werewolf film that focuses on a working-class character with few opportunities for advancement. And it is made abundantly clear, too, that Joe identifies with those living in financial hardship. Before agreeing to work a double shift, he is approached by David (Brett Goldstein) – who snidely reveals that he has been promoted to the supervisor position Joe applied for – and criticised for failing to issue penalty notices to passengers without a ticket. The implication here, of course, is that David is valued by his company for generating income from the poor and vulnerable, while Joe's compassion ensures that he will be kept in a low-paid position.

The film then establishes a class hierarchy within the train carriages where its main action takes place, and saves much of its ire for those of status and privilege. It does this firstly by illustrating how the wealthier passengers interact with Joe as he checks their tickets: Kate (Shauna Macdonald), a stressed businesswoman, belittles him when he issues her with a penalty fare ('why don't you get a proper job?'); Nina (Rosie Day), an entitled teenage socialite, treats him with utter contempt; Ged (Duncan Preston) and Jenny (Ania Marson), a retired upper-class couple respectively dressed in a sharp three-piece suit and a fur-lined coat, look on in silence as Nina insults him; and Adrian (Elliot Cowan), an arrogant middle-aged city worker, ignores him completely. Importantly, most of these characters do very little but panic when the werewolves attack. The apparent leaders of British society are quickly proven to be utterly ineffectual, and all of them meet gruesome deaths before the film's end.

Adrian is the only one of these characters with any real agency – he forcefully tries to lead the group, but he is ultimately motivated only by self-interest. His character is, in fact, an embodiment of the film's overarching concern with austerity: as a man of wealth, power and status, he cares very little about the suffering of others. His efforts to ensure his own survival indirectly result in a number of deaths, and he frequently attempts to sacrifice other passengers; his most abhorrent act occurs when he throws Kate to the werewolves to save himself. As he says to Joe (in a line of dialogue that reveals his classist attitudes), he views the situation as nothing other than 'survival of the fittest'. In contrast, the film's less privileged characters – primarily Joe, Ellen and trainee engineer Billy (Sam Gittins) – proactively work together in the hope of getting the entire group to safety. *Howl* suggests, then, that the working class strive for the betterment of their entire community, while the elite serve only themselves.

However, the film does not just punish its wealthy characters: Billy is dead before the climax, for example, as are Paul (Calvin Dean), a drunken football fan, and Matthew (Amit Shah), a shy young professional. *Howl*'s werewolves kill indiscriminately, which might seem to undermine the film's class commentary. But, in fact, its creatures are perhaps the most important contributor to its themes – and the reason for this lies in their departure from established werewolf lore. When the group kills the first werewolf to break into their carriage, *Howl* reveals that the nature of its creatures differs from tradition in two ways. First, it frames werewolfism as a disease rather than a supernatural affliction (as Matthew suggests, 'Perhaps it's a disease, like a mutation'). Second, as is revealed when the group notices that the creature is wearing a wedding ring ('It used to be like us,' Joe comments), its werewolves irreversibly transform into monsters, becoming increasingly lupine over time. In fact, its werewolves pointedly appear more human than wolf (Figure 8.3).

These werewolves are outcasts who have contracted a terrible disease and retreated to the wilderness, their human characteristics functioning as a reminder that they were once ordinary people. *Howl*'s pack thus represents an economic group of its own in the film's microcosm of austerity Britain: a disenfranchised underclass wilfully ignored by mainstream society. They function, then, as a particularly potent metaphor for austerity's victims: those who have found themselves unemployed, destitute, homeless or dependent on food banks as a direct result of cuts to public spending – and those who

Figure 8.3 In *Howl* (2015), werewolves slowly transform into monsters over a prolonged period of time, giving them a distinctly human appearance.

have died as a direct result of government policy.[27] As is shown explicitly in the film, these creatures eat their victims; the reason they kill indiscriminately, then, is simply because they are starving. While there is certainly a hierarchy amongst those on board the train, none of them represent those at the very bottom of the economic ladder; that role is filled by the film's 'monsters'. Apart from their hulking alpha male – the first werewolf to enter the train – they are gaunt and malnourished creatures, their bones visible through their skin.

The film's final indictment of austerity politics comes at its climax. With the vast majority of the train's passengers dead, Joe sacrifices himself for Ellen and is bitten by one of the creatures. Sometime after sunrise, Adrian encounters a partially transformed Joe in the woods, his humanity lost. The implication of this ending is enormously important to the film's indictment of Cameron's Britain: Joe, who at the narrative's beginning is desperately worried for his financial security and long-term prospects, has – perhaps inevitably – become a monster by its end. In this, *Howl* suggests that working people are never far away from becoming just another victim of austerity: 'It used to be like us.'

The American *Late Phases* also arises, at least in part, from a recessionary context. It concentrates on a blind Vietnam veteran, Ambrose McKinley (Nick Damici), as he transitions to life in a retirement community following the death of his wife. Bitter, dysfunctional and disconnected from his son Will (Ethan Embry), Ambrose resists the move even before he discovers that Crescent Bay is the feeding ground for a werewolf; on his first night in his new home, both his neighbour, Dolores (Karen Lynn Gorney), and his guide dog, Shadow, are slaughtered by a towering lupine creature. The film then sees Ambrose use the last of his savings to purchase a tombstone for Shadow and enough silver bullets to wage all-out war on the werewolf when it returns on the night of the next full moon.

Ambrose is an ageing man on the verge of destitution who has lost all will to live. While there are many reasons for his desire to die, it is definitively connected with his financial situation on several occasions throughout the film – including in its very first scene, where he is bartering with a sardonic salesman, O'Brien (Larry Fessenden), for a gravestone. As the veteran attempts to negotiate on price, it becomes apparent that he is a man of meagre means; even the cheapest options are more than he can afford. We discover just how desperate his circumstances are when he returns to make a purchase later in the narrative. As he picks out a grandiose stone cross for Shadow, Will pleads with him to reconsider: 'You don't have that much money left, okay? I mean, how can you justify spending it all on a headstone?' The answer is because Ambrose doesn't intend on living for much longer – and, as these scenes reveal, his descent into poverty is a primary reason for that.

The film also attacks fiscal inequality in America through its depiction of Crescent Bay, a community largely occupied by wealthy retirees. On the surface, it is perfect: a quiet village filled with well-tended gardens and quaint wooden houses. But it is quickly revealed that its residents ostracise anyone of low economic status. On his first day, Ambrose is visited by three of the community's leaders: Emma (Caitlin O'Heaney), Gloria (Rutanya Alda) and Clarissa (Tina Louise). All three of these women are dressed in clothing that identifies them as members of the elite (fashionable dresses, grandiose sunhats and pearl necklaces), and they immediately take offense at Ambrose's uncouth manner. When he later visits Gloria in her well-kept home, an immaculate house filled with antiques and expensive furniture, she calls the police as soon as he leaves – obviously desperate to distance herself from a man unbefitting of her lifestyle. Later, the elite women of Crescent Bay insist that Ambrose be barred from travelling on the shuttle bus that ferries them to church.

The werewolf lurking in Crescent Bay replicates their classist attitudes. While the village's wealthier occupants have clearly been living in the community unscathed for quite some time, dialogue reveals that at least one resident is killed every full moon. Its victims, the film subtly tells us, are those with the least financial means; when Ambrose first meets Dolores, she is raising money by selling her belongings from a stall on her front drive. And once the werewolf has gutted her later that evening, it sets its sights on Ambrose: the community's most recent resident, and perhaps its poorest. Like Emma, Gloria and Clarissa, the monster wants to maintain Crescent Bay as a haven for rich conservatives.

This is another film that borrows many of its narrative, aesthetic and thematic elements from the community horror cycle of the 1980s, and particularly from *Silver Bullet* (1985). In fact, writer Eric J. Stolze acknowledged this influence in an interview with *Collider*: 'I appreciated that they utilized that fundamental concealed identity of the werewolf to make it into this really interesting story of who in this town is not who they say they are?'[28] A connection between *Late Phases* and *Silver Bullet* is immediately apparent. Both films feature protagonists living with a disability attempting to uncover a werewolf's identity; both are mysteries in which the monster's true face is not revealed until the third act; both are set in seemingly idyllic rural American communities; and, above all, both ultimately reveal that their monsters are men of faith. *Late Phases* works to create this thematic connection to *Silver Bullet* as it hints that, as in the earlier film, the werewolf might be a religious leader: Father Roger Smith (Tom Noonan). However, the werewolf is not the pastor but a member of his flock: James Griffin (Lance Guest), a resident of the retirement community and, ostensibly, a staunch believer.

Late Phases, then, sets itself apart from the rest of the films in this cycle in that it is not just concerned with fiscal conservatism, but also with social and religious conservatism. Just as on the surface Crescent Bay appears to be an idyllic community, Griffin presents the image of a charitable and committed Christian: for example, he drives Ambrose to church after he is removed from the bus service. But beneath Griffin's civilised veneer dwells a monster who feeds on his less fortunate neighbours. And, like *Silver Bullet*'s Reverend Lowe, while he would like to appear remorseful (he claims to be carrying out 'acts of contrition' by torturing himself), even in human form he is willing to indulge terrible impulses. When he begins to fear that Ambrose might kill him as the full moon approaches, Griffin reveals his true nature when he infects several of his wealthy neighbours to ensure that the veteran will be outnumbered, even leading two of his closest friends in a heartfelt prayer before biting them. *Late Phases* thus uses the dual nature of the werewolf to allegorise the falsehood of religious fanaticism, suggesting that just as a wolf can hide beneath human skin, faith can conceal an insidious agenda. This idea is literalised in the film's transformation scene, which sees Griffin tear away his human flesh to reveal the demonic creature beneath.

Late Phases thus attacks the central pillars of conservative America: capitalism, the church and, through its tragic protagonist, militarism. Ambrose is a man who has been both physically and mentally scarred by a life of service and an existence defined by violence and discipline. He finds it impossible to maintain a relationship with his son, and has lost any faith he might once have had (as he tells Father Smith, 'God don't want anything to do with me, Father, and I don't want anything to do with Him'). In addition to his financial insecurity, Ambrose's scars have given him a death wish; in buying a tombstone, he is declaring his steadfast determination to kill or be killed – or, as it transpires at the climax, both.

By the film's end – following a violent battle – Ambrose, Griffin and several of Crescent Bay's residents are all lying dead in its idyllic streets and gardens, and *Late Phases* has come to deconstruct every foundation of American conservatism. In this, *Late Phases* is one of the most interesting and multifaceted American werewolf films of the Obama era. In its indictment of fiscal inequality, rampant militarism and religious fundamentalism, it is the product of a period in the nation's history defined by the Great Recession, the ongoing War on Terror and the resurgence of populist conservatism in the years building up to the 2016 presidential election – which, of course, would see America embrace Donald Trump and the openly right-wing ideologies espoused by his administration.

The modern werewolf film, then, has continued to adapt to new social, cultural and political contexts in the twenty-first century. The case studies discussed here – a handful of the dozens of werewolf films produced since the year 2000 – have engaged with a range of issues, including 9/11 and the War on Terror, gender politics, the Great Recession and resurgent conservatism. Several of these thematic preoccupations have transnational relevance, and thus are evident in werewolf films produced by several indigenous film industries. It is likely that, as we move into the 2020s, the werewolf will increasingly proliferate in international horror cinema – and continue to transform with its times.

Conclusion: Who's Afraid of the Big Bad Wolf?

As explored in the introduction to this book, studies of the cinematic werewolf have often associated the creature with the concept of the beast within. With the exception of a handful of examples – notably *I Was a Teenage Werewolf* (1957), *An American Werewolf in London* (1981) and particularly *Ginger Snaps* (2000) – the majority of werewolf films have yet to be discussed outside of this framework, and few studies have paid attention to the cultural dimensions of the creature. This study has been designed to show that the werewolf does not always need to be understood as a psychologised monster; it can also be interpreted as a product of its historical moment. My aim here has been to establish a cultural understanding of one of our oldest and most enduring monsters as a diverse and constantly transforming metaphor – one that has come to carry many different meanings over the last century.

Alternative approaches to the werewolf film are needed now perhaps more than ever before, if only to encourage further scholarship; while there has been a renewed interest in werewolves in recent years, their place in cinema remains a neglected area of study. For example, the most recent work on the subject, *In the Company of Wolves: Werewolves, Wolves, and Wild Children* (2020), contains scant material on film and television.[1] This is a common phenomenon. A 2016 special issue of online journal *Revenant* dedicated to the werewolf features only one piece on werewolf films amongst its nine articles.[2] In 2019, *Gothic Studies* dedicated a special issue to 'Werewolves and Wildness'; it also offers only one article on cinema, which discusses the figure of the feral child rather than the werewolf.[3] The edited collection *Werewolves, Wolves and the Gothic* (2017) contains two pieces focused on screen media; of those, one concentrates on *Ginger Snaps* – increasingly the most studied werewolf film – while Hannah Priest's contribution analyses a number of films and television shows, principally *The Wolf Man* (1941) and *An American Werewolf in London*.

But Priest's contribution is symptomatic of a sort of pack mentality in the scholarly study of the werewolf that also suggests there is a need to propose new ways of studying the monster: it perpetuates Chantal Bourgault du Coudray's notion that modern werewolf media primarily articulates a fear of repressed masculine aggression.[4] The chapter suggests that the male werewolf is doomed to become a symbol of the 'grotesque, disfigured and impotent masculine' through the werewolf's bite, which Priest argues is a metaphor for paternal inheritance of damaging male traits.[5] This is an interesting reading of the werewolf in cinema – and one that resonates with my own analyses of films such as *The Boy Who Cried Werewolf* (1973), *Bad Moon* (1996) and *Big Bad Wolf* (2006) – but what is often missing from such discussions is a sense of historical context. And, furthermore, there is still a commonly held assumption that werewolves are simply not capable of communicating any other theme. For example, in Carys Crossen's *The Nature of the Beast: Transformations of the Werewolf from the 1970s to the Twenty-First Century* (2019), the author suggests:

> The cinematic werewolf differs from the contemporary werewolf in fiction in that it is unable to move beyond this inheritance and the past. The cinematic werewolf is still trapped in the classic representation of the werewolf as a (male) monster continually at war with itself, unable to find a socially acceptable form of masculinity. And also, as in fiction the cinematic werewolf has never been able to compete with the vampire in terms of popularity, and there are simply fewer films produced about werewolves, still fewer that allow for any kind of innovation concerning their lycanthropes.[6]

This statement is refuted by the numerous case studies provided here, and it is puzzling given that Crossen states, a few pages earlier, that the 'risk of being fatally reductive in labelling the werewolf as merely the beast within, in cultural and critical terms, is more than apparent'.[7] And there is mounting evidence that this traditional conception of the werewolf as a manifestation of the beast within has not only taken hold in the academy, but is now beginning to filter out of academic discourse and into critical and popular discussions of the werewolf's place in contemporary media. For example, in the introduction I draw attention to Craig Anderson's article for what has historically been one of the most popular magazines for fans of horror cinema, *Fangoria*. The piece – titled 'Where Are the Wolves?' – examines the apparently low critical reputation of werewolf films in the twenty-first century, attempts to posit several explanations for a seeming lack of quality in films featuring the monster, and interviews several individuals – including *WolfCop* (2014) director Lowell Dean – to obtain their opinions on the subject.

Anderson begins with a nostalgic musing on the many qualities of *An American Werewolf in London* and *The Howling* (1981), before pointing out that Universal Pictures chose to follow a marginally successful werewolf film, *The Wolfman* (2010), with a poorly reviewed straight-to-video effort: *Werewolf: The Beast Among Us* (2012). Shortly before Anderson asks whether the monster is 'infertile', its apparent meaning – a 'conflicting nature' derivative of Jekyll and Hyde – having proven too limiting for contemporary filmmakers, he asks 'are werewolves, as central characters, passé, particularly when it concerns the more well-heeled companies?' He continues: 'And, as horror-movie content often tends to reflect generalized cultural fears in a given time, are current phobias – such as the media-generated panic around viral pandemics – holding sway, and the ancient and once legitimate fear of wolves – along with the expansive mythology behind them – simply not all that salient anymore?'[8]

Anderson argues that although the werewolf has been prolific in the twenty-first century (and he is correct, as its popularity as a subject for horror cinema has exploded since the year 2000), the overall quality of the werewolf film has declined. This book, of course, is not concerned with determining the aesthetic value of werewolf cinema and explores many meanings for the monster beyond an apparently 'conflicting nature'.[9] However, in regard to the werewolf's cultural significance, Anderson's questions do reveal something of great importance to this study: as a critic of horror films and a contributor to a popular publication dedicated to the genre, Anderson assumes the werewolf's status as a limited metaphor – little more than an extension of the Jekyll and Hyde story – and suggests that it is simply not relevant to the contemporary cultural moment. It would seem, then, that the view of the werewolf as beast within has entered into popular discourse on the horror film. The notion is so ingrained, in fact, that it seems unfathomable to Anderson that the werewolf might have multiple meanings in multiple contexts. This is an idea, then, that has been perpetuated both in scholarly work and in more mainstream writing on horror. Even Dean – the director of a werewolf film with a rich subtext relevant to its historical moment – compares the werewolf to Jekyll and Hyde, suggesting that it is essentially a 'dual identity character'.[10]

Anderson's suggestion that the werewolf has become 'passé' has been reinforced by critics and scholars alike; Anne Billson's remark that the werewolf is 'basically just the beast within' in an article for *The Guardian* is just one example.[11] Similarly, in his study of films adapted from Stephen King's work, Mark Browning opens his discussion of *Silver Bullet* (1985) with a diatribe on the werewolf film, stating 'in cinematic terms the werewolf subgenre seems all but played out . . . anachronistic and largely exhausted'.[12]

Writing in 2009, he draws attention to the critical and commercial failure of films such as *An American Werewolf in Paris* (1997) and *Cursed* (2005) to prove the werewolf's irrelevance in modern times.

Of course, Browning's argument is problematic; he claims that the werewolf film has become 'exhausted' in recent years, and then applies the same logic to *Silver Bullet*, a picture released only four years after *An American Werewolf in London* and *The Howling*, two of the most highly regarded of all werewolf movies. Nonetheless, he expresses an opinion that is in step with comments made by Anderson, Billson and Crossen in their assessments of the monster's place in contemporary popular culture: that the cinematic werewolf has limited metaphorical potential. This is unfortunate. After all, for every contemporary werewolf film that embraces period settings and gothic aesthetics (see *Romasanta: The Werewolf Hunt* [2004], *The Wolfman*, *Red Riding Hood* [2011] or *Werewolf: The Beast Among Us*) or veers into spoof or pastiche (see *Cursed*, *House of the Wolf Man* [2009] or *The Snarling* [2018]), there is another that updates the monster for ever-changing times and new cultural contexts.

This study, then, has primarily aimed to illustrate that the werewolf is not, to borrow Anderson's phrases, 'passé' or 'infertile'. These terms are inextricably tied to the notion of the werewolf as the beast within. It is notable that the beast within relies entirely on conceptions of the cinematic werewolf as both protagonist and antagonist: Larry Talbot is also the Wolf Man; Tony Rivers is also a teenage werewolf; David Kessler is also an American werewolf in London. Although it is limiting to assume that these films are solely representative of the werewolf as a psychologised creature concerned with repressed masculine aggression, it is not difficult to see why such readings are popular: these films muddy the distinction between hero and monster, and pit their central characters against the creatures that dwell inside of them. However, these readings fail to account for films featuring she-wolves – which can perhaps explain the growing body of work on *Ginger Snaps* – and werewolf films that cast their monsters as villains. For example, in *The Howling* (and many of its sequels), *Silver Bullet*, *Dog Soldiers* (2002), *Big Bad Wolf* and *Late Phases* (2014), werewolves are not framed as sympathetic, tortured souls but as ravenous monsters to be defeated by human adversaries. Clearly, there are many werewolf films to which the concept of the beast within simply does not apply.

That is not to say that the werewolf film has never expressed a fear of unchecked masculine aggression or sexual violence; it would be exceptionally problematic to make such a claim and many of the case studies here would refute it. But any analysis of films in which these themes are apparent is deeply enriched by an understanding of cultural context. *Wolf* (1994) serves as a pertinent example: a film about an ageing man choosing to embrace typically masculine traits in order to take control of his life (and having to face the consequences of that decision), it clearly engages with the notion of the werewolf as beast within. But it is also a product of its time – one that arises from a culture deeply concerned with changing perceptions of the masculine role and its depiction in popular media. Many other films discussed here that might be seen to articulate a generalised fear of the beast within are also bound to the cultural moment in which they were produced and received.

To reiterate just a few examples, *The Wolf Man*'s psychologised depiction of the werewolf can be interpreted as a manifestation of the horrors of war; *I Was a Teenage Werewolf*'s tale of adolescent revolt is inextricable from the moral panic surrounding the rise of teen culture in the 1950s; *An American Werewolf in London* plays on male monstrosity to explore tensions between popular perceptions of physical and mental illness in the early 1980s; and the grotesque sexual imagery in several Reaganite werewolf films can be linked to the era's conception of normative sexuality and the onset of the AIDS crisis. And, of course, an entire cycle of European werewolf films in the 1960s and 1970s is concerned with sexually aggressive monsters. From *The Curse of the Werewolf* (1961) to Paul Naschy's many outings as the werewolf Waldemar Daninsky, all of these films have sexual subtexts. Yet they are not indicative of an overbearing obsession with masculine aggression in the werewolf film, but rather the cultural consequences of the sexual revolution; the werewolf becomes a figure through which to explore – and, in some cases, to condemn – the societal changes ushered in by significant shifts in Western conceptions of male and female sexuality.

Furthermore, the evidence provided here would suggest that above and beyond the beast within, the werewolf film's most enduring thematic preoccupation is with youth culture and the many cultural, social and political issues that surround it. Since the release of *I Was a Teenage Werewolf*, this has been a consistent theme across the countercultural films of the 1970s, the teen wolf revival of the 1980s, the pack films of the 1990s and the youth-orientated werewolf films of the twenty-first century. *The Wolf Man* is often cited as the progenitor of the modern werewolf myth, and Curt Siodmak certainly popularised – even canonised – many of the werewolf film's generic tropes: the idea that a werewolf's transformations are tied to a full moon; that it can be destroyed with silver; that metamorphosis is a source of pain, stress and anguish for the afflicted individual. But in thematic terms, *I Was a Teenage Werewolf* has proven to be the more influential film. Its story of a teenager refusing to play by society's rules while literally transforming into a wild animal paved the way for the likes of *Werewolves on Wheels* (1971), *The Boy Who Cried Werewolf, Full Moon High* (1981), *Teen Wolf* (1985), *Teen Wolf Too* (1987), *An American Werewolf in Paris, Ginger Snaps, Ginger Snaps 2: Unleashed* (2004), *Big Bad Wolf, Blood and Chocolate* (2007), *The Howling: Reborn* (2011), *When Animals Dream* (2014), *Wolves* (2014) and *Wildling* (2018).

As a versatile and ever-evolving metaphor, the werewolf has also expressed cultural fears related to: racial tension and xenophobia; war, weapons development and the military-industrial complex; nuclear annihilation; identity politics; the rise of the counterculture, Vietnam and Watergate; infection and disease; and economics, conservative values and social injustice. The werewolf film has addressed issues that range from the national to the global and can often be interpreted from progressive, conservative or neutral points of view. That the werewolf has been reimagined in so many different contexts and in relation to numerous ideological and cultural shifts is the best evidence that it is a monster with vast potential as a cultural metaphor.

This study has provided an indication of that potential, but there are many more werewolf narratives still to explore. For the sake of brevity and to allow for adequate discussion of case studies, the history of werewolf cinema constructed here is comprehensive but not exhaustive; there are a number of films that remain unexplored in this book, particularly in the twenty-first century. While I have endeavoured to cover some of the most interesting werewolf movies produced since the turn of the millennium, there are a great many films still in need of cultural analysis – and yet more that are set to be released in 2020 and beyond, including the American *Hunter's Moon* and *I Am Lisa*, the Canadian *Bloodthirsty*, the French *Teddy* and Andy Muschietti's remake of *The Howling* for Netflix.[13] Perhaps, then, a comprehensive study of the werewolf film in the twenty-first century is needed to shed further light on what exactly the monster has meant to us since the release of *Ginger Snaps* in 2000.

This book also concentrates exclusively on case studies produced in North America and Europe, the parts of the world that have traditionally been the most prolific consumers of werewolf fiction. But werewolf films have also been produced by indigenous film industries all over the world. What is the cultural context of, to provide just a few examples, Mexico's *The She-Wolf* (1965), Japan's *Wolf Guy* (1975), Thailand's *Werewolf* (1987), India's *Junoon* (1992) or Brazil's *Good Manners* (2017)? While nations outside of North America and Europe may not have produced concentrated and sustained cycles of werewolf movies, these individual films are nonetheless extremely interesting and deserving of cultural analysis. Further study of these films and others like them would reveal a great deal about the creature's varied meanings across a number of specific national contexts, and thus enrich our understanding of the werewolf narrative as a whole.

Furthermore, there are many cinematic werewolf narratives to be found beyond the realms of the horror film. This book has investigated some of them in analysing teen-orientated comedies such as *Full Moon High*, *Teen Wolf* and *Teen Wolf Too*, for example; these are films that have drawn on narrative and aesthetic elements traditionally associated with horror cinema, but transferred them into very different generic contexts. There are many more examples to be found in fantasy, romance and action-adventure films such as *Van Helsing* (2004), *Red Riding Hood*, the *Harry Potter* series (2001–11), the *Twilight* saga (2008–12), the *Chronicles of Narnia* adaptations (2005–10) and *The Mortal Instruments: City of Bones* (2013). There is still much work to be done, then, before the werewolf film is understood in the same way that the academy has come to understand the cinematic vampire or zombie genres.

And, of course, the werewolf is now increasingly present in other forms of screen media and particularly television. While this book has covered a handful of movies produced for television broadcast, space has not allowed for a discussion of the vast number of live-action shows and animated series to feature werewolves, including (but not limited to) *The Munsters* (1964–66), *Dark Shadows* (1968–71), *Kolchak: The Nightstalker* (1974–5), *Fangface* (1978–80), *Tales from the Darkside* (1983–8), *Teen Wolf* (1986–7), *Werewolf* (1987–8), *Monsters* (1988–91), *Tales from the Crypt* (1989–96), *She-Wolf of London* (1990–1), *Eerie, Indiana* (1991–2), *Are You Afraid of the Dark?* (1992–2000), *The X-Files* (1993–2018), *Goosebumps* (1995–8), *The Nightmare Room* (2000–1), *Buffy the Vampire Slayer* (1997–2003), *Angel* (1999–2004), *Big Wolf on Campus* (1999–2002), *Wolf Lake* (2001), *Supernatural* (2005–20), *Doctor Who* (2005–), *Being Human* (2008–13) and its 2011 American remake, *True Blood* (2008–14), *Fear Itself* (2008), *The Vampire Diaries* (2009–17), *Teen Wolf* (2011–17), *Death Valley* (2011), *Wolfblood* (2012–17), *Hemlock Grove* (2013–15), *The Originals* (2013–18), *Penny Dreadful* (2014–16), *Bitten* (2014–16), *The Order* (2018–), *Wellington Paranormal* (2018–), *What We Do in the Shadows* (2019–) and *Creepshow* (2019–).

There are many werewolf narratives left to explore before we will fully understand the lupine monster's cultural dimensions: contemporary werewolf films, the international werewolf film, the fantasy werewolf and the werewolf on television are particularly interesting areas for further study. For my part, it has been my aim to offer a new approach to cinematic

werewolves. In doing so, I have constructed the broadest cultural history
for the werewolf film possible within the confines of a single monograph.
This study covers films made over a century on two continents, and often
provides multiple interpretations of given films in relation to their historical moment. For example, *The Howling* could be read as a conservative
film at the point of consumption: it contains several scenes that explicitly
link sex and monstrosity at a time in American history when dominant
conceptions of sexuality were changing. However, given the thematic preoccupations of John Sayles and Joe Dante, the film is clearly satire: an
indictment of the increasingly capitalist psychotherapy industry. It has
been my aim, then, to provide the clearest possible view of the werewolf
film's cultural significance by exploring a multiplicity of meanings where
appropriate.

   To further explore the werewolf film as a product of its historical
moment, the analyses contained in this study are often accompanied by
investigations of the values held by the individuals involved in producing them. This has sometimes been achieved through direct commentary, as in the case of John Landis's comments on *An American Werewolf
in London*, and sometimes through a consideration of how a film relates
to their body of work. In the case of *Werewolf of London* (1935) and *The
Howling*, for example, the wider thematic preoccupations of the films'
screenwriters have informed my analyses. In some cases, this has both
complicated and enriched a discussion of a given film in relation to its
immediate cultural moment. See *An American Werewolf in London*, a film
written by its creator as a personal response to a brush with the supernatural, but released a decade later in a specific context that colours its
meaning – even for Landis, who has come to look back on the film as one
tied up in a culture consumed by a fear of disease.

   I have also endeavoured to identify connections between individual
films in order to create a clear picture of thematic cycles and the cultural, social and political landscapes in which they were produced and
released. This has revealed that the werewolf has experienced a number
of dramatic revisions over a period of more than 100 years: silent werewolf cinema is preoccupied with skinwalkers and Native American myth;
the she-wolf cycle of the 1940s arises from shifting gender politics during wartime; the monstrous new werewolf of the 1980s is a product of
changing perceptions of disease, physical health and mental wellbeing;
and the first cycle of pack films engages with a rising fear of criminal
youth. So while individual werewolf films can tell us a great deal about
their cultural moment, the larger shifts in the depiction of wolf-men and
she-wolves across several decades are equally revealing.

The werewolf is one of civilisation's oldest mythical monsters. Like the vampire, zombie or Frankenstein's monster, it has evolved over many years, in various incarnations and in several media to function as an ample metaphor for any number of social, cultural or political issues in relation to a specific historical moment. Unlike those other monsters, though, the study of the werewolf has been slowed by a widely held assumption regarding its limitations. However, this has begun to change over the last decade. Bourgault du Coudray's *The Curse of the Werewolf: Fantasy, Horror and the Beast Within* (2006) remains the major touchstone for writers with an interest in werewolves and pop culture, but scholars have begun to propose alternative approaches to the monster since its publication.

Leslie A. Sconduto's *Metamorphoses of the Werewolf: A Literary Study from Antiquity through the Renaissance* (2008) considers important examples of werewolf literature as the products of specific cultural moments; Kimberley McMahon-Coleman and Roslyn Weaver's *Werewolves and Other Shapeshifters in Popular Culture: A Thematic Analysis of Recent Depictions* (2012) considers the social and cultural significance of contemporary werewolf narratives; Matthew Beresford's *The White Devil: The Werewolf in European Culture* (2013) places the folkloric werewolf in historical and cultural context, as does Willem de Blécourt's edited collection *Werewolf Histories* (2015); Priest's edited collection *She-Wolf: A Cultural History of Female Werewolves* (2015) refocuses academic attention solely on werewolf women; and while Crossen's *The Nature of the Beast* unfortunately dismisses cinematic werewolf narratives for the most part, it does offer new and extremely illuminating interpretations of werewolves in literature.

These works are symptomatic of a renewed scholarly interest in werewolf fiction since the publication of *The Curse of the Werewolf*. *She-Wolf*, for example, was the result of the UK's first academic conference dedicated to the study of the werewolf. Titled 'Female Werewolves, Shapeshifters and Other Horrors in Art, Literature and Culture', the conference considered the diverse cultural meanings of she-wolves and took place on 9–10 September 2010. The papers presented there form the basis of Priest's collection, and included a keynote on the development and significance of the cinematic she-wolf by eminent horror scholar Peter Hutchings.

This first conference was followed by the University of Hertfordshire's 'The Company of Wolves – Sociality, Animality and Subjectivity in Literary and Cultural Narratives – Werewolves, Shapeshifters and Feral Humans', a three-day event held on 3–5 September 2015. A number of papers presented here reveal a slow but clear shift towards considering werewolf films in their historical and cultural contexts: Irene Baena-Cuder's paper places Spanish werewolf films – from Naschy to *Game of Werewolves* (2012) – in the context of Francisco Franco's fascist regime, and has since been published in the collection *Gender and Contemporary Horror in Film* (2019); Simon Brown's paper consciously moves away from the concept of the beast within to place *Silver Bullet* in the context of Stephen King's larger thematic concerns; and Colette Balmain's contribution suggests that the South Korean production *A Werewolf Boy* (2012) uses the werewolf to engage with residual national trauma related to the Korean War.[14]

It is clear that perceptions of the werewolf film are slowly beginning to change, and it is important that new approaches to the monster are found – particularly in film studies, where the continued dominance of the beast within seems to have stifled debate. The werewolf can be – is and has been – far more than the beast within. By analysing a century of werewolf films, this study has provided evidence that, from *The Werewolf* (1913) to *Wildling*, wolf-men and she-wolves are products of their time – ever-evolving monsters that can tell us a great deal about society's deepest cultural anxieties. 'Who's afraid of the big bad wolf?' is a question, then, with many answers. At the dawn of narrative cinema, the werewolf was used for an unfortunate purpose: to demonise the Native American, rendered superstitious strangers on their own land. It has since shifted across several decades, adapting to our deepest fears. Today, as the werewolf continues to transform in contemporary horror media, it has unbound potential.

Notes

Introduction

1. Anne Billson, 'The werewolf howls again', *The Guardian, Film and Music*, 5 February 2010, p. 7.
2. Reynold Humphries, *The American Horror Film: An Introduction* (Edinburgh: Edinburgh University Press, 2002), p. 21.
3. Ibid. p. 22.
4. James B. Twitchell, *Dreadful Pleasures: An Anatomy of Modern Horror* (Oxford and New York: Oxford University Press, 1985), p. 205.
5. Chantal Bourgault du Coudray, *The Curse of the Werewolf: Fantasy, Horror and the Beast Within* (London and New York: I. B. Tauris, 2006), p. 79.
6. Ibid. p. 81.
7. Ibid. p. 86.
8. Ibid. p. 1.
9. Leslie A. Sconduto. *Metamorphoses of the Werewolf: A Literary Study from Antiquity through the Renaissance* (Jefferson: McFarland, 2008), p. 7.
10. Sconduto, *Metamorphoses of the Werewolf*, p. 15.
11. Ibid. pp. 15–25.
12. Ibid. pp. 26–38.
13. Ibid. p. 30.
14. See: Daniel 4:33; Daniel 5:21 (KJV).
15. Sconduto, *Metamorphoses of the Werewolf*, pp. 39–56.
16. Ibid. pp. 57–75, 76–89, 90–126.
17. Brian P. Levack, *The Witch-Hunt in Early Modern Europe*, 3rd edn (Harlow: Pearson Education, 2006), p. 1.
18. Sconduto, *Metamorphoses of the Werewolf*, p. 128.
19. Ibid. p. 128.
20. Ibid. p. 128.
21. Ibid. p. 127.
22. Montague Summers, *The Werewolf in Lore and Legend* (Mineola: Dover Publications, 2003 [1933]), pp. 253–9.
23. Matthew Bunson, *The Vampire Encyclopedia* (New York: Gramercy Books, 2001), p. 279.
24. Ian Woodward, *The Werewolf Delusion* (London: Paddington Press, 1979), p. 12.

25. Paul E. Keck et al., 'Lycanthropy: alive and well in the twentieth century', *Psychological Medicine* 18, no. 1 (1988): 113.

26. Woodward, *The Werewolf Delusion*, p. 2.

27. Sabine Baring-Gould, *The Book of Werewolves* (London: Senate, 1995 [1865]), p. 31.

28. Woodward, *The Werewolf Delusion*, p. 11.

29. Bourgault du Coudray, *The Curse of the Werewolf*, p. 2.

30. Ibid. p. 14.

31. Ibid. p. 44.

32. Ibid. p. 54.

33. Ibid. p. 53.

34. Ibid. p. 53

35. Ibid. p. 65.

36. Ibid. p. 6.

37. Ibid. pp. 47–9.

38. Stefan Dziemianowicz, 'The werewolf', in S. T. Joshi (ed.), *Icons of Horror and the Supernatural: An Encyclopedia of Our Worst Nightmares*, vols 1 and 2 (Westport, CT: Greenwood Press, 2007), p. 658.

39. Ibid. p. 659.

40. Billson, 'The werewolf howls again', p. 7.

41. Craig Anderson, 'Where are the wolves?: with their rich history on screen, we should be seeing lycanthropes there more often', *Fangoria* 329 (2014): 74.

42. Willem de Blécourt (ed.), *Werewolf Histories* (New York: Palgrave Macmillan, 2015).

43. David J. Skal, *The Monster Show: A Cultural History of Horror* (London: Plexus Publishing, 1994), 211–18.

44. See: Peter Biskind, *Seeing Is Believing: Or How Hollywood Taught Us to Stop Worrying and Love the Fifties* (New York: Pantheon Books, 1983), pp. 217–23; Mark Jancovich, *Rational Fears: American Horror in the 1950s* (Manchester: Manchester University Press, 1996), pp. 207–12.

45. See: Robert Spadoni, 'Strange botany in *Werewolf of London*', *Horror Studies* 1, no. 1 (2010): 49–71; Simon Bacon, 'Dirty, wild beasts! Representations of the homeless as werewolves in films from *Werewolf of London* (1935) to *Underworld: Rise of the Lycans* (2009)', *Revenant* 2 (2016): 73–90; Lorna Jowett, 'White trash in wife-beaters? U.S. Television werewolves, gender, and class', in Linda Belau and Kimberley Jackson (eds), *Horror Television in the Age of Consumption: Binging on Fear* (New York: Routledge, 2018), pp. 76–89.

46. See: Brigid Cherry, *Horror* (New York: Routledge, 2009), pp. 167–211; Adam Lowenstein, *Shocking Representation: Historical Trauma, National Cinema, and the Modern Horror Film* (New York: Columbia University Press, 2005), pp. 1–16.

47. Andrew Tudor, 'Why horror? The peculiar pleasures of a popular genre', in Mark Jancovich (ed.), *Horror the Film Reader* (New York: Routledge, 2002), p. 50.

48. Andrew Tudor, *Monsters and Mad Scientists: A Cultural History of the Horror Movie* (Oxford: Blackwell, 1989), p. 1.
49. See: Biskind, *Seeing Is Believing*, pp. 217–23; Jancovich, *Rational Fears*, pp. 207–12.
50. Andrew Tudor, *Decoding Culture: Theory and Method in Cultural Studies* (Thousand Oaks: SAGE Publications, 1999), p. 194.
51. Andrew Tudor, 'Sociology and film', in John Hill and Pamela Church Gibson (eds), *Film Studies: Critical Approaches* (Oxford: Oxford University Press, 2000), p. 192.

Chapter 1

1. Stephen Jones, *The Essential Monster Movie Guide* (New York: Billboard Books, 2000), p. 409.
2. See: Anon., 'Data from manufacturers' list of releases', *Motion Picture News*, 29 October 1913, p. 58; Anon., 'Releases', *New York Clipper*, 12 December 1913, p. 10.
3. See: Jeremy Dyson, *Bright Darkness: The Lost Art of the Supernatural Horror Film* (London: Cassell, 1997), p. 2; James B. Twitchell, *Dreadful Pleasures: An Anatomy of Modern Horror* (Oxford and New York: Oxford University Press, 1985), p. 216.
4. Anon., 'Punished for hundred year old crime', *Universal Weekly* 3, no. 24 (1913): 16.
5. Ibid. p. 16.
6. Stephen Jones, *The Essential Monster Movie Guide*, p. 410.
7. Anon., 'Nestor – *The White Wolf*', *Moving Picture World* 21, no. 13 (1914): 1818.
8. Stefan Dziemianowicz, 'The werewolf', in S. T. Joshi (ed.), *Icons of Horror and the Supernatural: An Encyclopedia of Our Worst Nightmares*, vols 1 and 2 (Westport, CT: Greenwood Press, 2007), p. 660.
9. Angela Aleiss, *Making the White Man's Indian: Native Americans and Hollywood Movies* (Westport, CT: Praeger, 2005), pp. 2–4.
10. Dziemianowicz, 'The werewolf', p. 9.
11. Jones, *The Essential Monster Movie Guide*, p. 409.
12. Aleiss, *Making the White Man's Indian*, p. 4.
13. Anon., 'Punished for hundred year old crime', p. 16.
14. Andrew Tudor, *Monsters and Mad Scientists: A Cultural History of the Horror Movie* (Oxford: Blackwell, 1989), p. 98.
15. Robert Spadoni, 'Strange botany in *Werewolf of London*', *Horror Studies* 1, no. 1 (2010): 49.
16. Ibid. p. 50.
17. Dziemianowicz, 'The werewolf', p. 683.
18. Darryl Jones, *Horror: A Thematic History in Fiction and Film* (London: Bloomsbury Academic, 2002), p. 171.

19. Alison Peirse, *After Dracula: The 1930s Horror Film* (London and New York: I. B. Tauris, 2013), p. 157.

20. Gina Marchetti, *Romance and the 'Yellow Peril': Race, Sex and Discursive Strategies in Hollywood Fiction* (Berkeley: University of California Press, 1993), p. 2.

21. Jenny Clegg, *Fu Manchu and the 'Yellow Peril': The Making of a Racist Myth* (Stoke-on-Trent: Trentham Books, 1994), p. ix.

22. John Soister, *Up from the Vault: Rare Thrillers of the 1920s and 1930s* (Jefferson: McFarland, 2004), p. 67.

23. Marchetti, *Romance and the 'Yellow Peril'*, p. 3.

24. Ibid. p. 3.

25. Anon., '*Werewolf of London*', *Variety*, 15 May 1935, p. 19.

26. Karla Rae Fuller, 'Creatures of Good and Evil: Caucasian Portrayals of the Chinese and Japanese during World War II,' in *Classic Hollywood, Classic Whiteness*, ed. Daniel Bernardi (Minneapolis: University of Minnesota Press, 2001), 281.

27. See: Spadoni, 'Strange botany', pp. 51–2; Peirse, *After Dracula*, p. 157.

28. Anon., 'The *Werewolf of London*', *Motion Picture Herald*, 4 May 1935, pp. 38–9.

29. Marchetti, *Romance and the 'Yellow Peril'*, p. 3.

30. Amnon Kabatchnik, *Blood on the Stage 1925–1950: Milestone Plays of Crime, Mystery and Detection* (Lanham: Scarecrow Press, 2010), p. 25.

31. Ibid. p. 23.

32. Ibid. p. 24.

33. Spadoni, 'Strange botany', pp. 49–50.

34. Colin Shindler, *Hollywood Goes to War: Films and American Society 1939–1952* (New York: Routledge, 1979), p. 40.

35. David J. Skal, *The Monster Show: A Cultural History of Horror* (London: Plexus Publishing, 1994), p. 217.

36. Melvin E. Matthews Jr, *Fear Itself: Horror on Screen and in Reality during the Depression and World War II* (Jefferson: McFarland, 2009), p. 132.

37. Ibid. pp. 214–15.

38. Ibid. p. 217.

39. Curt Siodmak in Dennis Fischer, 'Curt Siodmak: the idea man', in Patrick McGilligan (ed.), *Backstory 2: Interviews with Screenwriters of the 1940s and 1950s* (Berkeley: University of California Press, 1991), 255–6.

40. Fischer, 'Curt Siodmak', p. 247.

41. Siodmak in Fischer, 'Curt Siodmak', p. 256.

42. Ibid. p. 256.

43. Ibid. pp. 257–8.

44. Skal, *The Monster Show*, pp. 211–12.

45. Siodmak in Fischer, 'Curt Siodmak', p. 258.

46. Sylvia Whitman, *V is for Victory: The American Home Front during World War II* (Minneapolis: Lerner Publications, 1993), pp. 11–12.

47. Dziemianowicz, 'The werewolf', p. 683.

48. Chantal Bourgault du Coudray, *The Curse of the Werewolf: Fantasy, Horror and the Beast Within* (London and New York: I. B. Tauris, 2006), p. 77.
49. Siodmak in Fischer, 'Curt Siodmak', p. 258.
50. Siodmak in Matthews Jr, *Fear Itself*, p. 133.
51. Matthews Jr, *Fear Itself*, p. 133.
52. Ibid. p. 145.
53. Skal, *The Monster Show*, p. 215.
54. Matthews Jr, *Fear Itself*, p. 143.
55. Whitman, *V is for Victory*, p. 49.
56. Bernard Schubert, 'Wolfman vs. Dracula', in Philip J. Ridley (ed.), *Wolfman vs. Dracula* (Albany: BearManor Media, 2010), pp. 116–33.

Chapter 2

1. Kim Newman, *Cat People* [BFI Classics] (London: BFI Publishing, 2001), p. 11.
2. Tim Snelson, *Phantom Ladies: Hollywood Horror and the Home Front* (New Bruswick: Rutgers University Press, 2015), p. 22.
3. Ibid. p. 10.
4. Melvin E. Matthews Jr, *Fear Itself: Horror on Screen and in Reality during the Depression and World War II* (Jefferson: McFarland, 2009), p. 146.
5. Newman, *Cat People*, p. 24.
6. Marie LaTour is a wholly fictional character created by screenwriter Griffin Jay. However, she may be named for Marie Louise de La Tour d'Auvergne, an eighteenth-century French noblewoman descended from French and Polish royalty notable for an extramarital affair with her first cousin.
7. Snelson, *Phantom Ladies*, p. 87.
8. Ibid. p. 87.
9. Ibid. p. 17.
10. Frank Krutnik, *In a Lonely Street: Film Noir, Genre, Masculinity* (New York: Routledge, 1991), p. 63.
11. Jennifer Fay and Justus Nieland, *Film Noir* (New York: Routledge, 2010), p. 148.
12. Janey Place, 'Women in film noir', in E. Ann Kaplan (ed.), *Women in Film Noir*, 2nd edn (London: BFI Publishing, 1998), p. 56.
13. Newman, *Cat People*, pp. 30–1.
14. Ibid. p. 26.
15. Mark Jancovich, 'Phantom ladies: the war worker, the slacker and the femme fatale', *New Review of Film and Television Studies* 8, no. 2 (2010): 176.
16. Ibid. p. 169.
17. Jon Towlson, *Subversive Horror Cinema: Countercultural Messages of Films from* Frankenstein *to the Present* (Jefferson: McFarland, 2014), p. 48.
18. Snelson, *Phantom Ladies*, p. 28.
19. Ibid. pp. 28–9.
20. Newman, *Cat People*, p. 26.
21. Snelson, *Phantom Ladies*, p. 87.

22. Ibid. p. 86.

23. Ibid. p. 84.

24. Peter Hutchings, 'The she-wolves of horror cinema', in Hannah Priest (ed.), *She-Wolf: A Cultural History of Female Werewolves* (Manchester: Manchester University Press, 2015), p. 171.

25. Jancovich, 'Phantom ladies', p. 175.

26. Rick Worland, *The Horror Film: An Introduction* (Oxford: Blackwell, 2007), p. 73.

27. Andrew Tudor, *Monsters and Mad Scientists: A Cultural History of the Horror Movie* (Oxford: Blackwell, 1989), p. 133.

28. Ibid. p. 98.

29. Matthews Jr, *Fear Itself*, p. 154.

30. Worland, *The Horror Film*, p. 72.

31. Matthews Jr, *Fear Itself*, p. 154.

32. Ibid. p. 155.

33. Joseph Maddrey, *Nightmares in Red, White and Blue: The Evolution of the American Horror Film* (Jefferson: McFarland, 2004), p. 30.

34. Cyndy Hendershot, *Paranoia, the Bomb and 1950s Science Fiction Films* (Bowling Green: Bowling Green State University Popular Press, 1999), p. 127.

35. Though *How to Make a Monster* (1958) would feature a killer dressed as a werewolf: an actor in makeup who is mind-controlled by a maniacal special effects artist.

Chapter 3

1. Peter Biskind, *Seeing Is Believing: Or How Hollywood Taught Us to Stop Worrying and Love the Fifties* (New York: Pantheon Books, 1983), pp. 197–8.

2. Mark Jancovich, *Rational Fears: American Horror in the 1950s* (Manchester: Manchester University Press, 1996), p. 198.

3. Ibid. p. 212.

4. James Gilbert, *A Cycle of Outrage: America's Reaction to the Juvenile Delinquent in the 1950s* (Oxford and New York: Oxford University Press, 1986), p. 13.

5. Ibid. p. 1.

6. Biskind, *Seeing Is Believing*, p. 197.

7. Bryan Senn, 'Twin bill terrorama!: *Invasion of the Saucer Men* and *I Was a Teenage Werewolf*', *Filmfax* 93/4 (2002): 80.

8. Ibid. p. 130.

9. Jancovich, *Rational Fears*, p. 211.

10. Ibid. p. 212.

11. Biskind, *Seeing Is Believing*, p. 220.

12. Ibid. p. 218.

13. Jancovich, *Rational Fears*, p. 210.

14. Ibid. p. 200.

15. Biskind, *Seeing Is Believing*, pp. 222–3.

16. Jancovich, *Rational Fears*, p. 210.

17. Biskind, *Seeing Is Believing*, p. 223.

18. Leslie H. Abramson, '1968: movies and the failure of nostalgia', in Barry Keith Grant (ed.), *American Cinema of the 1960s: Themes and Variations* (New Brunswick, NJ: Rutgers University Press, 2008), p. 193.

19. Kendall R. Phillips, *Projected Fears: Horror Films and American Culture* (Westport, CT: Praeger, 2005), p. 108.

20. Jason Zinoman, *Shock Value: How a Few Eccentric Outsiders Gave Us Nightmares, Conquered Hollywood and Invented Modern Horror* (London: Duckworth Overlook, 2012), pp. 8–9.

21. Joseph Maddrey, *Nightmares in Red, White and Blue: The Evolution of the American Horror Film* (Jefferson: McFarland, 2004), p. 52.

22. Gregory A. Waller, 'Introduction', in Waller (ed.), *American Horrors: Essays on the Modern American Horror Film* (Urbana and Chicago: University of Illinois Press, 1987), p. 4.

23. Phillips, *Projected Fears*, p. 107.

24. The group was founded in 1948 as the 'Hells Angels Motorcycle Club' but is often stylised as 'Hell's Angels' by journalists and scholars. Officially the name should not include an apostrophe.

25. Thomas Barker, *Biker Gangs and Organised Crime* (Cincinnati: Anderson Publishing, 2007), 37.

26. John Wood, 'Hell's Angels and the illusion of the counterculture', *Journal of Popular Culture* 37, no. 2 (2003): 336.

27. Randall Clark, *At a Theater or Drive-In Near You: The History, Culture and Politics of the American Exploitation Film*, library edn (New York: Routledge, 2014), p. 115.

28. Ibid. pp. 115–16.

29. Ibid. p. 116.

30. Ibid. p. 120.

31. Wood, 'Hell's Angels', p. 336.

32. Clark, *At a Theater or Drive-In Near You*, p. 120.

33. Jon Towlson, *Subversive Horror Cinema: Countercultural Messages of Films from* Frankenstein *to the Present* (Jefferson: McFarland, 2014), p. 135.

34. Michel Levesque, 'Commentary by director Michel Levesque and co-writer David M. Kaufman', *Werewolves on Wheels*, DVD. Directed by Michel Levesque (Orland Park: Dark Sky Films, 2006).

35. See: R. H. W. Dillard, '*Night of the Living Dead*: it's not like just a wind that's passing through', in Gregory A. Waller (ed.), *American Horrors: Essays on the Modern American Horror Film* (Urbana and Chicago: University of Illinois Press, 1987), p. 27; Jonathan L. Crane, 'Come on-a my house: the inescapable legacy of Wes Craven's *The Last House on the Left*', in Xavier Mendik (ed.), *Shocking Cinema of the Seventies* (Hereford: Noir Publishing, 2002), p. 172; Phillips, *Projected Fears*, pp. 116–17.

36. Phillips, *Projected Fears*, p. 109.
37. Ibid. p. 109.
38. Ibid. p. 109.
39. Ibid. pp. 109–10.
40. Crane, 'Come on-a my house', pp. 172–3.
41. Barna William Donovan, *Conspiracy Films: A Tour of Dark Places in the American Conscious* (Jefferson: McFarland, 2011), p. 75.
42. Ginsberg in Brian Albright, *Regional Horror Films, 1958–1990: A State-by-State Guide with Interviews* (Jefferson: McFarland, 2012), p. 67.
43. Ibid. p. 67.
44. Ibid. p. 67.
45. S. S. Prawer, *Caligari's Children: The Film as a Tale of Terror* (New York: Da Capo Press, 1980), pp. 15–16.

Chapter 4

1. Denis Meikle, *A History of Horrors: The Rise and Fall of the House of Hammer*, revised edn (Lanham: Scarecrow Press, 2009), p. 31.
2. Marcus K. Harmes, *The Curse of Frankenstein* [Devil's Advocates] (Leighton Buzzard: Auteur Publishing, 2015), p. 28.
3. *I Vampiri* was released in international markets under the alternative titles *The Devil's Commandment* and *Lust of the Vampire*.
4. Roberto Curti, *Italian Gothic Horror Films, 1957–1969* (Jefferson: McFarland, 2015), p. 30.
5. *Black Sunday* is the film's best-known title, used for its American release in 1961. In Italy, it is known as *La maschera del demonio*, or *The Mask of Satan*.
6. Curti, *Italian Gothic Horror Films, 1957–1969*, pp. 47–8.
7. The Soviet film *Viy* (1967) shares aesthetic commonalities with the gothic horror cinema produced in Western Europe during this period.
8. Danny Shipka, *Perverse Titillation: The Exploitation Cinema of Italy, Spain and France, 1960–1980* (Jefferson: McFarland, 2011), p. 5.
9. Andrew M. Francis, 'The wages of sin: how the discovery of penicillin reshaped modern sexuality', *Archives of Sexual Behavior* 42, no. 1 (2013): 5–13.
10. David Allyn, *Make Love, Not War – The Sexual Revolution: An Unfettered History* (New York: Routledge, 2001), pp. 4–5.
11. Ibid. p. 4.
12. Ibid. p. 4.
13. Peter Hutchings, *Dracula* [British Film Guide] (London: I. B. Tauris, 2003), p. 83.
14. Peter John Dyer, '*Dracula*', *Films and Filming* 47, no. 9 (1958): 27.
15. Meikle, *A History of Horrors*, p. 52.
16. Ibid. p. 52.
17. Peter Hutchings, *Hammer and Beyond: The British Horror Film* (Manchester: Manchester University Press, 1993), p. 67.

18. Anon., 'The Curse of the Werewolf,' Monthly Film Bulletin 28, no. 329 (1961): 81.

19. John Trevelyan in Wayne Kinsey, Hammer Films: The Bray Studios Years (Richmond: Reynolds and Hearn, 2002), p. 198.

20. Jonathan Rigby, English Gothic: A Century of Horror Cinema (Richmond: Reynolds and Hearn, 2004), p. 67.

21. Rick Worland, The Horror Film: An Introduction (Oxford: Blackwell, 2007), p. 84.

22. Andrew Tudor, Monsters and Mad Scientists: A Cultural History of the Horror Movie (Oxford: Blackwell, 1989), pp. 174–5.

23. Ibid. p. 99.

24. Hutchings, Hammer and Beyond, p. 69.

25. Laura Hubner, Fairytale and Gothic Horror: Uncanny Transformations in Film (New York: Palgrave Macmillan, 2018), p. 133.

26. Michael Carreras, The Werewolves of Moravia (n.d.) [unproduced screenplay], pp. 1–7.

27. Ibid. p. 10.

28. Ibid. p. 26.

29. Ibid. p. 55.

30. Ibid. p. 72.

31. Ibid. p. 82.

32. Ibid. p. 84.

33. Peter Hutchings, 'The Amicus House of Horror', in Steve Chibnall and Julian Petley (eds), British Horror Cinema (London: Routledge, 2002), p. 134.

34. Though Legend of the Werewolf does not give Endore an on-screen credit.

35. Anthony Hinds used the pseudonym John Elder for much of his screenwriting work, including his two werewolf films.

36. Allyn, Make Love, Not War, p. 5.

37. Paul Newland, British Films in the 1970s (Manchester: Manchester University Press, 2013), p. 38.

38. Hubner, Fairytale and Gothic Horror, p. 136.

39. Ibid. p. 136.

40. Ibid. p. 136.

41. Curti, Italian Gothic Horror Films, 1957–1969, p. 40.

42. Martyn Conterio, Black Sunday [Devil's Advocates] (Leighton Buzzard: Auteur Publishing, 2015), pp. 42–5.

43. Shipka, Perverse Titillation, p. 35.

44. Lycanthropus was released in America as Werewolf in a Girls' Dormitory in 1963 and in Britain as I Married a Werewolf in 1964.

45. Curti, Italian Gothic Horror Films, 1957–1969, p. 65.

46. Ibid. p. 65.

47. Ibid. p. 65.

48. Werewolf Woman is a literal translation of the original Italian; several alternative titles were used for international markets.

49. Shipka, Perverse Titillation, p. 169.

50. Rino di Silvestri in Roberto Curti, *Italian Gothic Horror Films, 1970–1979* (Jefferson: McFarland, 2017), p. 165.

51. Curti, *Italian Gothic Horror Films, 1970–1979*, p. 165.

52. Nicholas G. Schlegel, *Sex, Sadism, Spain, and Cinema: The Spanish Horror Film* (Lanham: Rowman and Littlefield, 2015), p. 90.

53. All of the English titles provided here are literal translations of the original Spanish; these films also went under several different titles in international markets. According to Naschy, another Daninsky film titled *Nights of the Wolfman* was written and filmed in 1968. If it exists at all, it is now lost.

54. Irene Baena-Cuder, '*Game of Werewolves*: XXI Century Spanish werewolves and the conflict of masculinity', in Samantha Holland, Robert Shail and Steven Gerrard (eds), *Gender and Contemporary Horror Film* (Bingley: Emerald Publishing, 2019), p. 40.

55. Ibid. p. 39.

56. Ibid. p. 40.

57. Mary Nash, 'Pronatalism and motherhood in Franco's Spain', in Gisela Block and Pat Thane (eds), *Maternity and Gender Policies: Women and the Rise of the European Welfare States 1880s–1950s* (New York: Routledge, 1991), p. 160.

58. Aurora G. Morcillo, *The Seduction of Modern Spain: The Female Body and the Francoist Body Politic* (Lewisburg: Brucknell University Press, 2010), p. 192.

59. Ibid. p. 172.

60. Ibid. p. 180.

61. Todd Tjersland, 'Cinema of the doomed: the tragic horror of Paul Naschy', in Steven Jay Schneider (eds), *Fear without Frontiers: Horror Cinema across the Globe* (Godalming: FAB Press, 2003), p. 70.

62. Antonio Lázaro-Reboll, *Spanish Horror Film* (Edinburgh: Edinburgh University Press, 2012), p. 76.

63. Mary T. Hartson, 'Voracious vampires and other monsters: masculinity and the terror genre in Spanish cinema of the *Transición*', *Romance Notes* 55, no. 1 (2015): 132.

Chapter 5

1. *Wolfen* was also released in 1981, but its monsters are a hyper-intelligent breed of wolf rather than werewolves in a traditional sense.

2. Steve Neale, '"You've got to be fucking kidding!"' Knowledge, belief and judgement in science fiction', in Annette Kuhn (ed.), *Alien Zone: Cultural Theory and Contemporary Science Fiction Cinema* (New York: Verso, 1990), p. 161.

3. Ernest Mathijs, 'They're here!: special effects in horror cinema of the 1970s and 1980s', in Ian Conrich (ed.), *Horror Zone: The Cultural Experience of Contemporary Horror* (London and New York: I. B. Tauris, 2010), p. 154.

4. Ibid. p. 153.

5. Susan Jeffords, *Hard Bodies: Hollywood Masculinity in the Reagan Era* (New Brunswick, NJ: Rutgers University Press, 1994), p. 24.

6. Philip Brophy, 'Horrality – the textuality of the contemporary horror film', *Screen* 27, nos 1/2 (1986): 8.

7. Pete Boss, 'Vile bodies and bad medicine', *Screen* 27, nos 1/2 (1986): 17.

8. Brophy, 'Horrality', p. 8.

9. Boss, 'Vile bodies and bad medicine', p. 14.

10. Deborah Lupton, *Medicine as Culture: Illness, Disease and the Body*, 3rd edn (Thousand Oaks: SAGE Publications, 2012), p. 38.

11. Rick Baker in Jovanka Vuckovic, 'Four-legged hound from hell', *Rue Morgue* 93 (2009): 20.

12. Brophy, 'Horrality', p. 9.

13. Bob Batchelor and Scott Stoddart, *The 1980s* (Westport, CT: Greenwood Press, 2007), p. 81.

14. Ibid. pp. 81–2.

15. Michael Schaller, *Reckoning with Reagan: America and its President in the 1980s* (Oxford and New York: Oxford University Press, 1992), p. 93.

16. Frank Furedi, *Therapy Culture: Cultivating Vulnerability in an Uncertain Age* (New York: Routledge, 2004), p. 84.

17. Ibid. pp. 40–1.

18. John Landis in Jason Lapeyre, 'The bad moon rises again', *Rue Morgue* 93 (2009): 18–19.

19. Ibid. p. 18.

20. It is worth noting that the episode of *The Muppet Show* briefly seen in *An American Werewolf in London* was filmed specifically for Landis and was never broadcast.

21. John Landis in Adam Savage, 'Adam Savage interviews John Landis – The Talking Room', YouTube video, 01:02:42, posted by 'Tested', 29 August 2013. Available at <https://www.youtube.com/watch?v=Q7RoL1FUR1g>.

22. Ibid.

23. Landis in Lapeyre, 'The bad moon rises again', p. 18.

24. Ibid. p. 18.

25. Robin Wood, 'an introduction to the American horror film,' in Barry Keith Grant (ed.), *Planks of Reason: Essays on the Horror Film* (Lanham: Scarecrow Press, 2004), pp. 107–41.

26. Mark Bould, *The Cinema of John Sayles: Lone Star* (New York: Wallflower Press, 2009), p. 34.

27. John Kenneth Muir, *Horror Films of the 1980s* (Jefferson: McFarland, 2007), p. 37.

28. Ibid. pp. 34–9.

29. Craig Ian Mann, 'America, down the toilet: urban legends, American society and *Alligator*', in Katarina Gregersdotter, Johan Höglund and Nicklas Hållén (eds), *Animal Horror Cinema: Genre, History and Criticism* (New York: Palgrave Macmillan, 2015), pp. 110–25.

30. James Kinsella, *Covering the Plague: AIDS and the American Media* (New Brunswick, NJ: Rutgers University Press, 1989), p. 56.

31. Ibid. pp. 56–7.
32. Schaller, *Reckoning with Reagan*, pp. 22–3.
33. Ibid. p. 23.
34. Sandra Scanlon, 'Ronald Reagan and the Conservative movement', in Andrew L. Johns (ed.), *A Companion to Ronald Reagan* (Maiden: Wiley Blackwell, 2015), p. 594.
35. Schaller, *Reckoning with Reagan*, p. 25.
36. Ibid. p. 94.
37. Marcy J. Wilder, 'The rule of law, the rise of violence and the role of morality: reframing America's abortion debate', in Rickie Solinger (ed.), *Abortion Wars: A Half Century of Struggle, 1950–2000* (Berkeley: University of California Press, 1998), p. 82.
38. Schaller, *Reckoning with Reagan*, p. 93.
39. Kinsella, *Covering the Plague*, pp. 144–5.
40. Ibid. p. 94.
41. Ibid. p. 95.
42. David J. Skal, *The Monster Show: A Cultural History of Horror* (London: Plexus Publishing, 1994), p. 334.
43. Kim Newman, *Horror! The Definitive Guide to the Most Terrifying Movies Ever Made* (London: Carlton Books, 2006), p. 236.
44. Reynold Humphries, *The American Horror Film: An Introduction* (Edinburgh: Edinburgh University Press, 2002), p. 109.
45. Muir, *Horror Films of the 1980s*, p. 11.
46. Ibid. p. 37.
47. Andrew Tudor, *Monsters and Mad Scientists: A Cultural History of the Horror Movie* (Oxford: Blackwell, 1989), p. 99.

Chapter 6

1. Reynold Humphries, *The American Horror Film: An Introduction* (Edinburgh: Edinburgh University Press, 2002), pp. 97–112.
2. Sandra Scanlon, 'Ronald Reagan and the Conservative movement', in Andrew L. Johns (ed.), *A Companion to Ronald Reagan* (Maiden: Wiley Blackwell, 2015), p. 594.
3. Michael Schaller, *Reckoning with Reagan: America and its President in the 1980s* (Oxford and New York: Oxford University Press, 1992), p. 42.
4. Ibid. p. 76.
5. Lawrence Mishel and David M. Frankel, *The State of Working America 1990–1991 Edition* (London: M. E. Sharpe, 1991), p. 34.
6. Schaller, *Reckoning with Reagan*, p. 70.
7. Graham Thompson, *American Culture in the 1980s* (Edinburgh: Edinburgh University Press, 2007), p. 11.
8. Schaller, *Reckoning with Reagan*, p. 70.
9. Ibid. p. 75.

10. Ibid. p. 77.
11. Doug Rossinow, *The Reagan Era: A History of the 1980s* (New York: Columbia University Press, 2015), pp. 5–6.
12. Simon Brown, *Screening Stephen King: Adaptation and the Horror Genre in Film and Television* (Austin: University of Texas Press, 2018), p. 12.
13. Tony Magistrale, *Landscape of Fear: Stephen King's American Gothic* (Bowling Green: Bowling Green State University Popular Press, 1988), pp. 25–6.
14. Michael R. Collings, *The Films of Stephen King* (Rockville: Wildside Press, 1986), p. 139.
15. Ibid. p. 139.
16. Ibid. p. 139.
17. Mark Browning, *Stephen King on the Big Screen* (Bristol: Intellect Books, 2009), p. 88.
18. Ibid. p. 89.
19. Tom Newhouse, 'A blind date with disaster: adolescent revolt in the fiction of Stephen King,' in Gary Hoppenstand (ed.), *Stephen King* (Pasadena and Hackensack: Salem Press, 2011), p. 267.
20. Browning, *Stephen King on the Big Screen*, p. 88.
21. Ibid. p. 88.
22. Schaller, *Reckoning with Reagan*, p. 90.
23. Chris Jordan, *Movies and the Reagan Presidency: Success and Ethics* (Westport, CT: Praeger, 2003), pp. 15–16.
24. Ibid. p. 92.
25. Jazmina Cininas, 'Fur girls and wolf women: fur, hair and subversive female lycanthropy', in Hannah Priest (ed.), *She-Wolf: A Cultural History of Female Werewolves* (Manchester: Manchester University Press, 2015), p. 80.
26. Tony Williams, *Larry Cohen: The Radical Allegories of an Independent Filmmaker*, revised edn (Jefferson: McFarland, 2014), p. 122.
27. Joseph Maddrey, *Nightmares in Red, White and Blue: The Evolution of the American Horror Film* (Jefferson: McFarland, 2004), p. 147.
28. Williams, *Larry Cohen*, p. 126.
29. Of course, this may also be a reference to Ford's 1975 trip to Austria, during which he famously stumbled and fell down a set of stairs while departing Air Force One.
30. Williams, *Larry Cohen*, p. 127.
31. Ibid. p. 126.
32. Susan Jeffords, *Hard Bodies: Hollywood Masculinity in the Reagan Era* (New Brunswick, NJ: Rutgers University Press, 1994), p. 25.
33. Ibid. p. 25.
34. Catherine Driscoll, *Teen Film: A Critical Introduction* (New York: Continuum, 2011), p. 97.
35. Stefan Dziemianowicz, 'The werewolf', in S. T. Joshi (ed.), *Icons of Horror and the Supernatural: An Encyclopedia of Our Worst Nightmares*, vols 1 and 2 (Westport, CT: Greenwood Press, 2007), p. 684.
36. Williams, *Larry Cohen*, p. 126.

Chapter 7

1. Stacey Abbott, 'High concept thrills and chills: the horror blockbuster', in Ian Conrich (ed.), *Horror Zone: The Cultural Experience of Contemporary Horror Cinema* (New York: I. B. Tauris, 2010), p. 29.
2. Ibid. p. 31.
3. Ibid. p. 33.
4. There are, of course, some scenes in *Interview with the Vampire* which take place in contemporary San Francisco, but the larger part of the film is made up of flashbacks to the years 1791–1988.
5. Jude Davies, 'Gender, ethnicity and cultural crisis in *Falling Down* and *Groundhog Day*', *Screen* 36, no. 3 (1995): 214–32.
6. Philip Kemp, '*Wolf*', *Sight and Sound* 4, no. 9 (1994): 52.
7. Susan Jeffords, 'The big switch: Hollywood masculinity in the nineties', in Jim Collins, Hilary Radner and Ava Preacher Collins (eds), *Film Theory Goes to the Movies* (New York: Routledge, 1993), p. 196.
8. Ibid. p. 197.
9. Kemp, '*Wolf*', p. 52.
10. Denis Duclos, *The Werewolf Complex: America's Fascination with Violence* (Oxford: Berg Publishers, 1998), p. 5.
11. J. W. Whitehead, *Mike Nichols and the Cinema of Transformation* (Jefferson: McFarland, 2014), p. 184.
12. Ibid. p. 189.
13. Ibid. p. 186.
14. Ibid. p. 184.
15. Peter Biskind, 'Who's afraid of the big bad wolf?', *Premiere* 81 (1994): 58.
16. Whitehead, *Mike Nichols*, p. 184.
17. Biskind, 'Who's afraid of the big bad wolf?', p. 58.
18. Jeffrey Fagan, 'Gangs, drugs and neighborhood change', in C. Ronald Huff (ed.), *Gangs in America*, 2nd edn (Thousand Oaks: SAGE Publications, 1996), pp. 40–1.
19. Paul Robinson, 'Race, space and the evolution of black Los Angeles', in Darnell Hunt and Ana-Christina Ramon (eds), *Black Los Angeles: American Dreams and Racial Realities* (New York: New York University Press, 2010), p. 50.
20. Yvonne Tasker, *Spectacular Bodies: Gender, Genre and the Action Cinema* (New York: Routledge, 1993), pp. 47–53.
21. Stacey Abbott, *Celluloid Vampires: Life after Death in the Modern World* (Austin: University of Texas Press, 2007), p. 188.
22. Robinson, 'Race, space and the evolution of black Los Angeles', p. 50.
23. Tasker, *Spectacular Bodies*, p. 48.
24. Kim Newman, '*An American Werewolf in Paris*', *Sight and Sound* 7, no. 12 (1998): 37.
25. Ibid. p. 37.
26. Fagan, 'Gangs, drugs and neighborhood change', p. 46.

27. Eric D. Wish, 'PCP and crime: just another illicit drug?', *NIDA Research Monograph* 64 (1986): 174.
28. Fagan, 'Gangs, drugs and neighborhood change', p. 47.
29. Ibid. p. 46.
30. Ronald M. Holmes, Richard Tewksbury and George E. Higgins, *Introduction to Gangs in America* (Boca Raton: CRC Press, 2012), p. 114.
31. Ibid. p. 115.
32. Estella Ticknell, 'Feminine boundaries: adolescence, witchcraft and the new gothic cinema and television', in Ian Conrich (ed.), *Horror Zone: The Cultural Experience of Contemporary Horror Cinema* (London and New York: I. B. Tauris, 2010), p. 253.
33. See: Martin Barker, Ernest Mathijs and Xavier Mendik, 'Menstrual monsters: the reception of the *Ginger Snaps* cult horror franchise', in Ernest Mathijs and Xavier Mendik (eds), *The Cult Film Reader* (Maidenhead: Open University Press, 2008), pp. 482–94; Brigid Cherry, *Horror* (New York: Routledge, 2009), pp. 113–15.
34. Paula Devonshire in Barker, Mathijs and Mendik, 'Menstrual monsters', p. 487.
35. John Fawcett in Barker, Mathijs and Mendik, 'Menstrual monsters', p. 487.
36. Linda Ruth Williams, 'Blood sisters', *Sight and Sound* 11, no. 7 (2001): 37.
37. Benjamin Frymer, 'The media spectacle of Columbine: alienated youth as an object of fear', *American Behavioral Scientist* 52, no. 10 (2009): 1387.
38. Ibid. pp. 1391–2.
39. Ernest Mathijs, *John Fawcett's* Ginger Snaps (Toronto: University of Toronto Press, 2013), p. 19.
40. Frymer, 'The media spectacle of Columbine', p. 1402.
41. Mathijs, *John Fawcett's* Ginger Snaps, p. 20.
42. See: Bianca Nielsen, 'Something's wrong, like more than you being female: transgressive sexuality and discourses of reproduction in *Ginger Snaps*', *Thirdspace* 3, no. 2 (2004): 55–69; Barbara Creed, '*Ginger Snaps*: the monstrous feminine as *femme animale*', in Hannah Priest (ed.), *She-Wolf: A Cultural History of Female Werewolves* (Manchester: Manchester University Press, 2015), 180–95.
43. This does not include Trina Sinclair, whose death in the Fitzgerald family home is a grotesque accident.
44. Katherine S. Newman et al., *Rampage: The Social Roots of School Shootings* (New York: Basic Books, 2004), pp. 60–1.
45. Ibid. p. 15.
46. Jacqueline A. Sparks and Barry L. Duncan, 'The ethics and science of medicating children', *Ethical Human Psychology and Psychiatry* 6, no. 1 (2004): 25.
47. Anon., 'Columbine Copy Plot Discovered,' *Newsday*, 14 January 2004, A34.
48. Augusto de Vananzi, 'School shootings in the USA: popular culture as risk, teen marginality, and violence against peers', *Crime, Media, Culture* 8, no. 3 (2012): 262.
49. Frymer, 'The media spectacle of Columbine', pp. 1388–9.

50. Sunnie Rothenburger, '"Welcome to civilisation": colonialism, the gothic, and Canada's self-protective irony in the *Ginger Snaps* werewolf trilogy', *Journal of Canadian Studies* 44, no. 3 (2010): 96–117.

Chapter 8

1. However, the idea of weaponised werewolves served as a minor plot point in both *The Werewolf of Washington* (1973) and *Howling III: The Marsupials* (1987) in the interim.

2. Peter Lavoy, 'Pyridostigmine bromide', in Eric A. Croddy and James J. Wirtz (eds), *Weapons of Mass Destruction: An Encyclopedia of Worldwide Policy, Technology, and History* (Santa Barbara: ABC-CLIO, 2005), p. 232.

3. Ella Shohat, 'The media's war', in Susan Jeffords and Lauren Rabinovitz (eds), *Seeing Through the Media: The Persian Gulf War* (New Brunswick, NJ: Rutgers University Press, 1994), p. 150.

4. Neil Marshall, 'Audio commentary with director Neil Marshall', *Dog Soldiers*, collectors edn, Blu-ray and DVD. Directed by Neil Marshall (Los Angeles: Scream Factory, 2015).

5. bell hooks, *Feminism is for Everybody: Passionate Politics* (London: Pluto Press, 2000), p. ix.

6. Ealasaid Munro, 'Feminism: A Fourth Wave?' *Political Insight* 4, no. 2 (2013): 24–5.

7. Ibid. p. 23.

8. David Arter, *Democracy in Scandinavia: Consensual, Majoritarian or Mixed?* (Manchester: Manchester University Press, 2006), p. 71.

9. Jazmina Cininas, 'Fur girls and wolf women: fur, hair and subversive female lycanthropy', in Hannah Priest (ed.), *She-Wolf: A Cultural History of Female Werewolves* (Manchester: Manchester University Press, 2015), p. 80.

10. Jonas Alexander Arnby in Per Juul Carlsen, 'The werewolf within', *Danish Film Institute*, 9 May 2014. Available at <https://www.dfi.dk/en/english/werewolf-within>.

11. Bel Powley in Jordan Crucchiola, 'Bel Powley wants to make men uncomfortable', *Vulture*, 13 April 2018. Available at <https://www.vulture.com/2018/04/bel-powley-is-here-for-the-roles-that-make-men-uncomfortable.html>.

12. Leigh Gallagher, *The End of the Suburbs: Where the American Dream is Moving* (London: Penguin, 2013), p. 5.

13. Peter Hough, *Understanding Global Security*, 3rd edn (New York: Routledge, 2013), p. 106.

14. Ibid. p. 192.

15. Michael Hout, Asaf Levanon and Erin Cumberworth, 'Job loss and unemployment', in David B. Grusky, Bruce Western and Christopher Wimer (ed.), *The Great Recession* (New York: Russell Sage Foundation, 2011), p. 60.

16. Atif Mian and Amir Sufi, *House of Debt: How They (and You) Caused the Great Recession and How We Can Prevent It from Happening Again* (Chicago: University of Chicago Press, 2014), p. 27.

17. Aaron Reeves, Martin McKnee and David Stuckler, 'Economic suicides in the Great Recession in Europe and North America', *British Journal of Psychiatry* 205, no. 3 (2014): 246.
18. Ibid. p. 246.
19. Ibid. pp. 313–14.
20. Christopher Stoney and Tamara Krawchencko, 'Crisis and opportunism: public finance trends from stimulus to austerity in Canada', *Alternative Routes: A Journal of Critical Social Research* 24 (2013): 39.
21. Toby Sanger, 'Canada's conservative class war: using austerity to squeeze labour at the expense of economic growth', *Alternative Routes: A Journal of Critical Social Research* 24 (2013): 59.
22. Craig Berry, *Austerity Politics and UK Economic Policy* (New York: Palgrave Macmillan, 2016), p. 2.
23. Sarah Wharton, 'Welcome to the (neo) grindhouse!', in Geoff King, Claire Molloy and Yannis Tzioumakis (eds), *American Independent Cinema: Indie, Indiewood and Beyond* (London and New York: Routledge, 2015), p. 198.
24. Ibid. p. 198.
25. Ibid. pp. 203–4.
26. Lowell Dean in Sean Plummer, 'Howl of justice', *Rue Morgue* 145 (2014): 21.
27. See: Danny Dorling, 'Austerity and mortality', in Vickie Cooper and David Whyte (eds), *The Violence of Austerity* (London: Pluto Press, 2017), pp. 44–50.
28. Eric J. Stolze in Evan Dickson, 'Writer Eric Stolze talks *Late Phases*, the film's unique setting, practical effects, and his favorite werewolf films', *Collider*, 5 December 2014. Available at <https://collider.com/eric-stolze-late-phases-interview/>.

Conclusion

1. Samantha George and Bill Hughes (eds), *In the Company of Wolves: Werewolves, Wolves and Wild Children* (Manchester: Manchester University Press, 2020).
2. Simon Bacon, 'Dirty, wild beasts! Representations of the homeless as werewolves in films from *Werewolf of London* (1935) to *Underworld: Rise of the Lycans* (2009)', *Revenant* 2 (2016): 73–90.
3. Michael Brodski, 'The cinematic representation of the wild child: considering *L'enfant sauvage* (1970)', *Gothic Studies* 21, no. 1 (2019): 100–13.
4. Chantal Bourgault du Coudray, *The Curse of the Werewolf: Fantasy, Horror and the Beast Within* (London and New York: I. B. Tauris, 2006), p. 79.
5. Hannah Priest, 'Like father like son: wolf-men, paternity and the male gothic', in Robert McKay and John Miller (eds), *Werewolves, Wolves and the Gothic* (Cardiff: University of Wales Press, 2017), p. 21.
6. Carys Crossen, *The Nature of the Beast: Transformations of the Werewolf from the 1970s to the Twenty-First Century* (Cardiff: University of Wales Press, 2019), p. 49.

7. Ibid. p. 47.

8. Craig Anderson, 'Where are the wolves?: with their rich history on screen, we should be seeing lycanthropes there more often', *Fangoria* 329 (2014): 74.

9. Ibid. p. 74

10. Dean in Anderson, 'Where are the wolves?', p. 75.

11. Anne Billson, 'The werewolf howls again', *The Guardian, Film and Music*, 5 February 2010, p. 7.

12. Mark Browning, *Stephen King on the Big Screen* (Bristol: Intellect Books, 2009), p. 87.

13. Jeff Sneider, '*It* filmmaker Andy Muschietti in early talks to direct *The Howling* for Netflix', *Collider*, 9 January 2020. Available at <https://collider.com/andy-muschietti-the-howling-netflix/>.

14. Irene Baena-Cuder, 'Spanish werewolves and the conflict of masculine identity in *Game of Werewolves*'. Paper presented at *The Company of Wolves: Sociality, Animality and Subjectivity in Literary and Cultural Narratives – Werewolves, Shapeshifters and Feral Humans*, University of Hertfordshire, Hatfield, 3–5 September 2015; Simon Brown, 'An American werewolf in America: Stephen King's *Cycle of the Werewolf* and *Silver Bullet*' (paper presented at *The Company of Wolves*); Colette Balmain 'Through the eyes of a child: hybridity and morbidity in Jo Sung-hee's *A Werewolf Boy*' (paper presented at *The Company of Wolves*).

Bibliography

Abbott, Stacey, *Celluloid Vampires: Life after Death in the Modern World* (Austin: University of Texas Press, 2007).

Abbott, Stacey, 'High concept thrills and chills: the horror blockbuster', in Ian Conrich (ed.), *Horror Zone: The Cultural Experience of Contemporary Horror Cinema* (London and New York: I. B. Tauris, 2010), pp. 27–44.

Abbott, Stacey, *Undead Apocalypse: Vampires and Zombies in the 21st Century* (Edinburgh: Edinburgh University Press, 2016).

Abramson, Leslie H., '1968: movies and the failure of nostalgia', in Barry Keith Grant (ed.), *American Cinema of the 1960s: Themes and Variations* (New Brunswick, NJ: Rutgers University Press, 2008), pp. 193–216.

Albright, Brian, *Regional Horror Films 1958–1990: A State-by-State Guide with Interviews* (Jefferson: McFarland, 2012).

Aleiss, Angela, *Making the White Man's Indian: Native Americans and Hollywood Movies* (Westport, CT: Praeger, 2005).

Allyn, David, *Make Love, Not War – The Sexual Revolution: An Unfettered History* (New York: Routledge, 2001).

Anderson, Craig, 'Where are the wolves?: with their rich history on screen, we should be seeing lycanthropes there more often', *Fangoria* 329 (2014): 74–6.

Anon., 'Columbine copy plot discovered', *Newsday*, 14 January 2004, p. A34.

Anon., 'Data from manufacturers' list of releases', *Motion Picture News*, 29 October 1913, p. 58.

Anon., 'Nestor – *The White Wolf*', *Moving Picture World* 21, no. 13 (1914): 1818.

Anon., 'Punished for hundred year old crime', *Universal Weekly* 3, no. 24 (1913): 16.

Anon., 'Releases', *The New York Clipper*, 12 December 1913, p. 10.

Anon., '*The Curse of the Werewolf*', *Monthly Film Bulletin* 28, no. 329 (1961): 80–1.

Anon., 'The *Werewolf of London*', *Motion Picture Herald*, 4 May 1935, pp. 38–9.

Anon., '*Werewolf of London*', *Variety*, 15 May 1935, p. 19.

Arter, David, *Democracy in Scandinavia: Consensual, Majoritarian or Mixed?* (Manchester: Manchester University Press, 2006).

Auerbach, Nina, *Our Vampires, Ourselves* (Chicago: University of Chicago Press, 1995).

Bacon, Simon, 'Dirty, wild beasts! Representations of the homeless as werewolves in films from *Werewolf of London* (1935) to *Underworld: Rise of the Lycans* (2009)', *Revenant* 2 (2016): 73–90.

Baena-Cuder, Irene, '*Game of Werewolves*: XXI Century Spanish werewolves and the conflict of masculinity', in Samantha Holland, Robert Shail and Steven Gerrard (eds), *Gender and Contemporary Horror Film* (Bingley: Emerald Publishing, 2019), pp. 39–51.

Baena-Cuder, Irene, 'Spanish werewolves and the conflict of masculine identity in *Game of Werewolves*'. Paper presented at *The Company of Wolves: Sociality, Animality and Subjectivity in Literary and Cultural Narratives – Werewolves, Shapeshifters and Feral Humans*, University of Hertfordshire, Hatfield, 3–5 September 2015.

Balmain, Colette, 'Through the eyes of a child: hybridity and morbidity in Jo Sung-hee's *A Werewolf Boy*'. Paper presented at *The Company of Wolves: Sociality, Animality and Subjectivity in Literary and Cultural Narratives – Werewolves, Shapeshifters and Feral Humans*, University of Hertfordshire, Hatfield, 3–5 September 2015.

Baring-Gould, Sabine, *The Book of Werewolves* (London: Senate, [1865] 1995).

Barker, Martin, Ernest Mathijs and Xavier Mendik, 'Menstrual monsters: the reception of the *Ginger Snaps* cult horror franchise', in Ernest Mathijs and Xavier Mendik (eds), *The Cult Film Reader* (Maidenhead: Open University Press, 2008), pp. 482–94.

Barker, Thomas, *Biker Gangs and Organised Crime* (Cincinnati: Anderson Publishing, 2010).

Batchelor, Bob and Scott Stoddart, *The 1980s* (Westport, CT: Greenwood Press, 2007).

Beresford, Matthew, *The White Devil: The Werewolf in European Culture* (London: Reaktion Books, 2013).

Berry, Craig, *Austerity Politics and UK Economic Policy* (New York: Palgrave Macmillan, 2016).

Billson, Anne, 'The werewolf howls again', *The Guardian, Film and Music*, 5 February 2010, p. 7.

Bishop, Kyle William, *American Zombie Gothic: The Rise and Fall (and Rise) of the Walking Dead in Popular Culture*.Jefferson: McFarland, 2010.

Biskind, Peter, 'Who's afraid of the big bad wolf?', *Premiere* 81 (1994): 57–63.

Biskind, Peter, *Seeing is Believing: Or How Hollywood Taught Us to Stop Worrying and Love the Fifties* (New York: Pantheon Books, 1983).

Boss, Pete, 'Vile bodies and bad medicine', *Screen* 27, nos 1/2 (1986): 14–24.

Bould, Mark, *The Cinema of John Sayles: Lone Star* (New York: Wallflower Press, 2009).

Bourgault du Coudray, Chantal, *The Curse of the Werewolf: Fantasy, Horror and the Beast Within* (London and New York: I. B. Tauris, 2006).

Brandner, Gary, *The Howling* (New York: Fawcett, [1977] 1986).

Brodski, Michael, 'The cinematic representation of the wild child: considering *L'enfant sauvage* (1970)', *Gothic Studies* 21, no. 1 (2019): 100–13.

Brophy, Philip, 'Horrality – the textuality of the contemporary horror film', *Screen* 27, nos 1/2 (1986): 2–13.

Brown, Simon, 'An American werewolf in America: Stephen King's *Cycle of the Werewolf* and *Silver Bullet*'. Paper presented at *The Company of Wolves: Sociality, Animality and Subjectivity in Literary and Cultural Narratives – Werewolves, Shapeshifters and Feral Humans*, University of Hertfordshire, Hatfield, 3–5 September 2015.

Brown, Simon, *Screening Stephen King: Adaptation and the Horror Genre in Film and Television* (Austin: University of Texas Press, 2018).

Browning, Mark, *Stephen King on the Big Screen* (Bristol: Intellect Books, 2009).

Bunson, Matthew, *The Vampire Encyclopedia* (New York: Gramercy Books, 2001).

Carlsen, Per Juul, 'The werewolf within', *Danish Film Institute*, 9 May 2014, <https://www.dfi.dk/en/english/werewolf-within/>.

Carreras, Michael, *The Werewolves of Moravia*, n.d. [unproduced screenplay].

Cherry, Brigid, *Horror* (New York: Routledge, 2009).

Cininas, Jazmina, 'Fur girls and wolf women: fur, hair and subversive female lycanthropy', in Hannah Priest (ed.), *She-Wolf: A Cultural History of Female Werewolves* (Manchester: Manchester University Press, 2015), pp. 77–95.

Clark, Randall, *At a Theater or Drive-In Near You: The History, Culture and Politics of the American Exploitation Film*, library edn (New York: Routledge, 2014).

Clegg, Jenny, *Fu Manchu and the 'Yellow Peril': The Making of a Racist Myth* (Stoke-on-Trent: Trentham Books, 1994).

Collings, Michael R., *The Films of Stephen King* (Rockville: Wildside Press, 1986).

Conterio, Martyn, *Black Sunday* [Devil's Advocates] (Leighton Buzzard: Auteur Publishing, 2015).

Crane, Jonathan L., 'Come on-a my house: the inescapable legacy of Wes Craven's *The Last House on the Left*', in Xavier Mendik (ed.), *Shocking Cinema of the Seventies* (Hereford: Noir Publishing, 2002), pp. 166–77.

Creed, Barbara, '*Ginger Snaps*: the monstrous feminine as *femme animale*', in Hannah Priest (ed.), *She-Wolf: A Cultural History of Female Werewolves* (Manchester: Manchester University Press, 2015), pp. 180–95.

Crossen, Carys, *The Nature of the Beast: Transformations of the Werewolf from the 1970s to the Twenty-First Century* (Cardiff: University of Wales Press, 2019).

Crucchiola, Jordan, 'Bel Powley wants to make men uncomfortable', *Vulture*, 13 April 2018, <https://www.vulture.com/2018/04/bel-powley-is-here-for-the-roles-that-make-men-uncomfortable.html/>.

Curti, Roberto, *Italian Gothic Horror Films, 1957–1969* (Jefferson: McFarland, 2015).

Curti, Roberto, *Italian Gothic Horror Films, 1970–1979* (Jefferson: McFarland, 2017).

Davies, Jude, 'Gender, ethnicity and cultural crisis in *Falling Down* and *Groundhog Day*', *Screen* 36, no. 3 (1995): 214–32.

de Blécourt, Willem (ed.), *Werewolf Histories* (New York: Palgrave Macmillan, 2015).

de France, Marie, 'Bisclavret', in *The Lais of Marie de France*, trans. Glyn S. Burgess, revised edn (London: Penguin, 1999), pp. 68–72.

de Vananzi, Augusto, 'School shootings in the USA: popular culture as risk, teen marginality, and violence against peers', *Crime, Media, Culture* 8, no. 3 (2012): 261–78.

Dickson, Evan, 'Writer Eric Stolze talks *Late Phases*, the film's unique setting, practical effects, and his favorite werewolf films', *Collider*, 5 December 2014, <https://collider.com/eric-stolze-late-phases-interview/>.

Dillard, R. H. W., '*Night of the Living Dead*: it's not like just a wind that's passing through', in Gregory A. Waller (ed.), *American Horrors: Essays on the Modern American Horror Film* (Urbana and Chicago: University of Illinois Press, 1987), pp. 14–29.

Donovan, Barna William, *Conspiracy Films: A Tour of Dark Places in the American Conscious* (Jefferson: McFarland, 2011).

Dorling, Danny, 'Austerity and morality', in Vickie Cooper and David Whyte (eds), *The Violence of Austerity* (London: Pluto Press, 2017), pp. 44–50.

Driscoll, Catherine, *Teen Film: A Critical Introduction* (New York: Continuum, 2011).

Duclos, Denis, *The Werewolf Complex: America's Fascination with Violence* (Oxford: Berg Publishers, 1998).

Dyer, Peter John, '*Dracula*', *Films and Filming* 47, no. 9 (1958): 27.

Dyson, Jeremy, *Bright Darkness: The Lost Art of the Supernatural Horror Film* (London: Cassell, 1997).

Dziemianowicz, Stefan, 'The werewolf', in S. T. Joshi (ed.), *Icons of Horror and the Supernatural: An Encyclopedia of Our Worst Nightmares*, vols 1 and 2 (Westport, CT: Greenwood Press, 2007), pp. 653–88.

Endore, Guy, *The Werewolf of Paris* (Cambridge: Pegasus, [1933] 2013).

Fagan, Jeffrey, 'Gangs, drugs and neighborhood change', in C. Ronald Huff (ed.), *Gangs in America*, 2nd edn (Thousand Oaks: SAGE Publications, 1996), pp. 39–74.

Fay, Jennifer and Justus Nieland, *Film Noir* (New York: Routledge, 2010).

Fischer, Dennis, 'Curt Siodmak: the idea man', in Patrick McGilligan (ed.), *Backstory 2: Interviews with Screenwriters of the 1940s and 1950s* (Berkeley: University of California Press, 1991), pp. 246–73.

Francis, Andrew M., 'The wages of sin: how the discovery of penicillin reshaped modern sexuality', *Archives of Sexual Behavior* 42, no. 1 (2013): 5–13.

Frymer, Benjamin, 'The media spectacle of Columbine: alienated youth as an object of fear', *American Behavioral Scientist* 52, no. 10 (2009): 1387–404.

Fuller, Karla Rae, 'Creatures of good and evil: Caucasian portrayals of the Chinese and Japanese during World War II', in Daniel Bernardi (ed.), *Classic Hollywood, Classic Whiteness* (Minneapolis: University of Minnesota Press, 2001), pp. 281–300.

Furedi, Frank, *Therapy Culture: Cultivating Vulnerability in an Uncertain Age* (New York: Routledge, 2004).

Gallagher, Leigh, *The End of the Suburbs: Where the American Dream is Moving* (London: Penguin, 2013).

George, Andrew (trans.), *The Epic of Gilgamesh*, revised edn (London: Penguin, 2003).

George, Samantha and Bill Hughes (eds), *The Company of Wolves: Werewolves, Wolves and Wild Children* (Manchester: Manchester University Press, 2020).

Gilbert, James, *A Cycle of Outrage: America's Reaction to the Juvenile Delinquent in the 1950s* (Oxford and New York: Oxford University Press, 1986).

Harmes, Marcus K., *The Curse of Frankenstein* [Devil's Advocates] (Leighton Buzzard: Auteur Publishing, 2015).

Hartson, Mary T., 'Voracious vampires and other monsters: masculinity and the terror genre in Spanish cinema of the *Transición*', *Romance Notes* 55, no. 1 (2015): 125–36.

Hendershot, Cyndy, *Paranoia, the Bomb and 1950s Science Fiction Films* (Bowling Green: Bowling Green State University Popular Press, 1999).

Hitchcock, Susan Tyler, *Frankenstein: A Cultural History* (New York: W. W. Norton, 2008).

Holmes, Ronald M., Richard Tewksbury and George E. Higgins, *Introduction to Gangs in America* (Boca Raton: CRC Press, 2012).

hooks, bell, *Feminism is for Everybody: Passionate Politics* (London: Pluto Press, 2000).

Hough, Peter, *Understanding Global Security*, 3rd edn (New York: Routledge, 2013).

Housman, Clemence, *The Were-Wolf* (Chicago: Way and Williams, 1896).

Hout, Michael, Asaf Levanon and Erin Cumberworth, 'Job loss and unemployment', in David B. Grusky, Bruce Western and Christopher Wimer (eds), *The Great Recession* (New York: Russell Sage Foundation, 2011), pp. 59–81.

Hubner, Laura, *Fairytale and Gothic Horror: Uncanny Transformations in Film* (New York: Palgrave Macmillan, 2018).

Humphries, Reynold, *The American Horror Film: An Introduction* (Edinburgh: Edinburgh University Press, 2002).

Hutchings, Peter, *Dracula* [British Film Guide] (London: I. B. Tauris, 2003).

Hutchings, Peter, *Hammer and Beyond: The British Horror Film* (Manchester: Manchester University Press, 1993).

Hutchings, Peter, 'The Amicus house of horror', in Steve Chibnall and Julian Petley (eds), *British Horror Cinema* (London: Routledge, 2002), pp. 131–44.

Hutchings, Peter, 'The she-wolves of horror cinema', in Hannah Priest (ed.), *She-Wolf: A Cultural History of Female Werewolves* (Manchester: Manchester University Press, 2015), pp. 166–79.

Jancovich, Mark, 'Phantom ladies: the war worker, the slacker and the femme fatale', *New Review of Film and Television Studies* 8, no. 2 (2010): 164–78.

Jancovich, Mark, *Rational Fears: American Horror in the 1950s* (Manchester: Manchester University Press, 1996).

Jeffords, Susan, 'The big switch: Hollywood masculinity in the nineties', in Jim Collins, Hilary Radner and Ava Preacher Collins (eds), *Film Theory Goes to the Movies* (New York: Routledge, 1993), pp. 196–208.

Jeffords, Susan, *Hard Bodies: Hollywood Masculinity in the Reagan Era* (New Brunswick, NJ: Rutgers University Press, 1994).

Jones, Darryl, *Horror: A Thematic History in Fiction and Film* (London: Bloomsbury Academic, 2002).

Jones, Stephen, *The Essential Monster Movie Guide* (New York: Billboard Books, 2000).

Jordan, Chris, *Movies and the Reagan Presidency: Success and Ethics* (Westport, CT: Praeger, 2003).

Jowett, Lorna, 'White trash in wife-beaters? U.S. television werewolves, gender, and class', in Linda Belau and Kimberley Jackson (eds), *Horror Television in the Age of Consumption: Binging on Fear* (New York: Routledge, 2018), pp. 76–89.

Kabatchnik, Amnon, *Blood on the Stage 1925–1950: Milestone Plays of Crime, Mystery and Detection* (Lanham: Scarecrow Press, 2010).

Keck, Paul E., Harrison G. Pope, James I. Hudson, Susan L. McElroy and Aaron R. Kulick, 'Lycanthropy: alive and well in the twentieth century', *Psychological Medicine* 18, no. 1 (1988): 113–20.

Kemp, Philip, '*Wolf*', *Sight and Sound* 4, no. 9 (1994): 52.

King, Stephen, *Cycle of the Werewolf* (Plymouth: Land of Enchantment, 1983).

Kinsella, James, *Covering the Plague: AIDS and the American Media* (New Brunswick, NJ: Rutgers University Press, 1989).

Krutnik, Frank, *In a Lonely Street: Film Noir, Genre, Masculinity* (New York: Routledge, 1991).

Krzywinska, Tanya, *A Skin for Dancing In: Possession, Witchcraft and Voodoo in Film* (Trowbridge: Flicks Books, 2000).

Lapeyre, Jason, 'The bad moon rises again', *Rue Morgue* 93 (2009): 16–19, 22–4.

Lavoy, Peter, 'Pyridostigmine bromide', in Eric A. Croddy and James J. Wirtz (eds), *Weapons of Mass Destruction: An Encyclopedia of Worldwide Policy, Technology, and History* (Santa Barbara: ABC-CLIO, 2005), pp. 231–3.

Lázaro-Reboll, Antonio, *Spanish Horror Film* (Edinburgh: Edinburgh University Press, 2012).

Levack, Brian P., *The Witch-Hunt in Early Modern Europe*, 3rd edn (Harlow: Pearson Education, 2006).

Levesque, Michel, 'Commentary by director Michel Levesque and co-writer David M. Kaufman', *Werewolves on Wheels*, 1971, DVD. Directed by Michel Levesque (Orland Park: Dark Sky Films, 2006).

Lowenstein, Adam, *Shocking Representation: Historical Trauma, National Cinema, and the Modern Horror Film* (New York: Columbia University Press, 2005).

Luckhurst, Roger, *The Mummy's Curse: The True History of a Dark Fantasy* (Oxford: Oxford University Press, 2012).

Luckhurst, Roger, *Zombies: A Cultural History* (London: Reaktion Books, 2015).

Lupton, Deborah, *Medicine as Culture: Illness, Disease and the Body*, 3rd edn (Thousand Oaks: SAGE Publications, 2012).

Mackay, Christopher S. (trans.), *The Hammer of Witches: A Complete Translation of the Malleus Maleficarum* (Cambridge: Cambridge University Press, 2009).

McMahon-Coleman, Kimberley and Roslyn Weaver, *Werewolves and other Shape-shifters in Popular Culture: A Thematic Analysis of Recent Depictions* (Jefferson: McFarland, 2012).

Maddrey, Joseph, *Nightmares in Red, White and Blue: The Evolution of the American Horror Film* (Jefferson: McFarland, 2004).

Magistrale, Tony, *Landscape of Fear: Stephen King's American Gothic* (Bowling Green: Bowling Green State University Popular Press, 1988).

Mann, Craig Ian, 'America, down the toilet: urban legends, American society and *Alligator*', in Katarina Gregersdotter, Johan Höglund and Nicklas Hållén (eds), *Animal Horror Cinema: Genre, History and Criticism* (New York: Palgrave Macmillan, 2015), pp. 110–25.

Marchetti, Gina, *Romance and the 'Yellow Peril': Race, Sex and Discursive Strategies in Hollywood Fiction* (Berkeley: University of California Press, 1993).

Marshall, Neil, 'Audio commentary with director Neil Marshall', *Dog Soldiers*, 2002, collectors edition, Blu-ray and DVD. Directed by Neil Marshall (Los Angeles: Scream Factory, 2015).

Mathijs, Ernest, 'They're here!: special effects in horror cinema of the 1970s and 1980s', in Ian Conrich (ed.), *Horror Zone: The Cultural Experience of Contemporary Horror* Cinema (London and New York: I. B. Tauris, 2010), 153–72.

Mathijs, Ernest, *John Fawcett's* Ginger Snaps (Toronto: University of Toronto Press, 2013).

Matthews Jr, Melvin E., *Fear Itself: Horror on Screen and in Reality during the Depression and World War II* (Jefferson: McFarland, 2009).

Meikle, Denis, *A History of Horrors: The Rise and Fall of the House of Hammer*, revised edn (Lanham: Scarecrow Press, 2009).

Mian, Atif and Amir Sufi, *House of Debt: How They (and You) Caused the Great Recession and How We Can Prevent It from Happening Again* (Chicago: University of Chicago Press, 2014).

Mishel, Lawrence and David M. Frankel, *The State of Working America 1990–1991 Edition* (London: M. E. Sharpe, 1991).

Morcillo, Aurora G., *The Seduction of Modern Spain: The Female Body and the Francoist Body Politic* (Lewisburg: Brucknell University Press, 2010).

Muir, John Kenneth, *Horror Films of the 1980s* (Jefferson: McFarland, 2007).

Munro, Ealasaid, 'Feminism: a fourth wave?', *Political Insight* 4, no. 2 (2013): 22–5.

Nash, Mary, 'Pronatalism and motherhood in Franco's Spain', in Gisela Block and Pat Thane (eds), *Maternity and Gender Policies: Women and the Rise of the European Welfare States 1880s–1950s* (New York: Routledge, 1991), pp. 160–77.

Neale, Steve, '"You've got to be fucking kidding!" Knowledge, belief and judgement in science fiction', in Annette Kuhn (ed.), *Alien Zone: Cultural Theory and Contemporary Science Fiction* (New York: Verso, 1990), pp. 160–8.

Newhouse, Tom, 'A blind date with disaster: adolescent revolt in the fiction of Stephen King', in Gary Hoppenstand (ed.), *Stephen King* (Pasadena and Hackensack: Salem Press, 2011), pp. 267–75.

Newland, Paul, *British Films in the 1970s* (Manchester: Manchester University Press, 2013).

Newman, Katherine S., Cybelle Fox, David J. Harding, Jal Mehta and Wendy Roth, *Rampage: The Social Roots of School Shootings* (New York: Basic Books, 2004).

Newman, Kim, '*An American Werewolf in Paris*', *Sight and Sound* 7, no. 12 (1998): 37.

Newman, Kim, *Cat People* [BFI Classics] (London: BFI Publishing, 2001).

Newman, Kim, *Horror! The Definitive Guide to the Most Terrifying Movies Ever Made* (London: Carlton Books, 2006).

Nielsen, Bianca, 'Something's wrong, like more than you being female: transgressive sexuality and discourses of reproduction in *Ginger Snaps*', *Thirdspace* 3, no. 2 (2004): 55–69.

Ovid, *Metamorphoses*, trans. David Raeburn, revised edn (London: Penguin, 2004).

Peirse, Alison, *After Dracula: The 1930s Horror Film* (London and New York: I. B. Tauris, 2013).

Petronius, *The Satyricon*, trans. J. P. Sullivan, revised edn (London: Penguin, 2011).

Phillips, Kendall R., *Projected Fears: Horror Films and American Culture* (Westport, CT: Praeger, 2005).

Place, Janey, 'Women in film noir', in E. Ann Kaplan (ed.), *Women in Film Noir*, 2nd edn (London: BFI Publishing, 1998), 47–68.

Plummer, Sean, 'Howl of justice', *Rue Morgue* 145 (2014): 16–22.

Prawer, S. S., *Caligari's Children: The Film as a Tale of Terror* (Oxford and New York: Oxford University Press, 1980).

Priest, Hannah (ed.), *She-Wolf: A Cultural History of Female Werewolves* (Manchester: Manchester University Press, 2015).

Priest, Hannah, 'Like father like son: wolf-men, paternity and the male gothic', in Robert McKay and John Miller (eds), *Werewolves, Wolves and the Gothic* (Cardiff: University of Wales Press, 2017), pp. 19–36.

Reeves, Aaron, Martin McKnee and David Stuckler, 'Economic suicides in the great recession in Europe and North America', *British Journal of Psychiatry* 205, no. 3 (2014): 246–7.

Rigby, Jonathan, *English Gothic: A Century of Horror Cinema*, revised edn (Richmond: Reynolds and Hearn, 2004).

Robinson, Paul, 'Race, space and the evolution of black Los Angeles', in Darnell Hunt and Ana-Christina Ramon (eds), *Black Los Angeles: American Dreams and Racial Realities* (New York: New York University Press, 2010), 21–59.

Rossinow, Doug, *The Reagan Era: A History of the 1980s* (New York: Columbia University Press, 2015).

Rothenburger, Sunnie, '"Welcome to civilisation": colonialism, the gothic, and Canada's self-protective irony in the *Ginger Snaps* werewolf trilogy', *Journal of Canadian Studies* 44, no. 3 (2010): 96–117.

Sanger, Toby, 'Canada's conservative class war: using austerity to squeeze labour at the expense of economic growth', *Alternative Routes: A Journal of Critical Social Research* 24 (2013): 59–83.

Savage, Adam, 'Adam Savage interviews John Landis – The Talking Room', YouTube video, 01:02:42, posted by 'Tested', 29 August 2013, <https://www.youtube.com/watch?v=Q7RoL1FUR1g>.

Scanlon, Sandra, 'Ronald Reagan and the conservative movement', in Andrew L. Johns (ed.), *A Companion to Ronald Reagan* (Malden, MA: Wiley Blackwell, 2015), pp. 585–607.

Schaller, Michael, *Reckoning with Reagan: America and its President in the 1980s* (Oxford and New York: Oxford University Press, 1992).

Schlegel, Nicholas G., *Sex, Sadism, Spain, and Cinema: The Spanish Horror Film* (Lanham: Rowman and Littlefield, 2015).

Schubert, Bernard, 'Wolfman vs. Dracula', in Philip J. Ridley (ed.), *Wolfman vs. Dracula* (Albany: BearManor Media, 2010), pp. 116–33.

Sconduto, Leslie A., *Metamorphoses of the Werewolf: A Literary Study from Antiquity through the Renaissance* (Jefferson: McFarland, 2008).

Senn, Bryan, 'Twin bill terrorama!: *Invasion of the Saucer Men* and *I Was a Teenage Werewolf*', *Filmfax* 93/4 (2002): 80–1, 128–30.

Shindler, Colin, *Hollywood Goes to War: Films and American Society 1939–1952* (New York: Routledge, 1979).

Shipka, Danny, *Perverse Titillation: The Exploitation Cinema of Italy, Spain and France, 1960–1980* (Jefferson: McFarland, 2011).

Shohat, Ella, 'The media's war', in Susan Jeffords and Lauren Rabinovitz (eds), *Seeing Through the Media: The Persian Gulf War* (New Brunswick, NJ: Rutgers University Press, 1994), 147–54.

Skal, David J., *The Monster Show: A Cultural History of Horror* (London: Plexus Publishing, 1994).

Smith, Wayne, *Thor* (New York: Ballantine Books, 1994).

Sneider, Jeff, '*It* filmmaker Andy Muschietti in early talks to direct *The Howling* for Netflix', *Collider*, 9 January 2020, <https://collider.com/andy-muschietti-the-howling-netflix/>.

Snelson, Tim, *Phantom Ladies: Hollywood Horror and the Home* Front (New Brunswick, NJ: Rutgers University Press, 2015).

Soister, John, *Up from the Vault: Rare Thrillers of the 1920s and 1930s* (Jefferson: McFarland, 2004).

Spadoni, Robert, 'Strange botany in *Werewolf of London*', *Horror Studies* 1, no. 1 (2010): 49–71.

Sparks, Jacqueline A. and Barry L. Duncan, 'The ethics and science of medicating children', *Ethical Human Psychology and Psychiatry* 6, no. 1 (2004): 25–39.

Stoney, Christopher and Tamara Krawchencko, 'Crisis and opportunism: public finance trends from stimulus to austerity in Canada', *Alternative Routes: A Journal of Critical Social Research* 24 (2013): 33–58.

Summers, Montague, *The Werewolf in Lore and Legend* (Mineola: Dover Publications, [1933] 2003).

Tasker, Yvonne, *Spectacular Bodies: Gender, Genre and the Action Cinema* (New York: Routledge, 1993).

Thompson, Graham, *American Culture in the 1980s* (Edinburgh: Edinburgh University Press, 2007).

Ticknell, Estella, 'Feminine boundaries: adolescence, witchcraft and the new gothic cinema and television', in Ian Conrich (ed.), *Horror Zone: The Cultural Experience of Contemporary Horror Cinema* (London and New York: I. B. Tauris, 2010), 245–58.

Tjersland, Todd, 'Cinema of the doomed: the tragic horror of Paul Naschy', in Steven Jay Schneider (ed.), *Fears without Frontiers: Horror Cinema across the Globe* (Godalming: FAB Press, 2003), pp. 69–80.

Towlson, Jon, *Subversive Horror Cinema: Countercultural Messages of Films from Frankenstein to the Present* (Jefferson: McFarland, 2014).

Tudor, Andrew, *Decoding Culture: Theory and Method in Cultural Studies* (Thousand Oaks: SAGE Publications, 1999).

Tudor, Andrew, *Monsters and Mad Scientists: A Cultural History of the Horror Movie* (Oxford: Blackwell, 1989).

Tudor, Andrew, 'Sociology and film', in John Hill and Pamela Church Gibson (eds), *Film Studies: Critical Approaches* (Oxford and New York: Oxford University Press, 2000), pp. 188–92.

Tudor, Andrew. 'Why horror? The peculiar pleasures of a popular genre', in Mark Jancovich (ed.), *Horror, The Film Reader* (New York: Routledge, 2002), pp. 47–56.

Twitchell, James B., *Dreadful Pleasures: An Anatomy of Modern Horror* (Oxford and New York: Oxford University Press, 1985).

Vuckovic, Jovanka, 'Four-legged hound from hell', *Rue Morgue* 93 (2009): 20–1.

Waller, Gregory A., 'Introduction', in Gregory A. Waller (ed.), *American Horrors: Essays on the Modern American Horror Film* (Urbana and Chicago: University of Illinois Press, 1987), pp. 1–13.

Waller, Gregory A., *The Living and the Undead: Slaying Vampires, Exterminating Zombies* (Urbana: University of Illinois Press, 1986).

Wharton, Sarah, 'Welcome to the (neo) grindhouse!', in Geoff King, Claire Molloy and Yannis Tzioumakis (eds), *American Independent Cinema: Indie, Indiewood and Beyond* (New York: Routledge, 2015), pp. 198–209.

Whitehead, J. W., *Mike Nichols and the Cinema of Transformation* (Jefferson: McFarland, 2014).

Whitman, Sylvia, *V is for Victory: The American Home Front during World War II* (Minneapolis: Lerner Publications, 1993).

Wilder, Marcy J., 'The rule of law, the rise of violence and the role of morality: reframing America's abortion debate', in Rickie Solinger (ed.), *Abortion Wars: A Half Century of Struggle, 1950–2000* (Berkeley: University of California Press, 1998), pp. 73–94.

Williams, Linda Ruth, 'Blood sisters', *Sight and Sound* 11, no. 7 (2001): 36–7.

Williams, Tony, *Larry Cohen: The Radical Allegories of an Independent Filmmaker*, revised edn (Jefferson: McFarland, 2014).

Wish, Eric D., 'PCP and crime: just another illicit drug?', *NIDA Research Monograph* 64 (1986): 174–189.

Wood, John, 'Hell's Angels and the illusion of counterculture', *Journal of Popular Culture* 37, no. 2 (2003): 336–51.

Wood, Robin, 'An introduction to the American horror film', in Barry Keith Grant (ed.), *Planks of Reason: Essays on the Horror Film* (Lanham: Scarecrow Press, 2004), pp. 107–41.

Woodward, Ian, *The Werewolf Delusion* (London: Paddington Press, 1979).

Worland, Rick, *The Horror Film: An Introduction* (Oxford: Blackwell, 2007).

Zinoman, Jason, *Shock Value: How a Few Eccentric Outsiders Gave Us Nightmares, Conquered Hollywood and Invented Modern Horror* (London: Duckworth Overlook, 2012).

Index

CPSIA information can be obtained
at www.ICGtesting.com
Printed in the USA
LVHW060747201120
672095LV00004B/1